S0-BNK-674

Racial Formation in the United States

Critical Social Thought
Series editor: Michael W. Apple
Professor of Curriculum and Instruction and of Educational
Policy Studies, University of Wisconsin-Madison

Racial Formation in the United States
From the 1960s to the 1980s

Michael Omi and
Howard Winant

Routledge & Kegan Paul
New York and London

LIBRARY
COLBY-SAWYER COLLEGE
NEW LONDON, N.H. 03257

E
184
.A1
O46
1986

8/8

First published in the USA by
Routledge & Kegan Paul Inc.
in association with Methuen Inc.
29 West 35th Street, New York, NY 10001

and in the UK by
Routledge & Kegan Paul plc
11 New Fetter Lane, London EC4P 4EE

Set in Times, 10 on 12pt
by Inforum Ltd, Portsmouth
and printed in Great Britain
by Billing & Sons Ltd
Worcester

Copyright © Michael Omi and Howard Winant 1986

No part of this book may be reproduced in
any form without permission from the publisher
except for the quotation of brief passages
in criticism

Library of Congress Cataloging in Publication Data

Omi, Michael.
Racial formation in the United States.
(Critical social thought)
Bibliography: p.
Includes index.
1. United States—Race relations. 2. United States—
Social conditions—1960–1980. 3. United States—
Social conditions—1980–   . I. Winant, Howard.
II. Title. III. Series.
E184.A1046 1986   305.8'00973   86–3285

British Library CIP Data also available

ISBN 0–7102–0566–X (c)
      0–7102–0970–3 (p)

100008

Contents

Series editor's introduction

During the past decade, a good deal of progress has been made by leftist scholars in how we should think through the relationships between the actions of people as classed, raced and gendered subjects and the larger social formation. One of the major gains has been a rejection of economically determinist positions, where the economic "base" determines at each and every moment cultural and political structures.[1] A second, and just as significant, area of progress has also been partly built on a move away from past formulations. This has involved going beyond class reductionism. Feminist work has proven exceptionally important in enabling us to recognize the co-determinant status of sex/gender and class dynamics.[2] Subsequent work has not only increased our understanding of these two dynamics, but has also begun to argue that race should occupy a parallel position.[3]

Out of this anti-determinist and anti-reductive movement has come some truly outstanding work on politics and the state, on ideology and culture, and on the ways class, gender and race are interconnected. Though much of this scholarship has been exceptional, it has not tended to focus as much as it could have done *directly* on the specificities of race itself. What is needed at this time is a synthetic and creative treatment of racial formation, one that incorporates the progress made in the literature on politics and ideology, and one that uses it to interrogate the current and emerging conditions in the United States. *Racial Formation in the United States* is just such a book. Race is at its heart, but in a different way than the usual manner in which conservative or radical theories look at it.

An honest picture of how the United States has confronted its racially defined minorities needs to squarely face the following.

"Native Americans faced genocide, blacks were subjected to slavery, Mexicans were invaded and colonized, and Asians faced exclusion." These were not incidental elements in the history of the country, but go to the very center of its political, cultural and economic relations. These were often quite overt policies. Racist discourse was openly used, and made legitimate in different ways over time by specific religious texts, by economic "necessities," and by "neutral" scientific findings in anthropology, eugenics, and so on.[4] However, as Vincent Harding has so eloquently demonstrated in his treatment of the Afro-American struggle for freedom, these racist practices and discourses brought with them a vast river of protest and of cultural and political action on the part of blacks that continues to this day.[5]

The focus on "to this day" is of no small moment. There has again been a growth not only of overt racist tendencies in the United States, England and elsewhere, but of covert racial dynamics as well. The conservative restoration in these countries has brought with it a reassertion of racist policies that are hidden underneath their rhetorical devices of individual economic freedom. How this racial discourse operates politically and ideologically is part of the story Omi and Winant want to tell.

With the politics of the right now resurgent and with the growth of neoconservatism, it is essential that we think through what this means in terms of the class, gender and race inequalities of American society. The goals of the right are visible around us: resuscitation of economic and imperial power, containing and/or making illegitimate the demands and political visions of people of color, women, unions, and so many others, the restoration of "governability" to democracy, and restoring traditional cultural and social values to their "proper" place.

Racial Formation in the United States argues that behind these objectives is an underlying racial discourse, one that is partly hidden by the right's ability to appropriate previous democratic themes and language and use them in their current attempt to reconstruct America around its economic, political and moral principles. It is here that the authors go beyond previous attempts to deal with race.

Omi and Winant's program can be best seen in the following quote.

Most racial theory fails to capture the centrality of race in

American politics and American life. In general, theoretical work on race has not successfully grasped the shifting nature of racial dynamics in the postwar US, a failure which sparked important challenges as postwar racial events appeared to conflict with the predictions of theory. Most theories are marked by a tendency to *reduce* race to a mere manifestation of other supposedly more fundamental social and political relationships such as ethnicity and class. Our doubts about this literature derived from this reductionism – an inability to grasp the uniqueness of race, its historical flexibility and immediacy in everyday experience and social conflict.

Three themes guide their analysis: (1) the way new social movements have emerged that have rearticulated important political and cultural themes and in the process have been able to mobilize a mass base of adherents; (2) locating race at the very center of America's political and social history, in essence to make it co-determinate with class and sex/gender; and (3) how the state both shapes and is shaped "by the racial contours of society and the political demands emanating from them." In order to develop their own theory of racial formation, they critically examine previous attempts to theorize race. These include the more conservative approach organized under the umbrella of ethnicity theory where race was viewed as one form of ethnicity among many, and the more radical class- and nation-based theories of race that arose to challenge earlier viewpoints.

In the process, the authors make a number of telling points. For example, for them, rather than racial dynamics being understood as the results of class relationships, these dynamics are focused on as determinants *themselves* of class relationships. Thus, unlike those who see class as the primary determinant, Omi and Winant argue that race has been a major force in the creation of mass movements, in the formation of state policy, and in the acting out of foreign policy as well. At the same time that they argue for giving race a parallel position with class in explaining current and past social tendencies, underlying their analysis is an important claim about the relationship among the economic, political and cultural spheres of this society. Politics and culture play a truly significant role in the creation, recreation and destabilizing of hegemonic relations. "Racial meaning-systems are contested and racial ideologies mobilized in *political* relationships." The recognition of the efficacy of political and cultural action goes a long way beyond the economically reductive theories that are still too dominant on the left.

For Omi and Winant, race is not an essence. It is not "something fixed, concrete, and objective." Rather, race needs to be seen "as an unstable and 'decentered' complex of social meanings constantly being transformed by political struggle." The stress on race not as a thing but as a set of social meanings is a key here. So too is the emphasis on political contestation. Taken together, they point to the relationship between race and social movements on the one hand and between such social movements and the state on the other. Thus, the state becomes the *racial state*. In fact, one of the authors' major contributions is to provide us with the tools to analyze the role of the state in racial formation.[6]

How is the unstable equilibrium of the racial order maintained? How is it disrupted? How does the racial state respond to such disruptions? In essence, what is the *trajectory* of racial politics? These are some of the questions that guide their provocative analysis.

In demonstrating these relationships they draw on Gramsci's important distinction between war of maneuver and war of position. The former signifies an historical situation in which oppressed or subordinate groups turn inward, in which they "seek to preserve and extend a definite territory, to ward off violent assault, and to develop an internal society as an alternative to the repressive social system they confront." A war of position is often based on gains made by a war of maneuver, but is outward-turning. It is predicated on political struggle. Oppositional political projects are mounted on a variety of terrains to confront the racial state. The state itself becomes a site of ongoing struggle over racial meanings and power. In the process, both the social movements and the state are transformed. The state doesn't just intervene in racial conflicts. It is the pre-eminent site on which and over which such conflict occurs.

These are real theoretical advances. But Omi and Winant are not content to remain on that level. They analyze the profound changes in racial meanings and politics and in the racial state from 1960 to the present in a remarkably clear manner. They trace out in fascinating detail how the new social movements of the 1960s and 1970s challenged the existing dominant forms of power relations. Yet in their failure to consolidate a new radical democratic politics,

one with majoritarian aspirations, oddly these new social movements "provided the political space in which right-wing reaction
could incubate and develop its political agenda." These movements also engendered a reaction among the individuals and
groups whose cultural and political groundings they challenged, a
reaction so clear today for example in the emergence of the authoritarian populism of the new right and in the works of neoconservative authors.

Omi and Winant's contribution does not end there. What is also
impressive is their consistent attempt to link the micro and macro
levels of social relations together. Structure and agency, political
economy and consciousness, are interwoven so that the workings of
racial formation are seen in a new and integrative light. In so doing,
they demonstrate that what is at stake at this time is the very
meaning of racial equality. This is a continuation of that even longer
struggle over racial politics not only in the United States but
elsewhere as well that I mentioned earlier.

All of this requires a particular sensitivity to a whole nexus of
relationships. One must uncover the connections among the state,
ideologies and social movements, and at the same time be sensitive
to how class and race work off and sometimes contradict each
other. Above all, it requires an awareness of the historical variabil-
ity and complexity of the concrete.

Stuart Hall has argued exactly this point in his own discussion of
why race needs to be taken as a truly constitutive dynamic in society
and why it has to be seen in all its complexities.

> The task of a critical theory is to produce as accurate a
> knowledge of complex social processes as their functioning
> requires. It is not its task to console the left by producing simple
> but satisfying myths, distinguished only by their super-left wing
> credentials. . . . Most important of all, these differences and
> complexities have real *effects*, which ought to enter into any
> serious political calculation about how their tendencies might be
> resisted or turned.[7]

It is expressly these effects and how they can be thought about
and worked against with which *Racial Formation in the United States*
is concerned. It furthers our understanding of a complex political
reality in fresh and notable ways. As such, it deserves to be read by

Series editor's introduction

all people who recognize the power race continues to have on our social policies and on our very lives.

Michael W. Apple
The University of Wisconsin-Madison

Notes

1   This work is summarized in Michael W. Apple, *Education and Power* (Boston: Routledge & Kegan Paul, 1982) and Michael W. Apple ed., *Cultural and Economic Reproduction in Education: Essays on Class, Culture and the State* (Boston: Routledge & Kegan Paul, 1982).
2   See Michèle Barrett, *Women's Oppression Today* (London: New Left Books, 1980).
3   See Centre for Contemporary Cultural Studies, *The Empire Strikes Back: Race and Racism in 70s Britain* (London: Hutchinson, 1980), Michael W. Apple and Lois Weis, eds, *Ideology and Practice in Schooling* (Philadelphia: Temple University Press, 1983), and Lois Weis, *Between Two Worlds* (Boston: Routledge & Kegan Paul, 1985).
4   Stephen Jay Gould, *The Mismeasure of Man* (New York: Norton, 1981).
5   Vincent Harding, *There Is a River: The Black Struggle for Freedom in America* (New York: Vintage, 1981).
6   As such, it is complementary to the more class-based positions analyzed in Martin Carnoy, *The State and Political Theory* (Princeton: Princeton University Press, 1984).
7   Stuart Hall, "The Whites of Their Eyes: Racist Ideologies and the Media," in George Bridges and Rosalind Brunt, eds, *Silver Linings: Some Strategies for the Eighties* (London: Lawrence & Wishart, 1981), pp. 35–6.

Acknowledgments

To study race in the United States is to enter a world of paradox, irony and danger. In this world, arbitrarily chosen human attributes shape politics and policy, love and hate, life and death. All the powers of the intellect – artistic, religious, scientific, political – are pressed into service to explain racial distinctions, and to suggest how they may be maintained, changed, or abolished. The intellectual climate is anything but benign where racial studies are concerned. The ordinary competitiveness and isolation of academic work only adds to the peril.

In such an atmosphere, we have enjoyed a rare privilege: the opportunity to share a prolonged and difficult labor. For the past seven years, we have collaborated in the research and writing which have led to this book. The project has been a most demanding one. It has forced us to re-examine our beliefs, our politics, our lives. It has given us new respect, not only for the scholars whose work inspired us, but also for those with whom we most disagreed. Above all, it has taught us to love and trust each other.

We have drawn on the knowledge and skill of many friends and colleagues. Thanks to the following people for their tireless support, helpful comments and merciless criticisms: Robert Allen, Carol Baker, Harold Baron, Mario Barrera, Gary Delgado, Doug Dowd, Jeff Escoffier, William Friedland, Hardy Frye, Frances Goldin, Amber Hollibaugh, Jim Jacobs, Andres Jimenez, Michael Kazin, Robert Meeropol, James O'Connor, David Plotke, Juan Carlos Portantiero, Michael Rosenthal, Pamela Rosenthal, Alex Saragoza, Paul Scheifer, Gay Seidman, Nancy Shaw, Larry Shinagawa, Jim Shoch, Jere Takahashi, Ron Takaki, Dianne Yamashiro-Omi, and the West Coast editorial collective of *Socialist Review*.

Acknowledgments

The faculties and staffs of the Center for Latin American Studies and the Asian American Studies Program at the University of California, Berkeley, though aware that completion of this manuscript diverted the authors' attention from other duties, provided both tangible and emotional support for the project.

Finally, we would like to thank loved ones who made our work possible in more ways than we could ever express. We dedicate this book to Debbie Rogow and to Ben and Mabel Omi.

Michael Omi, University of California, Berkeley
Howard Winant, Temple University

Introduction

In January 1985, the chair of the US Commission on Civil Rights, Clarence Pendleton Jr, told President Reagan that members of the then recently reconstituted Commission were "working on a color blind society that has opportunities for all and guarantees success for none."[1] Pendleton's remarks echoed the President's own sentiments, which in turn have resonated with broad sectors of US populace. The notion of a colorblind society where no special significance, rights or privileges attach to one's "race" makes for appealing ideology. Taken at face value, the concept reaffirms values of "fair play" and "equal opportunity" – ideals, some would argue, which constitute the very essence of our democratic way of life.

Yet even a cursory glance at American history reveals that far from being colorblind, the United States has been an extremely "color-conscious" society. From the very inception of the Republic to the present moment, race has been a profound determinant of one's political rights, one's location in the labor market, and indeed one's sense of "identity." The hallmark of this history has been *racism*,[2] not the abstract ethos of equality, and while racial minority groups have been treated differently, all can bear witness to the tragic consequences of racial oppression. The US has confronted each racially defined minority with a unique form of despotism and degradation. The examples are familiar: Native Americans faced genocide, blacks were subjected to racial slavery, Mexicans were invaded and colonized, and Asians faced exclusion.[3]

Optimistic observers of this history often acknowledge past atrocities, but offer a vision of the contemporary US as an egalitarian society, one which is trying to live up to its original principles by slowly extending and applying them to the gnawing issue of race. In such a vision recent history is seen as a period of enlightened progress – an unfolding drama of the social, political and economic incorporation of minorities which will not be thwarted or reversed. The "colorblind" society, it is argued, will be the end result of this process.

Yet viewed more deeply, recent history – particularly the period from the 1960s to the 1980s – reveals a more complex and contradictory trajectory in which the pattern of race relations seems far less certain, and much less tranquil.

In the 1960s, race occupied the center stage of American politics in a manner unprecedented since the Civil War era a century earlier. Civil rights struggles and ghetto revolts, as well as controversies over state policies of reform and repression, highlighted a period of intense conflict where the very *meaning* of race was politically contested. The 1970s, by contrast, were years of racial quiescence when the racial minority movements of the previous period seemed to wane. Racial oppression had hardly vanished, but conflicts over race receded as past reforms were institutionalized.

Issues of race have once again been dramatically revived in the 1980s, this time in the form of a "backlash" to the political gains of racial minority movements of the past. Conservative popular movements, academics and the Reagan administration have joined hands to attack the legacy and logic of earlier movement achievements. They have done this, moreover, in a way which escapes obvious charges of "racism."

Such an intense ebb and flow in the politics of race truly begs for interpretation. This book developed from our desire to comprehend the recent tumultuous decades and to assess their meaning for a broader understanding of race in the United States. We address three broad topics. First, we consider and critique recent theories of race in the US. Second, we advance an alternative conception, based in the concept of *racial formation*. Finally, we apply our racial formation approach to postwar US racial history and politics.

Most racial theory fails to capture the centrality of race in American politics and American life. In general, theoretical work on race has not successfully grasped the shifting nature of racial dynamics in the postwar US, a failure which sparked important challenges as postwar racial events appeared to conflict with the predictions of theory. Most theories are marked by a tendency to *reduce* race to a mere manifestation of other supposedly more fundamental social and political relationships such as ethnicity or class. Our doubts about this literature derived from this reductionism – an inability to grasp the uniqueness of race, its historical flexibility and immediacy in everyday experience and social conflict.

Instead of exploring how groups become racially identified, how racial identities and meanings changed over time, or how racial conflicts shape the American polity and society, "mainstream" approaches consider race as a problem of policy, of social engineering, of state management. In the largest number of works, incorporation and assimilation of differences (or the problems involved in achieving this) is the principle governing not only social policy, but also theory construction and analysis. "Radical" theories embrace class or nationalist perspectives which, while critical of the existing racial order, are often no more appreciative of the uniqueness and irreducibility of their subject than were the "established" analyses. Thus radicals too often submerge race in other social relations – most frequently class- or nation-based conflicts – thought to operate as the "motor force of history." Often influenced by movements and traditions whose reference points were located outside the US, many radical perspectives simply fail to address specific US conditions.[4]

Part of the confusion resides in the fact that race in the United States is concurrently an obvious and complex phenomenon. Everyone "knows" what race is, though everyone has a different opinion as to how many racial groups there are, what they are called, and who belongs in what specific racial categories.

For example, consider the US census. The racial categories used in census enumeration have varied widely from decade to decade. Groups such as Japanese Americans have moved from categories such as "non-white," "Oriental," or simply "Other" to recent inclusion as a specific "ethnic" group under the broader category of "Asian and Pacific Islanders." The variation both reflects and in turn shapes racial understanding and dynamics. It establishes often contradictory parameters of racial identity into which both individuals and groups must fit.[5]

How one is categorized is far from a merely academic or even personal matter. Such matters as access to employment, housing or other publicly or privately valued goods, social program design and the disbursement of local, state, and federal funds, or the organization of elections (among many other issues) are directly affected by racial classification and the recognition of "legitimate" groups. The determination of racial categories is thus an intensely political process.[6] Viewed as a whole, the census's racial classification reflects prevailing conceptions of race, establishes boundaries by which one's racial "identity" can be understood, determines the allocation of resources, and frames diverse political issues and conflicts.

Such an example underscores the fact that race and racial logic are ubiquitous. Yet existing racial theory, both mainstream and radical, has not grasped this reality. Consequently it minimizes the importance of race in recent American political history. Our work is an effort to overcome these limitations.

We sought an approach that would remedy the defects of existing theory. Three crucial, and related, concerns shaped our theoretical orientation. The first was to assess the significance of the emergence of *new social movements* in the 1960s, heralded by the black movement. By challenging existing patterns of race relations, the black movement created new political subjects, expanded the terrain of political struggle beyond "normal" politics, and inspired and galvanized a range of "new" social movements[7] – student, anti-war, feminist, gay, environmental, etc. The black movement's ability to *rearticulate*[8] traditional political and cultural themes and in so doing mobilize a mass base of adherents is, we believe, a striking feature of racial politics in the postwar period.

The second concern was to locate race at the center of American political history, not in order to displace other important social relationships such as class and sex/gender, but to serve as a corrective to the reductionism characteristic of racial theory. Our theory of *racial formation* emphasizes the social nature of race, the absence of any essential racial characteristics, the historical flexibility of racial meanings and categories, the conflictual character of race at both the "micro-" and "macro-social" levels, and the irreducible political aspect of racial dynamics.

Our third concern was to suggest a new "expanded" model of the state and state activity, which would place socially based movements, rather than traditionally defined, economically based interest groups, at the center of contemporary political processes. In order to do this, we examined the *trajectory* of racial politics in the US – the processes by which the state shapes and is shaped in turn by the racial contours of society and the political demands emanating from them.

While not possessing the ability to resolve all the problems inherent in the field of racial theory, our effort does provide an analytic framework with which to view the racial politics of the past three decades. Our argument is advanced in three parts.

Part I is an analytic assessment of contemporary racial theory. In each epoch of US history, a certain school of racial theory has been dominant, serving as the racial "common sense" of its age. For much of our country's history, explicitly racist theories have played this role. During the postwar period, however, for the first sustained period in US history, the dominant racial theory has upheld a notion of racial equality, albeit in various versions. In Chapter 1 we explore the particular approach to race – *ethnicity theory* – which since the early 1940s has been the main (though by no means the only) source of American racial concepts and values. Guided by ethnicity theory, Americans have come to view race as a variety of ethnicity, and to apply to racially defined groups certain standards and values whose pioneers and exemplars were European immigrants.

During its long reign, ethnicity theory has frequently been modified as its proponents attempted to account for new empirical phenomena or to address competing theoretical approaches. In the early postwar period, the ethnicity model encountered its main opponents in conservative quarters. Explicitly racial (and racist) perspectives on race, rooted in the formerly dominant paradigm of the prewar era, lived on in the South (and to some extent the Southwest). The early civil rights movement in the South, and the mobilization of Mexican Americans in the Southwest, destroyed these vestiges by the mid-1960s. Subsequently, the most severe challenge to ethnicity theory's dominance came from radical viewpoints, particularly *class-* and *nation*-based theories of race. These challenging approaches are the subjects of Chapters 2 and 3 respectively.[9]

Based on our criticism of existing racial theory (and also drawing upon it for the many partial insights it provides), Part II advances an alternative theory of race and the racial state in the US context. This approach is based on our conception of *racial formation*, which we present in Chapter 4, and on the socially based *trajectory* of racial politics, which we discuss in Chapter 5.

With these theoretical premises in place, we proceed in Part III to analyze recent racial history, focusing on the expansion of politics to the terrain of social life, political competition among paradigms of race, postwar transformations of the racial state, and the nature of racial movements, both "radical democratic" and "reactionary."

The period from the 1960s to the 1980s represented anything but a slow, steady evolution to a "colorblind" society. It was a period of racial upsurge, failed consolidation and reaction which, we believe, demonstrated the centrality of race in shaping American politics and culture. Today, faced with the antics of a Clarence Pendleton or the outlandish claims of Ronald Reagan that racial equality has been achieved, it is all too easy to regard race as an issue of the past. It is all too easy, even for those opposed to the right's racial policies, to suggest that today the crucial confrontation over America's future is taking place on some other ground. This book's conclusions, for the 1980s as much as for the 1960s, suggest the opposite. Race will *always* be at the center of the American experience.

Part One

Introduction:
Paradigms of race: ethnicity, class and nation

Introduction

Theories of race – of its meaning, its transformations, the significance of racial events – have never been a top priority in social science. The great social theorists of the nineteenth century, towering figures such as Ferdinand Toennies, Auguste Comte, Karl Marx, Frederick Engels, Emile Durkheim and Max Weber, were all consumed with analyzing the transition from feudalism to capitalism and interpreting the dynamic forces shaping the emergent capitalist order. Although they shared this central intellectual concern, these men could not agree on which structural relationships were the most important factors in explaining the new bourgeois industrial society.[1] What they could agree upon, though, was the belief that racial and ethnic social bonds, divisions and conflicts were remnants of a preindustrial order which would decline in significance in the modern period. Marx and Engels, for example, predicted that as society split up into two great, antagonistic classes, social distinctions such as race and ethnicity would decrease in importance.

In the US, although the "founding fathers" of American sociology (men such as Lester Ward, William Graham Sumner and Edward A. Ross) were explicitly concerned with the state of domestic race relations, racial theory remained one of the least developed fields of sociological inquiry. The pioneers were greatly influenced, not only by the Europeans, but also by the Social Darwinist currents of the period. Their work contributed, sometimes inadvertently but often by intention, to the racist hysteria of the late nineteenth and early twentieth centuries. The epoch of the emergence of modern social science in the US coincided with a

sustained period of racial reaction, marked by the institutionalization of Jim Crow in the South and the success of the movement for
Asian exclusion. Especially in this atmosphere, adherence to biologistic perspectives on race severely limited innovation and social
scientific interest in this field.[2]

Starting in the 1920s, the Chicago school of sociology began to
rework social scientific approaches to race. The Chicago sociologists, led by Robert E. Park, were the first *modern* analysts of the
subject, and their thinking shaped the dominant theoretical and
methodological assumptions about race relations for the greater
part of this century. Park's *race-relations cycle*, with its four stages
of contact, conflict, accommodation and assimilation, is widely
regarded as one of the most important contributions to the field.
Park postulated the cycle as a law of historical development, a way
of analyzing group relations and assessing a "minority" group's
progress along a fixed continuum.[3]

Beginning with Park's concepts, a set of assumptions have
gradually come to characterize the field and serve as guides for
social scientists investigating the nature of race in the United States.
Blauner discusses these assumptions as follows:

> First, the view that racial and ethnic groups are neither central
> nor persistent elements of modern societies. Second, the idea
> that racism and racial oppression are not independent dynamic
> forces but are ultimately reducible to other causal determinants,
> usually economic or psychological. Third, the position that the
> most important aspects of racism are the attitudes and
> prejudices of Americans. And, finally, the so-called *immigrant
> analogy*, the assumption, critical in contemporary thought, that
> there are no essential long-term differences – in relation to the
> larger society – between the *third world* or racial minorities and
> the European ethnic groups.[4]

These assumptions are as much political and ideological as they
are theoretical. They neglect both the institutional and ideological
nature of race in America, and the systemic presence of racial
dynamics in such social spheres as education, art, social policy, law,
religion and science. Instead they focus attention on racial dynamics
as the irrational products of individual pathologies.[5] Such assumptions make it impossible to grasp the specificity of racism and racial
conflict in the US. They lead the analyst toward evolutionary

models which optimistically predict the gradual absorption of distinct groups into the mainstream of American political, economic and cultural life.[6] Theories based on these assumptions, therefore, reveal as much about the prevailing state of racial politics and racial ideology as they do about the nature of race relations.

Three approaches to race

Racial theory is shaped by actually existing race relations in any given historical period. Within any given historical period, a particular racial theory is dominant – despite often high levels of contestation. The dominant racial theory provides society with "common sense" about race, and with categories for the identification of individuals and groups in racial terms. Challenges to the dominant racial theory emerge when it fails to adequately explain the changing nature of race relations, or when the racial policies it prescribes are challenged by political movements seeking a different arrangement.

In Part I of this work, we examine recent racial theory in the United States. We argue that this theory is encompassed by three paradigmatic approaches to race and race relations – approaches based on the categories of ethnicity, class and nation. These approaches are *paradigms*[7] which have particular core assumptions and which highlight particular key variables. Racial paradigms serve as guides for research and have implicit and explicit policy and political action orientations.

There are, of course, limitations to this approach. We do not suggest that these three paradigms encompass all the racial theories generated during the period under consideration, but we do think that they embrace the vast bulk of them and demarcate the major lines of debate. Specific theories, and the paradigms themselves, are treated as *ideal types:* that is, the paradigms represent distillations for the purpose of analysis of complex and variegated theoretical arguments. A qualification to our approach, therefore, is the recognition that often a specific study cannot be neatly classified in one or the other paradigm. In many cases a particular work which we locate in one paradigm contains arguments which resemble those suggested by another paradigm. Any sophisticated theory, moreover, tries to take account of competing approaches by responding to particular elements – criticizing some, and integrating and synthesizing others.

Having made these qualifications, we suggest that in the contemporary period, race and racial dynamics in the United States have been theoretically understood by relying on one of three central categories: *ethnicity, class, or nation*. The dominant paradigm of race for the last half-century has been that of *ethnicity*. Ethnicity theory emerged in the 1920s as a challenge to then predominant biologistic and social Darwinist conceptions of race. Securing predominance by World War II, it shaped academic thinking about race, guided public policy issues, and influenced popular "racial ideology" well into the mid-1960s.

At that point ethnicity theory was challenged by *class*- and *nation*-based paradigms of race. These theoretical challenges originated with the black and other racial minority movements which rejected two central aspects of the ethnicity approach: the European immigrant analogy which suggested that racial minorities could be incorporated into American life in the same way that white ethnic groups had been, and the assumption of a fundamental, underlying American commitment to equality and social justice for racial minorities.

The appearance in the late 1970s and 1980s of a white "backlash" signalled the decline of these challenges and marked the resurgence of ethnicity theory. Although it has sustained major attacks and required reformulation in certain respects, the dominant paradigm of ethnicity has not been supplanted. Today ethnicity theory once again reigns supreme in the somewhat altered guise of *neoconservatism*.

In the following three chapters, we discuss the three paradigms of race as part of a broader understanding of the evolution of racial theory, ideology and politics from the 1960s to the 1980s. Our concern here is not to elaborate our own approach to racial theory. That theoretical viewpoint, advanced in the concept of *racial formation*, is presented in Chapter 4. Nor will we dwell on the political dynamics of race during the period in question. That subject is considered theoretically in Chapter 5, and historically in Chapters 6 and 7. Rather, our immediate purpose is to elaborate and evaluate the existing range of racial theory. By locating established approaches to race in the three paradigms and discussing the development of the dominant approach and its challengers, we shall set the stage for the introduction of our own perspective in the next section of the book.

We argue that, in the absence of a clear conception of race itself, studies of race developed during the postwar period had perforce to rely on one of the three central categories of ethnicity, class, or nation in their interpretations of racial dynamics in the United States. Race has not been afforded explicit theoretical primacy since the demise of the biologistic approaches of the previous eras. Thinking about race since that time has subordinated it to a supposedly "broader" category or conception. Thus the existing racial theories – both dominant and challenging – have all missed the manner in which race has been a *fundamental* axis of social organization in the United States. It is for this reason that, in the following chapters and in this book as a whole, we attempt to develop an alternative conception which does not treat race epiphenomenally or subsume it within a supposedly more fundamental category.

1
The dominant paradigm: ethnicity-based theory

The definition of the terms "ethnic group" and "ethnicity" is muddy. "The connotation of an ethnic 'group,' " William Peterson writes in the *Harvard Encyclopedia of American Ethnic Groups*,

> is that its members are at least latently aware of common interests. Despite the difficulty of determining at what point people become a group, that is, the point at which coherence becomes established, it is important to retain the fundamental distinction between a group and a category. . . .[1]

Theoretically, the ethnicity paradigm represents the mainstream of the modern sociology of race. The paradigm has passed through three major stages: a pre-1930s stage in which the ethnic group view was an insurgent approach, challenging the biologistic (and at least implicitly racist) view of race which was dominant at that time; a 1930s to 1965 stage during which the paradigm operated as the progressive/liberal "common sense" approach to race, and during which two recurrent themes – assimilationism and cultural pluralism – were defined; and a post-1965 phase, in which the paradigm has taken on the defense of conservative (or "neoconservative") egalitarianism against what is perceived as the radical assault of "group rights."

The ethnicity-based paradigm arose in the 1920s and 1930s as an explicit challenge to the prevailing racial views of the period. The pre-existing biologistic paradigm had evolved since the downfall of racial slavery to explain racial inferiority as part of a natural order of humankind. Whites were considered the superior race; white skin was the norm while other skin colors were exotic mutations which had to be explained.[2] Race was equated with distinct hereditary characteristics. Differences in intelligence, temperament and sex-

14

uality (among other traits) were deemed to be racial in character. Racial intermixture was seen as a sin against nature which would lead to the creation of "biological throwbacks." These were some of the assumptions in social Darwinist, Spencerist and eugenicist thinking about race and race relations.[3]

But by the early decades of the twentieth century biologism was losing coherence. It had come under attack by adherents of progressivism, and had also been called into question by the work of the "Chicago school" of sociology. The progressive attack was led by Horace Kallen, who also introduced the concept of *cultural pluralism*, which was to become a key current of ethnicity theory. The Chicago sociologists were led by Robert E. Park, who had been secretary to Booker T. Washington, and whose approach embodied the other major current of the ethnicity paradigm, *assimilationism*.[4]

In contrast to biologically oriented approaches, the ethnicity-based paradigm was an insurgent theory which suggested that race was a *social* category. Race was but one of a number of determinants of ethnic group identity or ethnicity. Ethnicity itself was understood as the result of a group formation process based on culture and descent.[5] "Culture" in this formulation included such diverse factors as religion, language, "customs," nationality and political identification.[6] "Descent" involved heredity and a sense of group origins, thus suggesting that ethnicity was socially "primordial," if not biologically given, in character. While earlier theorists did indeed assume this,[7] later ethnicity theory came to question the validity of any primordial sense of identity or attachment, arguing instead that these concepts too were socially constructed.[8]

Early ethnicity-based theory, considered in the US context, concentrated on problems of migration and "culture contact" (to use Park's phrase). The problems and foci generated by this approach have continued to preoccupy the school: incorporation and separation of "ethnic minorities," the nature of ethnic identity, and the impact of ethnicity on politics.[9]

With the advent of the vaguely egalitarian (racially speaking) vision of the New Deal[10] and of the anti-fascism of World War II (a war which was anti-racist on the Atlantic front but decidedly racist on the Pacific front), the ethnic paradigm definitively dislodged the biologistic view in what appeared to be a triumph of liberalism. There remained, to be sure, many survivals from the old theoretical system (Jim Crow retained its grip on the South, for example, which would prove crucial for racial events in the 1950s and 1960s), but in the main, cultural and intellectual acceptance of the inevitability and even desirability of integration was achieved. Politically, the 1948 confrontation between integrationists and segregationists within the Democratic Party – a battle won decisively if not absolutely by the integrationists – symbolized the consensual shift.

Yet this victory was a hollow one where racial minorities were concerned, for the new paradigm was solidly based in the framework of European (white) ethnicity, and could not appreciate the extent to which racial inequality differed from ethnic inequality. Were the historical experiences which racial minority groups encountered similar to those of white Europeans? Were the trajectories for their perceived eventual incorporation and assimilation the same? To these questions ethnicity theorists generally answered yes. Many minority activists and movement groups, though, disagreed.

Theoretical dominance

The chief debate between assimilationists and cultural pluralists *within* the ethnic group paradigm has been about the possibility of maintaining ethnic group identities over time, and consequently the viability of ethnicity in a society characterized by what one writer has labelled "Anglo-conformity,"[11] that is, the presence of a supposedly unitary majority culture. However, both currents agree on the existence of that culture, and both treat race as a component of ethnicity.

Insurgent ethnicity theory's main empirical reference point had been the study of immigration and the social patterns resulting from it. Park and his student Louis Wirth saw the development of ethnic enclaves and what Park called a "mosaic of segregated peoples" as stages in a cycle leading to assimilation.[12] Kallen's perspective, by contrast, had focused on the acceptance of different immigrant-based cultures. But both assimilationism and cultural pluralism had largely emphasized European, white immigrants, what Kallen called "the Atlantic migration." The origins of the concepts of "ethnicity" and "ethnic group" in the US, then, lay outside the experience of those identified (not only today, but already in Park's and Kallen's time), as *racial* minorities: Afro-Americans, Latin Americans, Native Americans and Asian Americans (blacks, browns, reds and yellows). The continuity of experience embodied in the application of the terms of ethnicity theory to both groups – to European immigrants and racial minorities – was not established; indeed it tended to rest on what we have labelled the *immigrant analogy*.

The appearance of Gunnar Myrdal's *An American Dilemma* in 1944 marked the ascent of the ethnicity paradigm to a position of theoretical dominance.[13] This monumental study, funded by the Carnegie Commission, was the product of the labors not only of its director and principal author, but also of an unequalled array of talented students of racial issues in the US.[14] Myrdal both challenged biologistic theories of racism and asserted the desirability of assimilation for blacks.[15] He argued that the "American Creed" of democracy, equality and justice had entered into conflict with black inequality, segregation and racial prejudice in general. In order to resolve this conflict, America would be called upon, sooner or later, to extend its "creed" to include blacks. Myrdal's assessment was optimistic about the ultimate resolution of this battle – the contradictions would give way to racial equality and the eventual integration of blacks into the mainstream of American life.

The positions of many of his American advisors (particularly Park's students such as E. Franklin Frazier and "enlightened" liberals such as Arnold Rose), and Myrdal's own views as well, were predicated on the European immigrant model of assimilation. The US had absorbed the immigrants, had eventually granted them their rights, and had seen them take their places as "Americans" despite the existence of considerable nativist hostility and prejudice against them. Was this not the essence of the "creed"? True, blacks presented this model with a stern challenge. Yet Myrdal and his associates firmly believed that black assimilation was an ineluctable imperative which presented the nation with a clear choice:

> If America in actual practice could show the world a progressive trend by which the Negro finally became integrated into modern democracy, all mankind would be given faith again – it would have reason to believe that peace, progress, and order are feasible. . . . *America is free to choose whether the Negro shall remain her liability or become her opportunity.*[16]

Assimilation was viewed as the most logical, and "natural,"

response to the dilemma imposed by racism. Indeed, Myrdal, drawing on the work of E. Franklin Frazier (as Daniel Patrick Moynihan was to do twenty years later) suggested that there was a "pathological" aspect to black culture which only full assimilation could cure.[17]

In its elevation to theoretical dominance with the Myrdal study, ethnicity theory derived its agenda from the political imperatives of the period: to condemn in the liberal terms of the war years the phenomenon of racial inequality, which smacked of the kinds of despotism the US was fighting; to modernize and mobilize American society in preparation for its postwar role of world leadership; and to distribute the seemingly limitless resources deriving from US hegemony – resources which were not only economic, but also political and cultural – to all at home, even as they were to be offered to the vanquished as well as American allies abroad. The ethnicity-based theoretical tradition, derived from the experiences of European immigrants, was extended in the conclusions of *An American Dilemma* so that it might apply as well to nonwhites, especially blacks.

In the 1960s Nathan Glazer and Daniel P. Moynihan attempted a further innovation in ethnicity theory, stimulated by the burgeoning civil rights movement. Glazer and Moynihan wished both to validate the assimilationist bent of previous ethnic group-based theory, and to reintroduce the theme of "ongoing ethnicity" or cultural pluralism. In *Beyond The Melting Pot* (1963) they sought to link *cultural* pluralism with *political* pluralism, the dominant construct in American political science, and thus seemingly to reconcile the paradigm's problem of ethnic group identity – assimilation vs. cultural pluralism, incorporation vs. preservation – at a stroke.[18] Glazer and Moynihan argued that immigrating groups were transformed, if hardly "melted," by their experiences in New York, emerging as communities distinct not only from each other and their pre-existing sociocultural milieux, but also from their communities of origin.

> Ethnic groups, then, even after distinctive language, customs, and culture are lost . . . are continually recreated by new experiences in America. The mere existence of a name itself is perhaps sufficient to form group character in new situations, for the name associates an individual, who actually can be anything, with a certain past, country, or race.[19]

Assimilation, they argued, does take place as individuals accultu-
rate and groups enter the political arena. Yet out of this very
process a separate identity emerges, which must sustain itself
culturally and deliver tangible political gains (as well as – ultimately
– economic gains, e.g. "upward mobility") to the group. It was thus
fundamental political interests, rather than factors such as primordial ties, cultural differences, or majoritarian resistance to incorporation which were ultimately decisive in the maintenance of
ethnic identities. Continuing with the same passage:

> But as a matter of fact, someone who is Irish or Jewish or Italian
> generally has other traits than the mere existence of the name
> that associates him [sic] with other people attached to the group.
> A man is connected to his group by ties of family and friendship.
> But he is also connected by ties of *interest*. The ethnic groups in
> New York are also *interest groups*.[20]

This political focus initially seemed quite compatible with the
racial conflicts of the 1950s and early 1960s. At that time ethnicity
theory was grappling with black attempts to achieve equality
through the civil rights movement. As seen through the lens of
ethnicity, the civil rights movement was a drive for black integration
and for the removal of any remaining forms of institutional/legal
discrimination. From the perspective of writers such as Glazer and
Moynihan or Milton Gordon, civil rights demands were intelligible
and comprehensible within the ethnicity framework, and deserved
the dominant paradigm's support. The civil rights movement was
trying to create for blacks the same conditions that white ethnics
had found: "opportunity" and relative equality (i.e. the absence of
formal discriminatory barriers, however much attitudinal prejudice
may have existed).[21] While debates about specific "affirmative"
measures such as busing existed,[22] the ethnicity school supported
such "negative" measures as the outlawing of discrimination to
create and maintain conditions of equality.[23]

Although virulent forms of racism persisted in the South, the
remedies for segregation were clear. The North, though, presented
a different set of problems for the ethnicity theorists. At first glance,
it was assumed that black equality had already been achieved there:

> One looked at the demands of the civil rights movement in 1963
> – equality in the vote, equality in the courts, equality in

representation in public life, equality in accommodations – saw that they existed more or less in New York City, and concluded that the political course of the Northern Negro would be quite different from that of the Southern Negro. He [sic] would become part of the game of accommodation politics – he already was – in which posts and benefits were distributed to groups on the basis of struggle, of course, but also on the basis of votes, money, and political talent, and one concluded that in this game Negroes would not do so badly.[24]

In other words, blacks already had equal opportunity in the North; what more could they demand? Once equal opportunity legislation along with its judicial and administrative enforcement were accomplished facts, it fell to blacks to follow in their "predecessors' " footsteps. Through hard work, patience, delayed gratification, etc., blacks could carve out their own rightful place in American society. In the North, where blacks were still recent "immigrants" (from the South), this would involve some degree of assimilation.[25] It would involve the development of a new post-immigration cultural identity, and it would require engagement in mainstream pluralist politics. Race relations would thus continue in what Nathan Glazer was later to call the "American ethnic pattern."

So, ethnicity theory assigned to blacks and other racial minority groups the roles which earlier generations of European immigrants had played in the great waves of the "Atlantic migration" of the nineteenth and early twentieth centuries. But racial minorities refused to play their assigned roles. Structural barriers continued to render the immigrant analogy inappropriate and the trajectory of incorporation did not develop as the ethnicity paradigm had envisioned. Many blacks (and later, many Latinos, Indians and Asian Americans as well) rejected *ethnic* identity in favor of a more radical *racial* identity which demanded group rights and recognition. Given these developments, ethnicity theory found itself increasingly in opposition to the demands of minority movements.[26] The ethnicity paradigm had to be reworked once again. The result was the phenomenon of *neoconservatism*.[27]

Remaining true to their earlier ideas, ethnicity theorists developed a conservative egalitarian perspective which emphasized the dangerous radicalism and (in their view) anti-democratic character of "positive" or "affirmative" anti-discrimination policies. State activities should be restricted, they argued, to guarantees of equality for individuals.

This position was not new. As we have noted, Gordon argued something similar as early as 1964. But the *doyens* of the ethnicity school, Glazer and Moynihan, were ambivalent about the group rights question in the 1960s. Indeed, Moynihan had *endorsed* positive anti-discrimination measures ("equality of result") in his famous "Report,"[28] though Glazer had warned about the principle's dangers early on.[29]

Some critical remarks on the ethnicity paradigm

Substantial criticism has been directed at the ethnicity school for its treatment of racially defined minorities as ethnically defined minorities, and for its consequent neglect of race *per se*. These arguments point to the limits of the immigrant analogy in addressing what was in many cases a qualitatively different historical experience – one which included slavery, colonization, racially based exclusion and, in the case of Native Americans, virtual extirpation. In addition, it has been argued, the paradigm tends to "blame the victims" for their plight and thus to deflect attention away from the ubiquity of racial meanings and dynamics. We share much of this critique, and will not recapitulate it here.[30] Instead we shall explore two less frequently noticed problems of the ethnicity approach to race: the social scientific, indeed methodological, limitations encountered by the ethnicity paradigm in its attempt to reduce race to an element of ethnicity, and the paradigm's consequent inability to deal with the particular characteristics of racial minority groups as a direct consequence of this reductionism. The first of these we call the "bootstraps model," the second we refer to as "they all look alike."

The "bootstraps model" As we have noted, substantial reworking of the ethnicity paradigm took place in the later 1960s and early 1970s. By 1975 Glazer and Moynihan felt themselves able to offer a general hypothesis on the dynamics of group incorporation: "Ethnic groups bring different norms to bear on common circumstances with consequent different levels of success – hence *group* differences in status."[31] The "group norms/common circumstances" correlation raises enormous problems, which can in turn

21

be traced back to the immigrant analogy. The key factor in explaining the success that an ethnic group will have in becoming incorporated into majority society (a goal whose desirability is unquestioned) is the values or "norms" which the group brings to bear on the general social circumstances it faces just as all other minorities have done. Since the independent variable is the "norms," the idea that "differences in status" could be affected by factors outside or even unrelated to the group is ruled out at the level of assumptions. Everything is mediated through "norms" internal to the group. If Chicanos don't do well in school, this cannot, even hypothetically, be due to low-quality education; it has instead to do with Chicano values. After all, Jews and Japanese Americans did well in inferior schools, so why can't other groups? Ongoing processes of discrimination, shifts in the prevailing economic climate, the development of a sophisticated racial ideology of "conservative egalitarianism" (or should we say "benign neglect"?) – in other words, all the concrete sociopolitical dynamics within which racial phenomena operate in the US – are ignored in this approach. It is the European immigrant analogy applied to all without reservation.[32]

"Common circumstances," by contrast, are relegated to the dependent variable. They are the universal conditions to which each ethnic group must accommodate. The assumption is made that each minority faces the majority society alone. Successful achievement of mobility – the achievement of high group status – reflects group willingness and ability to accept the norms and values of the majority. The "difference" that characterizes a minority group, once incorporated, will be outweighed by the "commonality" it shares with the majority.

In other words, something akin to Milton Gordon's notion of "structural assimilation"[33] is assumed to take place as immigrant groups pass beyond their "fresh off the boat" status and gain the acceptance of the majority. Yet this assumption is quite unwarranted with respect to racial minorities, whose distinctiveness from the white majority is often not appreciably altered by adoption of the norms and values of the white majority. It would in fact be just as plausible to assume the opposite: that in the case of racial minorities "common circumstances" consist in relatively permanent racial difference and nonincorporation.

The entire model for comparing and evaluating the success of ethnic groups in achieving higher status or in being incorporated into the majority society is limited by an unwillingness to consider whether there might be any special circumstances which racially defined minorities encounter in the US, circumstances which definitively distinguish their experiences from those of earlier European immigrants, and make the injunction to "pull yourselves up by your own bootstraps" impossible to fulfill.

"They all look alike" In what sense can racial minority groups be considered in ethnic group terms? In what sense is the category "black," for example, equivalent to the categories "Irish" or "Jewish"?

The ethnicity paradigm does acknowledge black "uniqueness" because of the particular historical experience of institutionalized discrimination rooted in slavery. Yet there is something awkward, something one-dimensional, about ethnicity theory's version of black exceptionalism. *"Blacks" in ethnic terms are as diverse as "whites."* They resist comparison to the Jews and Irish, and even to Mexican Americans or Japanese Americans. The notion of "uniqueness" doesn't go far enough because it is still posed within the ethnic group framework, while "black," like "white," is a palpably racial category.

In fact, with rare exceptions, ethnicity theory isn't very interested in ethnicity *among* blacks. The ethnicity approach views blacks as one ethnic group among others. It does not consider national origin, religion, language, or cultural differences among blacks, as it does among whites, as sources of ethnicity. It would be quite interesting to see how ethnicity theory might address the range of subgroupings represented in the US black community. What distinctions might it employ? Haitians? Jamaicans? Francophones? Georgians? Northern/southern? The black community has been intensively studied from an ethnographic standpoint, so there is no lack of materials for analysis.[34] But ethnicity theory has not delved to any significant extent into the meaning of these "ethnic" distinctions.

There is, in fact, a subtly racist element in this substitution – in which whites are seen as variegated in terms of group identities, but blacks "all look alike." In our view, this is nothing intentional, but simply the effect of the application of a paradigm based in white ethnic history to a racially defined group. Blacks are thus aggregated – and treated as the great exception – because they are so clearly racially identified in the US.

But this issue cannot be confined to blacks. Similar problems can be discerned in ethnicity-based treatments of other racially based categories: Native Americans, Latin Americans, and Asian Americans. The aggregation of Americans of Filipino, Japanese, Korean, Chinese and now Vietnamese, Laotian, Thai and Cambodian descent into the category "Asian American," for example, is clearly a racially based process. Ethnicity theorists might object that this is an improper exercise of "race-thinking," that there should be no recognition by the state of such a category, that these various groups should be able to maintain their ethnic identities and thus avoid "racialization."[35] But the majority of Americans cannot tell the difference between members of these various groups. They are racially identified – their identities are racially constructed – by processes far more profound than mere state policy formation.

2
The challenging paradigms: class-based theory

The class paradigm of race includes those approaches which, in Stuart Hall's characterization, argue that "Social divisions which assume a distinctively racial or ethnic character can be attributed or explained principally by reference to economic structures and processes."[1]

Our adoption of this formulation truly opens up a Pandora's box. To equate Hall's "economic structures and processes" with *class*, whether understood in the Marxian sense of relationship to the means of production, or in the Weberian sense of relationship to the mode of distribution (giving rise to particular "life chances"),[2] is to make a certain analytic leap. Indeed there is a significant economic literature on race, exemplified by the "neoclassical" approach of Gary Becker, which does not recognize the existence of classes at all, but confines itself narrowly to market relationships.

How, then, do we define the class paradigm of race, and how can the variety of approaches which emphasize "economic structures and processes" in their analyses of racial phenomena be categorized, linked and compared? Without entering into the theoretical complexities involved in specifying the nature of "the economic,"[3] it is possible to proceed simply by recognizing that class theories "principally" explain race by reference to economic processes, understood in the standard sense of the creation and use of material resources. Thus the inclusion of "neoclassical" approaches in the class paradigm does not create insurmountable problems, precisely because such treatments seek to establish the roots *in exchange relationships* of racial inequality. Once we are dealing with any sort of unequal exchange we have a "class" system, although particular analysts might prefer not to use this designation.[4]

Given this qualification of the class paradigm, we suggest that there are three general approaches contained within it. We designate these as the market, stratification and class-conflict approaches.[5] The three approaches look to different economic spheres – to market relations (exchange), systems of stratification (distribution), and processes of class conflict (production) – to provide their respective frameworks of analysis.

The market relations approach

In the 1950s and 1960s, debates around the nature of racial inequality in the United States revealed some glaring problems in neoclassical economic thought. Market-based economic models appeared to lack the capacity to explain racial discrimination. Race appears as an anomaly in an equilibrium-oriented theoretical system – an obstacle to market processes. Neoclassical theory suggested that the market itself, unhampered by an interventionist state, would eliminate racial discrimination. Writers such as Milton Friedman argued that this was in fact taking place.[6]

Three sources of disruption of market equilibrium, potentially capable of generating racial inequality, were recognized: an irrational prejudice or "taste for discrimination"; monopolistic practices, which grant "privileges" or "special benefits" to strategically placed groups, and hence create various interests and incentives for maintaining (or transforming) racial inequality; and disruptive state practices which interfere with the supposed equilibrating tendencies of the market.[7] Focus on each of these three destabilizing forces generated a particular account of the social dynamics of race.

The irrational prejudice or "taste for discrimination" model suggests that a society segregated into black and white[8] sectors, linked as "trading partners" but separated by white "distaste" for physical proximity to blacks, will indeed be gradually integrated by market pressures. In a model such as Becker's, however, this will take place only if countervailing irrationalities can be tamed by limited and judicious state interventionism.[9]

The monopolistic practices model suggests a society structured in the interests of all whites, who gain thereby through a systematic transfer of resources from nonwhites in a wide variety of fields. Whites, for example, can receive wages above the marginal utility rate for their labor and benefit from discriminatory pricing practices. Here too market forces are understood to be egalitarian, but the monopoly "cartel" which includes all whites is seen to impose inequalities in labor, capital and consumption goods markets in order to maximize white gain. The political and cultural dynamics of race are merely the expressions of these fundamental relationships, and various conflicts which are not immediately given in market-based terms (e.g. busing), can be explained by reference to imputed market-based interests.

The disruptive state interventionism model suggests a society in which inequality is in the interests of some, but not all whites. State policies such as minimum wage laws, labor law, licensing procedures in labor-intensive trades (barbering, taxi-driving, trucking, etc.), are undertaken in response to the demands of white workers (or, often, white-dominated trade unions) anxious to protect their jobs from open competition on the part of nonwhites. Thus the opportunities which white workers' immigrant parents and grand-parents seized to lift themselves out of poverty and to create viable ethnic community institutions (particularly small businesses and trades) are denied to minorities today. In this view, minorities and capital share an interest in free market economics, which the state and white workers act to obstruct. This perspective argues that racial politics and ideologies of equality often mask the fact that concrete economic avenues for advancement are blocked.[10]

Market exchange theories of race necessarily try to reconcile racial inequality with the equilibrium assumptions of their model. Accounting for racial phenomena in terms of market relations is an onerous task, which lends itself to a certain whimsicality in the formulation of hypotheses about why disequilibrating racially based interests arise. Market theories employ by far the purest form of economic determinism to be found in racial theory. These approaches conceive of racial phenomena rather monolithically in terms of (in)equality and discrimination in exchange. Racial interests are either cast in these terms or assumed to be irrational.

Certain elements of the market-based approach overlap with views deriving from other paradigms. For example, the disruptive state interventionism model of Sowell and Williams agrees with neoconservative ethnicity theories of race that racial policies should be guided by principles of individualism, and opposes demands for "equality of result." In similar fashion, the monopolistic practices model shares certain elements with nation-based analyses of race, especially those which stress the operation of "white skin privilege"[11] or of a "colonial labor principle" which allocates rights and resources differentially to groups on the basis of race. There are innumerable theoretical coincidences, along with patterns of agreement and influence, in the vast literature on race. These resemblances, however, should not be mistaken for theoretical accord. Market-based theories (which are class-oriented, economic theories) are based on quite different perceptions of what race *means* than are ethnicity- or nation-based approaches.

Stratification theory

Stratification approaches deal with the social distribution of resources – chiefly, though not exclusively, economic ones. Individuals receiving roughly equal incomes, or partaking of equal quantities of wealth, are deemed to have similar "life chances" and assigned to groups in a "status order" or ranked hierarchy of "classes." Various degrees of "mobility" are postulated among the ranks of the hierarchy and numerous noneconomic factors are analyzed as playing important roles in the stratification system's maintenance and modification over time.

Politics are also a crucial factor. In stratification theory the relationships of elites and masses, the dynamics of authority systems and forms of domination, and the overall shape of socio-political conflict are central preoccupations. In most respects these extra-economic factors reinforce the distribution dynamic. Patterns of elite rule, for example, are frequently "traced back" to the distribution of economic resources.

William J. Wilson's *The Declining Significance of Race* (1978) represents the most sophisticated application to date of stratification theory to racial issues – in this case, to the interpretation of emerging class cleavages within the black community. While Wilson accepts an economically determined stratification theory for previous epochs of US history (an "economic system," he suggests, shaped the "polity" and thereby structured and enforced "racial norms"), he argues that the contemporary period is one in which the state has developed "autonomy" in handling racial problems.[12] This does not negate the existence of an economically determined status order. Rather, it detaches "class" (i.e. status) categories from racial ones. According to Wilson, although black "life-chances" were formerly determined by racial stratification, since 1965 they have been shaped directly by "class" stratification. After state-enforced racial inequality was eliminated by civil rights legislation, blacks were admitted to the society-wide system of stratification, rather than being confined to a specific location by segregation. The results are a black community which is stratified into a small privileged "class" whose opportunities are equivalent to those of whites with similar high levels of training and skills, and a massive black "underclass" which is relegated to permanent marginality.

Wilson's book has been received by critics in a highly partisan fashion. Many radical writers have castigated the work, although some have found in it the justification for orthodoxy.[13] Conservative writers have appropriated Wilson's notion of a shift from racially based to class-based sources of black poverty to argue against egalitarian state interventionism itself. This is far from Wilson's own position. He appeals for state policies which will ameliorate the catastrophic impact of increased class cleavages in the black community, calling, for instance, for expansion of day care services available to low-income single mothers.[14]

Despite the many merits of Wilson's analysis, certain serious flaws remain. He appears to believe that since the mid-1960s a genuinely egalitarian racial state has existed in the United States, and further, that support for its policies is now a permanent feature of US politics. Yet one has only to consider electoral dynamics, or recent shifts in civil rights policy which legitimate a notion of "reverse discrimination" (that is, the supposedly invidious effects on *whites* of affirmative action and similar policies), to recognize that the ongoing (post-1965) racial contestation for and within the state is far from over.

Wilson's argument that the contemporary black community is stratified into a relatively small privileged "class" and a large black "underclass" suggests that race is no longer a salient linkage between those who have "made it" and their less fortunate "underclass" brethren. We consider, on the contrary, that the fate of the black middle class remains tied to the lower class precisely through racial dynamics which are structured into the US economy, culture and politics. First of all, personal, familial and community ties continue to interconnect the two strata despite attempts on the part of a few black intellectuals and some in the privileged strata to create a distinct "black bourgeois" community and culture.[15] Second, the very existence of educational and job opportunities of which middle-class blacks took advantage depended, and continues to depend, on the political action of the black majority.[16] Furthermore, many "privileged" blacks work in industries and economic sectors whose economic and political *raison d'être* is linked to the black "masses." Government workers, educators and other tertiary sector workers, for example, may have achieved middle-class status and incomes, but their employment relates directly to the management, marketing and servicing of the black community as a whole.[17] An extended period of reaction which included significant curtailment of the welfare state, underfunding of public education, restriction of health and social security benefits, etc., would prove massively detrimental, not only to the black "under-class" but to "middle-class" blacks as well.

As in the case of market-based theories, stratification theories overlap with viewpoints originating in other paradigms. Where they emphasize "caste," that is, the closing off of "mobility" in a status order with racial characteristics, they resemble certain nation-based views which deny the potential for integration across racial (or colonizer/colonized) lines.[18] Where they focus on those characteristics of the system which facilitate "mobility," such as the avenues available to various minority groups for economic advancement, they resemble ethnicity-based views. Within the class paradigm, there is also considerable variation among stratification analyses. For example, they may tend toward market-based approaches, if decisionistic models of trade and association are judged to generate status disparities relatively automatically;[19] or they may tend toward class-conflict perspectives, if segmentations or splits in the labor market are thought to play a major role in assigning particular locations in the status order to different racial groups.

Class conflict theory

"Classical" Marxism never explicitly addressed issues of race and racial conflict, but it did consider the problem of divisions within the working class and the nature of "national oppression." As such, the

Marxian legacy has had a profound impact on both class-based and nation-based paradigms of race.

Class conflict theories of race in the 1960s posed a fundamental challenge to ethnicity theory rooted in an idea central to Marxist analysis – the concept of *exploitation*. Exponents of this paradigm recognize the existence of racial oppression, but regard class divisions as the fundamental source of exploitation in society. Class conflict theory asserts the centrality of the "social relations of production" in structuring classes and class relationships.[20] This view then proceeds to situate racial conflict within the class dynamics of society as a whole. There are many ways of doing this, including crudely economic determinist as well as highly mediated "neo-Marxist" conceptions of the class-race relationship.

Effects of class conflict upon race relations are noted at all "levels" of society, but as in the market-based and stratification variants, class conflict theory infers racially oriented political interests from economic ones. An interest in shaping labor or immigration policy, for example, may be attributed to capitalists who seek higher profits and more effective controls over the labor process through strategies of "divide and rule"[21] or to white labor's efforts to limit competition from lower-paid minority workers.[22] Ideologies of racial inferiority are explained in a similar manner, as "grounded" in racially defined economic interests.

It is not coincidental that class conflict approaches strongly resemble market-based perspectives since both rely on conceptions of the *labor market* to situate their views of the race-class relationship. This emphasis on the labor market derives from the tendency, explicit in all "classical" and much "neo-" Marxism, to understand class as a production-relation. Within this framework it is quite difficult to specify *anything* about actual production relationships that is specifically racial.[23]

If we rule out mechanistic and dogmatic class conflict theories, the field can be understood as ranging from attempts, such as those of Cox and Reich, to establish a capitalist class interest in racial inequality,[24] to efforts, such as that of Bonacich and Prager, to demonstrate a working-class interest therein.[25]

Class conflict theories of race may be divided into two opposing tendencies, each focused on the labor market. These two viewpoints are, first, a "divide and rule" conception which rests on the notion of labor market *segmentation* as the key determinant of racially based inequalities in production relations; and second, an "exclusionism" perspective which suggests that a *split* labor market is the central source of these inequalities. Despite the diametric opposition of the two positions, there is agreement between them on the primacy of class conflict over racial conflict. But it must be stressed that in both of these approaches, racially differentiated relationships to the means of production are the result, not of production relationships themselves, but of market or exchange relationships.

Segmentation theory has been developed in the Marxian tradition most centrally by Michael Reich (in collaboration with David M. Gordon and Richard Edwards), and in the institutionalist or stratification tradition by Michael Piore and Peter Doeringer.[26]

Reich, Gordon and Edwards have developed the segmentation perspective in two basic ways: first, Reich has explored the microeconomics of racial inequality in a rigorous critique of the neoclassical or market-based approach.[27] Second, Gordon, Edwards and Reich have chronicled the historical evolution of labor control and labor market processes in the US, linking these to long-run trends or "swings" in the capitalist accumulation process. This evolution, they argue, has culminated in a segmented labor system in the contemporary period.[28]

In his micro-economic analysis, Reich develops evidence for the "divide and rule" hypothesis by measuring the effects of racial (in)equality on wage levels and on the distribution of social spending in such areas as education and welfare. He effectively demonstrates the limits of the market-based approach by introducing class variables (measurements of class cohesion and class segmentation across racial lines) which account far better for empirically observed inequalities than do pure market-based variables. Finally, he attempts to synthesize the class conflict and neoclassical modes of analysis. Concerned to emphasize the structural aspects of discrimination, Reich employs a "bargaining power theory." Because a working class which lacks unity will exercise less leverage over employers, Reich argues, "Capitalists benefit from racial divisions whether or not they have individually or collectively practiced racial discrimination."[29]

The problem with this is that it relegates subjectivity to the sidelines of the model. Class organization – across racial lines – is seen as the objective and primary necessity which all workers face.

Racially based organization and identification is implicitly a form of "false consciousness." This may work fine in the abstract, but concretely it would require the suppression of racially defined experience in order to operate. Historically speaking, the call for class unity across racial lines has amounted in practice to an argument that nonwhites give up their racially based demands in favor of "class" unity on white terms. This will not be achieved by appeals to "class unity" or by reliance on "bargaining power theory," which merely offer an abstraction to minorities confronted by racial inequities in the workplace.

In Reich's study, then, economic interests come strongly to the fore, and political/ideological factors appear as mere manifestations of underlying economic relationships. But in practice economic interests are defined politically and ideologically. The identities which social actors take on are defined ideologically; they are the essence of ideology. Am I a worker first or a Chicano first? By placing so much emphasis on the structural nature of racial inequality (which he does to combat conspiratorial and cartelization theories of discrimination), Reich upholds a rather strong economic determinism of his own. This problem is not limited to his treatment, of course, but is endemic to the class paradigm in general.

In *Segmented Work, Divided Workers*, Gordon, Edwards and Reich attempt a synthesis of a different sort: here accumulation processes and the dynamics of capitalist labor control are seen to be woven together. Two themes drawn from this ambitious work and essential to the segmentation framework are particularly relevant to the present study: the argument that labor market segmentation "played a major role in channeling the effects of past and present race and sex discrimination,"[30] and the contention that the segmentation system began to "decay" in the early 1970s. Because the authors focus their account on labor relations, processes and structures of control, it is quite understandable that they should seek to locate "black" labor within the segmentation model they defined earlier[31] (and refine substantially in this work). There should be no illusions, however, that this focus addresses the basic dynamics of race. Indeed when the authors assert that "black protest" in the 1960s placed strains on the segmentation system, this political intervention by blacks appears as entirely exogenous to their model. They note that "blacks became increasingly intolerant of low-wage

100008   LIBRARY
COLBY-SAWYER COLLEGE
NEW LONDON, N.H. 03257

labor and lack of opportunities for advancement,"[32] but *why* this should have occurred is not explained.

Although Gordon, Reich and Edwards place great emphasis on the role played by labor market segmentation in structuring the post-World War II accumulation process, they make no special effort to explore the racial dimensions of this segmentation. Race (along with sex) merely furnishes one of the major axes upon which the working class is assumed to be divided.

This line of argument carries less weight today than it might have in the past. In the contemporary US, as an analysis like Wilson's shows, race cuts *across* class lines as well as dividing classes internally. It is thus extremely important to understand the different axes along which "workers" (or if you prefer, "social actors") are organized, linked in the system of social reproduction, and "constructed" as ideological subjects. Only on the basis of such an analysis is it possible to understand how political opposition takes shape, how, for example, black struggles for integration of public facilities in the South during the 1950s could have expanded into the confrontation with the overall capitalist accumulation process which Gordon, Reich and Edwards themselves note.

Today it is more difficult than ever to understand race in terms of an economically determined formula of class belonging (for example, that class is determined by relationship to the means of production). It would be more accurate to say that race and class are competing modalities by which social actors may be organized.

Problems of this sort have led Gordon, Edwards and Reich to conclude that the segmentation system has begun a phase of "decay." "Decay," in their theory, is the breakdown phase into which each epochal arrangement of the capitalist accumulation/labor control system enters as internal conflicts and external pressures challenge its organizational and reproductive capacity. In the 1960s and early 1970s, Gordon, Edwards and Reich assert, the signs of decay were becoming apparent in the system of labor market segmentation. Although they previously informed us that "black protest" strained the system, the major reasons cited for the onset of decay are located at the point of production: productivity slowdowns, increased rank-and-file militance, etc.[33] The fact that the authors make no effort to interpret these phenomena in terms of the racial conflicts and protests which characterized this period, and which they recognize as a key source of political opposition at this time, testifies to the limited explanatory capacity of the segmentation model in accounting for racial dynamics.

The *split labor market* approach has been most effectively advanced by Edna Bonacich.[34] Her conception stresses the existence of a group of "dominant workers" which is threatened by the competition of "cheap labor." *Class* conflict takes place between capital and the "dominant" group, which seeks to maintain its wage levels, defend whatever control it may have of production processes, etc. *Racial/ethnic* conflict takes place between "dominant" and "subordinate" workers as the former seek to prevent the latter from bidding down the price of their labor.

The exclusionist movements that arise as a result are not racially motivated or "nationalist" *per se*, but "the product of historical accident which produced a correlation between ethnicity and the price of labor."[35] They are the result of pre-existing differences between the costs of racially (and ethnically) defined labor, differences which in turn stem from the existence of a worldwide division of labor, migration patterns, unequal exchange and uneven development processes, etc.[36]

Far from enhancing capitalist control over labor, as the segmented labor market is said by its theorists to do, the split labor market is seen as problematic for capital. Bonacich argues that while the existence of a cheap labor pool creates an obvious incentive for lowering wage costs and thus boosting profits, the resistance of dominant labor to these tactics forces capitalists into accommodations they would otherwise not choose to make:

> Capital turns toward the cheap labor pool as a more desirable work force, a choice consistent with the simple pursuit of higher profits. Higher priced labor resists being displaced, and the racist structures they erect to protect themselves are antagonistic to the interests of capital.[37]

Bonacich confronts the "divide and rule" approach of the segmentation theorists with the following counterarguments: (1) labor is already differentiated in price before employers can engage it; (2) offering a positive incentive to dominant workers would be inconsistent with the pronounced capitalist preference for tactics of virulent struggle; (3) indeed, cheap labor would be (and historically has been) a better target than "dominant" labor for "bribes" and similar tactics.[38]

The split labor market approach fares no better than the segmentation argument in accounting for the complexities of US race relations. While it recognizes that in practice class modalities of organization are often less salient than racial ones, the "exclusionism" perspective is as absolute as the "divide and rule" view in imputing political interests and ideological meanings to the various economically defined class and racial actors it depicts. This eliminates the possibility that "class unity" might prevail at one moment or on one terrain, while racial conflict might rule the day on another. The "split" labor market approach, as much as the "segmentation" one, refuses to engage concrete politics and ideologies of race, insisting instead on imposing a highly schematic and economically determined model of the race/class relationship.

Whether understood as "dual," "segmented," or "split," the labor market exhibits a great variety of forms and axes of differentiation: "internal labor markets,"[39] "monopoly, competitive, and state" sectors,[40] gender-based categories, undocumented workers' jobs, "upper primary" and "subordinate primary" categories, etc.[41] These overlap and cut across racial lines of division. It thus becomes problematic to assert for example that "dominant" (or "primary sector") labor is white, unionized, or even (given recent debates on the question) more "skilled." Segmented or split labor markets organized along racial lines cannot be demonstrated to exist in the US today with the same degree of definition they might have possessed in the past. As Lever-Tracy observes with respect to immigrant labor,

> To explain the finer contours of segmentation, the
> concentration of immigrant workers in some productive jobs or
> their exclusion from others, the formation or the avoidance of
> ethnic work groups, and so on, requires knowledge of the
> various strategies pursued by employers and by workers (both
> native and immigrant) in their conflicts with each other.[42]

In short, segmentations and splits must be understood politically and ideologically, rather than as "objective" systems of division within the labor market, and beyond this, within the working class as a whole.

If "strategies" (or more broadly, political and ideological factors) are recognized to be central to these conflicts, it is clear that any correspondence between racially defined groupings and sectors of the labor market – "dominant-subordinate," "core-peripheral," "primary-secondary," or "monopoly-competitive-state" – is at best highly inaccurate, and at worst quite spurious. Indeed it is rather obvious that racial categories cut across class lines and will not serve adequately to classify social actors even in terms of class membership, not to mention among classes.[43] Nor is the concept of "labor market" equivalent to that of "working class."

The "class conflict" perspective on race is thus no more workable than the market- or stratification-based approaches; it does, however, bring to the fore the necessity of understanding classes as the "effects of struggles."

Racial dynamics must be understood as determinants of class relationships and indeed class identities, not as mere consequences of these relationships. Recent analyses of class formation processes have suggested as much.[44] Once it is recognized that classes too are not objectively given entities, but formed and transformed over time, it becomes possible to view sectoral organization in production much more flexibly. We can then investigate how, at any historical point, sectoral lines of demarcation, both within and among classes, are themselves the objects of political struggle, how they are secured by "coercion" against challenge, and made flexible and adaptable by "consent."[45] Such an approach could explore the meaning of class for racial minorities in terms which avoid mere assimilation of racial categories into class ones.[46]

As the segmentation theorists have recognized, capitalist interests in profit maximization and (very importantly) in control of production processes have at times been furthered by "balkanization" of the labor force, at other times by its homogenization. Yet there is little in either the segmentation or the split labor market analyses which comprehends class formation in broad enough terms to suggest a theory of racial dynamics. Race remains an exogenous element to both conceptions. Both adopt a "zero-sum" approach in which either capitalists or white workers "gain" what minority workers "lose." On this economic "base," which has much more in common with market-based theory than with a class formation perspective, an epiphenomenal racial "superstructure" is quite easily erected, in which political interests and racial as well as subjective identities are assigned to the various actors (themselves defined in simplistic terms) in the more "fundamental" drama of class conflict. In our view, as will be seen, such an approach hardly begins to inquire into the sources and contours of racial dynamics.

3
The challenging paradigms: nation-based theory

The emergence of black nationalism in the mid-1960s ruptured the tenuous unity of liberal and radical factions within the civil rights movement and signalled a growing disillusionment with the moderate political agenda of nonviolence and integration. The rise and popularity of black nationalism initiated an intense theoretical and strategic debate about the nature of racism and the future of black politics in the US.

The nation-based analysis of black oppression and resistance had, of course, its historical antecedents. The refusal of integrationist solutions could be traced back at least to the repatriation movements of the mid-nineteenth century, led by men such as Martin Delany and Paul Cuffe.[1] The Pan-Africanist and Marxist-Leninist traditions had also elaborated nationalist analyses, and a substantial current of cultural nationalism existed whose components could be discerned in DuBois's *The Souls of Black Folk*,[2] in the Harlem Renaissance of the 1920s, and in the influential writings of Harold Cruse during the 1950s and 1960s.[3] Strong nationalist traditions could also be found in other minority communities, notably among Puerto Ricans, Mexican Americans, and Native Americans.

The nation-based paradigm, to a far greater extent than the ethnicity- or class-based approaches, is a theoretical convergence, a resultant of disparate currents. Nationalist currents have always existed in the US – in the form of minority-based political movements – responding to perceived failures of racial accommodation and integration. Nation-based approaches to race also have a long theoretical tradition, which analyzes in diverse ways the realities of racial separation and white supremacy. In the postwar period, nation-based approaches have taken on an additional theoretical dimension: the critical rejection of ethnicity-based racial theory.

Despite the wide range of specific approaches, nation-based theory is fundamentally rooted in the dynamics of *colonialism*. Colonialism in the age of capitalism differed from previous imperial systems in that it came to encompass the entire world. Launched from Europe in the fifteenth century, it reached its zenith in the nineteenth century, by which time all nations and territories had been assigned a place in "the modern world system."[4] Although in a state of disarray and breakdown today, the legacy of the colonial order remains in a variety of forms, extending from the position of international frontiers drawn in much of the colonized world by the ruling powers to the existence of spheres of influence descended from systems of colonial rule,[5] and indeed to the very contours of the international division of labor, based on unequal exchange and the domination of the "periphery" by the "core." In the nation-based paradigm, racial dynamics are understood as products of colonialism and, therefore, as outcomes of relationships which are global and epochal in character.

Framing the paradigm in this way has several advantages. First, it emphasizes the relationships among the different elements of racial oppression – inequality, political disenfranchisement, territorial and institutional segregation, cultural domination – in contrast to the ethnicity or class paradigms which focus on a few aspects (or even one "fundamental" aspect) of the social order in an attempt to explain racial dynamics. Recognition of the centrality of the colonial heritage also provides an alternative to other, more taxonomic approaches to nation-based theories of race. Many writers have delineated, for example, "varieties of black nationalism:" bourgeois, proletarian, reformist, revolutionary, cultural, religious, economic, educational, etc.[6] While efforts to catalog the range of nationalist positions within specific minority group traditions, and to trace debates within these traditions, obviously have merit,[7] they often reveal a notable lack of specificity about the *meaning* of nation-based categories in such approaches. Nationalism is easily reduced to minority militance or separatism, for example, if no effort is made to specify its historical and theoretical origins, in particular minority experiences of colonialism.

While not comparable in many respects, we include Pan-Africanism, cultural nationalism, Marxist debates on "The National Question," and perspectives focusing on internal colonialism as specific analyses of race and racism which take shape within the nation-based paradigm. What these approaches share is their reliance on elements derived from the dynamics of colonialism to demonstrate the continuity of *racial* oppression from its origins in the *national* oppression prevailing in colonialism's heyday. Chief among these is the use of racial categories to distinguish members of the oppressor and oppressed "nations" – the colonizers and the colonized. Several consequences of these arguments may be specified: the explicit demand for organizations and movements uniformly composed of the "colonized" (i.e. the victims of racial oppression), the need for "cultural autonomy" to permit the development of those unique characteristics which the colonized group has developed or preserved through the ordeal of subjugation, or the necessity of "national liberation" to uproot the colonial heritage and restructure society on a nonracial basis.

Pan-Africanism

The roots of Pan-Africanism can be traced back to the black repatriation movements of Martin Delany, Paul Cuffe, and others in the mid-nineteenth century. In the twentieth century, Pan-Africanism took shape on two fronts: the first was a series of international conferences held in Europe and the US from 1900 to 1945, most of them organized by W.E.B. DuBois.[8] These conferences were oriented primarily toward decolonization of Africa and had relatively little US domestic impact.

The second front of Pan-Africanist activity was the formation, largely in the US, of the Universal Negro Improvement Association, led by Marcus Garvey.[9] The UNIA had unprecedented success in mobilizing blacks, numbering millions of adherents at its height in the 1920s. Garvey sought to unite blacks throughout the world in a movement for the "redemption" of Africa, which he envisioned as a "racial empire." For him and his followers, Africa existed not only on the continent but also in the diaspora which slavery had visited on its inhabitants and their descendants. Thus the fates of blacks throughout the world were linked. The liberation and reconstruction of the African homeland would allow blacks finally to overcome the racial oppression which had sustained colonialism.

Garvey was greatly influenced by the doctrines of Booker T. Washington, specifically those promoting separate economic development. Garvey's economic argument, however, went beyond Washington's in two respects: first, he denounced the exploitation of Africa and African labor throughout the world.[10] Second, he saw the black population of the United States not only in the "self-help" terms of Washington, but as "a vanguard for Africa's redemption. . . . He believed that if the Negroes were economically strong in the United States, they would be able to redeem Africa and establish a worldwide confraternity of black people."[11]

For all its excesses and errors, the most notorious being its *rapprochement* with the Ku Klux Klan,[12] the Garvey movement represents one of the founding pillars of modern Pan-Africanism,[13] and stands as a crucial source for much other black nationalism as well.[14] Indeed it still represents the highwater mark of mass black political mobilization, rivalled only by the movements of the 1960s. In this respect it is entirely appropriate to treat Garveyism as the archetype of the Pan-Africanist tradition in the United States.[15]

Pan-Africanism maintained a limited foothold in the US through the contributions of DuBois, Padmore and C.L.R. James. When Malcolm X broke with the Nation of Islam in 1964 to form the Organization of Afro-American Unity, making a series of well-publicized trips to Africa and attempting to enlist the support of African governments in denouncing US racism at the United Nations, he dramatically stimulated black interest in African issues. With the advent of "black power," the contributions of Malcolm, Nkrumah, Frantz Fanon and, later, Amilcar Cabral and Walter Rodney received new attention in the US, and contributed to the Pan-African canon. Stokely Carmichael in particular moved to embrace Pan-Africanism after 1967.[16]

Pan-Africanism enjoyed a further resurgence in the early 1970s, providing what in retrospect can only be seen as an illusion of unity for many nationalists: the reference point of Africa. The precise character of the illusion was that US political reference points could be subordinated to African ones. In 1975 even this fell apart in debates over the Angolan revolution. "Left" Pan-Africanists supported the MPLA, thereby accepting (often dogmatically) some version of Marxism and rejecting the racial determinism of "right" Pan-Africanists, who sided with UNITA.[17]

The power of the Pan-Africanist perspective remains its ability to link the specific forms of oppression which blacks face in various societies with the colonialist exploitation and underdevelopment of Africa. The impact this theoretical current had in the US stemmed from its argument that black identity conferred membership in a single worldwide black "nation" – the African diaspora itself.

Cultural nationalism

Cultural nationalism has had a particularly strong hold in the black community, where its roots can be traced back at least to the Harlem Renaissance of the 1920s.[18] As a broader phenomenon, however, cultural nationalist perspectives have been enunciated and practiced in nearly all racially defined communities.[19] Cultural nationalism has focused less on the political and economic elements of the nation-based approach than it has on *cultural* elements which give rise to collective identity, community, and a sense of "people-hood."

Probably the most devoted and incisive cultural nationalist theorist has been Harold Cruse. In his early and highly original essay entitled "Rebellion or Revolution?" and his massive and controversial *The Crisis of the Negro Intellectual*,[20] Cruse argued that "The only observable way in which the Negro rebellion can become revolutionary in terms of American conditions is for the Negro movement to project the concept of Cultural Revolution."[21]

Cruse stressed the unique conditions facing American blacks, conditions which, while related to those encountered by other victims of colonialism, were unlike those of the African continent, the West Indies, or elsewhere. Cruse also accepted certain "domestic colonialism" concepts; indeed, he gave voice to them as early as 1962.[22] Anticipating the "black power" view, he criticized the civil rights movement in the early 1960s for being dominated by liberal ideas and demands: "This Negro rebellion, mistakenly called by some the Negro revolution, is not revolutionary because it projects no new ideas beyond what have already been ratified in the democratic philosophy of the American Constitution."[23]

He proposed that the movement "incorporate . . . a cultural program along with its economic, social and political programs."[24] A "cultural program," in Cruse's view, would recognize both the unique characteristics of black cultural traditions, and the essential part that these cultural elements – for example in music, art or language – played in the cultural life of the US. Cruse suggested that the black movement focus its demands on "the creation and distribution of cultural production in America."[25] The ultimate aim of this challenge, Cruse argued, was "the revolutionizing . . . of the entire apparatus of cultural communication and placing it under public ownership."[26]

This approach, needless to say, raised as many questions as it answered. How the cultural apparatus could be so transformed, how blacks could affect cultural production under the proposed new "revolutionary" conditions, and what would be the ultimate social and political impact of such a change, were only a few of the issues Cruse did not address. What was significant about his work, however, was not its immediate practical application. Rather, his accomplishment lay in the development of a culturally based radical perspective. His positions anticipated debates between integrationists and nationalists in the later 1960s and 1970s. He thus re-opened questions that had lain dormant for nearly half a century.[27] In many ways Cruse explored the terrain upon which later, lesser figures of this current, such as Ron Karenga, Imamu Amiri Baraka and Haki Madhubuti would stand.[28]

Many black nationalists embraced African values, traditions, culture and language through Pan-Africanism, while others became adherents of groups such as Karenga's US organization or Baraka's Spirit House in Newark, without becoming Pan-Africanists politically. Cultural nationalism had many indirect effects on black "lifestyle:" clothes, hair, language and art reflected the perspective's upsurge. African heritage was often invoked to support domestic ideological and political aims.[29]

Cultural nationalism was by no means limited to the black movement. In the Chicano movement, for example, it arose in the early 1970s, basing itself in the concept of *Aztlan*, particularly as developed in quasi-mythical form by Rodolfo "Corky" Gonzales. The appeal of *Aztlan*, the lost Mexico of the North, evoked traditional Mexican cultural values untainted by Anglo domination. This symbolism was then applied to present-day realities of Chicano life.[30] Such reference systems represented less any real possibility of forging a separate Afro-American or Chicano "nation" within the territorial boundaries of the US (despite occasional illusions to the contrary) than efforts to unify previously fragmented minority groups by forging collective cultural identities.

Black cultural nationalism degenerated in the late 1960s and early 1970s as its discourse and symbolism was increasingly coopted and commodified. There was, it turned out, nothing particularly radical about afros, dashikis or the concept of "soul." As Adolph L. Reed Jr. noted:

> [T]he intellectual climate which came to pervade the movement was best summarized in the nationalists' exhortation to "think black". . . . Truth became a feature of the speaker's "blackness," i.e. validity claims were to be resolved not through discourse but by the claimant's manipulation of certain banal symbols of legitimacy.[31]

Demographic, economic and political fissures within the black community – whose "unity" and "peoplehood" had been central features of cultural nationalist theory – increasingly became too obvious to ignore. In the face of these changes, leading adherents moved on to new political horizons. Some, notably Baraka, made spectacular and belated conversions to Marxism-Leninism and Maoism, subsuming their original "racial" projects under broader "class" ones.

Interestingly, cultural nationalists have always manifested a certain disdain for political activity, especially normal politics, whether reform-oriented or radical. Their preference has been for building "countercultural" institutions, and, where necessary, for elite-led negotiations with the white power structure. A willful neglect of key political determinants of race – the racial state, class conflict, the politics of alliance and coalitions – ultimately doomed many cultural nationalist projects to irrelevance as US racial formation processes overtook their models. Cultural nationalist projects which sought to create minority "nations" founded on common cultural reference points were never politically viable. The real accomplishment of cultural nationalist currents was in the nature of "consciousness-raising." They underscored the centrality of cultural domination in the logic of racial oppression, and stressed the importance of "cultures of resistance" in unifying and promoting collective identity among the oppressed.

The "national question" and Marxist debates

Classical Marxism viewed nations and national boundaries as increasingly meaningless as world capitalism inexorably penetrated every corner of the planet. Marx and Engels stated this perspective clearly in *The Communist Manifesto* and view it as a "progressive" feature of the unfolding capitalist order:

> National differences and antagonisms between peoples are daily more and more vanishing, owing to the development of the bourgeoisie, to freedom of commerce, to the world market, to uniformity in the mode of production and in the conditions of life corresponding thereto.[32]

It is far from clear that this view was their final word on the subject, for the idea of the abolition of national boundaries and antagonisms is contradicted by other writings of Marx during the same period.[33] When Marx begins to write on the national question (with specific reference to Ireland), he argues that the bourgeoisie not only maintains but *heightens* national antagonisms. National hostilities are engendered by: (1) the struggle to control world markets, which creates conflicts among capitalist powers; (2) the exploitation of colonies, which creates antagonism between "oppressed" and "oppressor" nations; and (3) the use of nationalism as an ideological tool to detract proletarian attention from class antagonisms.

This contradictory stance towards the persistence or demise of nations is further complicated by an implicit "stage" theory of development which views colonial penetration and plunder as "progressive" events in so far as they rupture traditional social relations and supplant them with capitalist ones.

The dilemma of what posture Marxists should take toward forms of oppression which were viewed in essentially nonclass terms was not resolved by Marx and Engels and formed the basis for significant debates on the "national question" during the Second International. The polemical exchange between Lenin and Luxemburg on the national question revolves around the "right of nations to self-determination." Lenin argued that all nations should be free from national oppression and enjoy the right to determine their own destiny.[34] Luxemburg was critical of this "right to self-determination," which led in her view to a certain pandering to the aspirations of the national bourgeoisies of the "oppressed" countries. Both Lenin and Luxemburg attempted to steer a course between positions which asserted an unqualified right to national/cultural autonomy, and a position which completely denied the legitimacy of nationalist aspirations.[35]

The legacy of these debates on the national question was subsequently invoked to analyze the situation of blacks in the United States. Prior to 1928, the Communist Party of the United States attributed no special role or status to blacks (or other "national minorities") within the general class struggle. Comintern discussions between 1928 and 1930, however, resulted in the thesis that blacks in the southern region known as the Black Belt (named for the soil) constituted a nation and were therefore entitled to "self-determination" – including the right of political secession. Blacks in the North were considered an oppressed "national minority" whose salvation was to be sought in solidarity with white workers in the struggle for socialism.

The criteria for this thesis were drawn from a pamphlet by Joseph Stalin, who in 1908 had proposed four defining characteristics of a nation: "A nation is a historically constituted, stable community of people, formed on the basis of a common language, territory, economic life, and psychological make-up manifested in a common culture."[36]

The "Black Nation Thesis" was meant to resolve contradictions within the party due to racism and to compete for black support with Garveyism and other supposedly "bourgeois" separatist trends.

The Communist Party adhered only fitfully to this increasingly marginal analysis. Between 1936 and the early 1950s, the right to self-determination was subordinated to the New Deal and the war against fascism. Between 1955 and 1959, the party moved to discard the thesis entirely, recognizing that black migration from the South had eroded its political viability. After dying this slow death, the thesis was exhumed by various Marxist-Leninist groups in the 1970s.[37]

There is no consensus about the application, or indeed the meaning, of the Black Nation Thesis on the Marxist-Leninist left. Thus, debates both recapitulate discussions in the Second (and Third) International, and overlap with ongoing academic debate. There has been discussion on: (1) the application of Stalin's criteria (Do blacks constitute a nation?); (2) the material basis of racism (Is racism merely a capitalist tool to divide the working class? Are blacks "superexploited"?); (3) the nature of nationalism (Is nationalism reactionary or revolutionary in character and in what instances?); and (4) the right of self-determination (Does this include separatism?).

Lacking an orthodox Marxist theory of racism, and unable to examine US society without a comforting pillow of citations from the "classics," Marxist-Leninist groups have performed some strenuous theoretical contortions in their efforts to apply the literature on the "national question" to racial dynamics in the US. In these approaches national categories are frequently substituted for racial ones. This done, the corresponding political rights (e.g. self-determination for "legitimate" nations) can be asserted. The result has been confusion and endless debate over the appropriate criteria for "nationhood."[38] For Marxist-Leninists, nation-based approaches became little more than a conventional way to deal with the messy and untheorized problem of race and racism.[39]

Internal colonialism

The internal colonialism perspective has been applied to national movements in many countries, among them France,[40] Peru,[41] South Africa[42] and Great Britain.[43] In the United States the concept achieved great currency in the late 1960s and early 1970s (although earlier formulations, such as that of Cruse, can be found), when various writers employed it to account for the upsurge in racial minority militance. Radical nationalist movements (re)surfaced in black, Chicano, Native American, Puerto Rican and even Asian American communities at this time; these groups generally rejected reform-oriented politics, preferring to link their struggles with those of such national liberation movements as the Vietnamese, Algerian or Chinese revolutions.

Internal colonialism approaches attempted the synthesis of different aspects of racial oppression: economic, political and cultural, through the invocation of a colonial model. In most cases they appealed as well to nationalist forms of mobilization against this generalized system of oppression. Among the elements of internal colonialism which analysts identified were:

   (1) a colonial *geography* emphasizing the territoriality or spatial arrangement of population groups along racial lines;

   (2) a dynamic of *cultural domination and resistance*, in which racial categories are utilized to distinguish between antagonistic colonizing and colonized groups, and conversely, to emphasize the essential cultural unity and autonomy of each;

   (3) a system of *superexploitation*, understood as a process by which extra-economic coercion is applied to the racially identified colonized group, with the aim of increasing the economic resources appropriated by the colonizers;

   (4) institutionalization of *externally based control*, such that the racially identified colonized group is organized in essential political and administrative aspects by the colonizers or their agents.

In some cases militant groups themselves adopted analyses of their conditions and demands based on internal colonialism arguments; in others, scholarly treatments brought these perspectives to bear. Notable studies were devoted to the black[44] and Chicano[45] communities.

Robert Blauner's *Racial Oppression in America* is probably the most familiar general discussion of race in the US written from an internal colonialism perspective, and the one most "tailored" to US conditions.[46] Blauner has two central preoccupations: the first is to provide theoretical arguments with which to counter the dominant ethnicity paradigm of race in the US. As we have seen, that approach sought to incorporate racial categories within ethnic ones, and thus to locate racial minorities in an analytical framework defined by the dynamics of assimilation and cultural pluralism. It generalized from European immigrant experiences in the US to formulate racial theory in ethnic terms. A critical dialogue with Nathan Glazer, the chief spokesperson for the ethnicity paradigm, punctuates several chapters of Blauner's book.[47]

The second overriding commitment in Blauner's work is a commitment to the radical nationalist politics of the 1960s, which Blauner admirably recognizes to have shaped his analysis in counterpoint with the sociological literature he seeks to criticize.[48] He explicitly seeks to provide radical nationalist practice with the theory that it lacks. In adopting the movements of his times, however, Blauner is also forced to transfer their weaknesses from the realm of practice to that of theory.

Blauner effectively employs the distinction between "colonized and immigrant minorities" to criticize the ethnic group paradigm. "Colonized" minorities are those whose presence in the United States was the result of "forced entry," a criterion that serves well in general (though not absolutely) to distinguish between those whose entry was the direct result of processes of colonialism and those (Europeans) who "became ethnic groups and minorities within the United States by the essentially voluntary movements of individuals and families."[49]

In respect to Blauner's second point of emphasis, derived chiefly from the militant black politics of the late 1960s (his "basic thesis that the most important expressions of protest in the black community reflect the colonized status of Afro-America"),[50] the internal colonialism approach fares poorly. None of the protest phenomena Blauner cites (ghetto riots, cultural nationalism, ghetto-based "community control" movements) necessitates the internal colonialism perspective as a framework of explanation. Rioting has been explained as an extension of "normal" politics when institutionalized channels of political expression are blocked.[51] What is "nationalist" about cultural movements among the oppressed is a matter of considerable ambiguity and debate. Ghetto community control demands have proved subject to quite moderate (or "reformist") interpretation, besides proving to be at best "too little, too late" as key decisions about the cities' fate are made elsewhere.[52] At worst such demands provide grounds for rearticulation in new right or neoconservative analyses and programs, for example to provide codewords for opposition to busing or welfare rights.[53]

Blauner's approach also neglects class cleavages within minority communities, inter-minority group rivalries, and the extensive interpenetration in the US of minority and majority societies, which, though hardly as complete as an ethnicity theorist like Glazer might wish to argue, cast into doubt the internal colonialism analogy in respect to territoriality, at the very least.[54] This interpenetration, in our view, also suggests limits to other elements of the nation-based paradigm in the US context. Cultural domination/cultural autonomy, for example, appears to be but one element of a broader cultural dynamic that includes both the distinctiveness and the interaction of majority- and minority-based cultural elements. Superexploitation does not encompass contemporary economic developments which include marginalization and permanent dependency for many on the one hand, and significant "upward mobility" for some on the other.

In many respects, then, the patent limitations of the analogy to Vietnam or Algeria, an analogy which was politically and not analytically grounded, doomed the internal colonialist version of nation-based racial theory.

Some critical remarks on the nation-based paradigm

How effectively does the nation-based paradigm account for racial dynamics? In fact, the connection is tenuous. The analogy between US conditions and colonial systems of discrimination composed of colonizers and colonized – systems which made use of racial distinctions – does not automatically carry over into post-colonial society. Even the specifically national aspects of the internal colonialism perspective (geography, culture, extra-economic coercion, and external political rule), are rather easily dispensed with, as Burawoy shows in his critique of Blauner.[55] As applied to the contemporary US (with significant exceptions such as Native American conditions or the case of Puerto Rico), the appeal of nationalism, in political practice or in theory, appears to be limited. Unlike many of the old colonial nations, and possibly because it was created out of a colony, the US political scene allows radical nationalism little space.[56] Even black nationalism, the most vibrant and multifaceted minority movement of this kind, has been mainly a refuge for activists and "intellectuals" disaffected by the intransigence of the racial order and disillusioned by moderate programs for change.

What is important in the nation-based account is the paradigm's retention of an explanatory framework *based* on race (even if race is seen through the distorted "national" lens). Nation-based theories of race, while not free of epiphenomenalism, contrast sharply with both the ethnicity and class approaches in this respect. Perhaps it is the very inability of the nation-based account to specify precisely what exactly is "national" about racial oppression in the United States which leads it to lend a certain "primacy" and integrity to racial phenomena. The ethnicity and class paradigms, working from more secure assumptions about the "primacy" of their paradig-matic categories, tend to dissolve the unity of racially constituted groups.

While the nation-based account fails to demonstrate the exist-ence of racial minority or colonized "nations" internal to the US and structurally separated from the majority society, some applica-tions of this paradigm do facilitate comprehensiveness in the study of racial dynamics. Nation-based approaches may unite the micro- and macro-levels of racially shaped experience, for example, or permit comparisons among different groups. Thus the nation-based approach serves in some ways as an inadequate but partial pro-totype for the approach we present in the following chapter in respect to "racial formation."

Conclusion:
Towards a racial formation
perspective

The ethnic group-, class-, and nation-based perspectives all neglect the specificity of race as an autonomous field of social conflict, political organization, and cultural/ideological meaning. Authors working within each paradigm locate the fundamental elements of race, not surprisingly, on their own home ground.

For ethnicity theory, this terrain is that of the *dynamics of incorporation* of minority groups into the dominant society. Ethnicity theory is therefore primarily concerned with questions of group identity; with the resolution of tensions between the twin pressures of assimilation (dissolution of group identity) and cultural pluralism (preservation of group identity); and with the prospects for political integration via normal political channels. The terrain of ethnicity was first explored in US history by immigrating Europeans, and later mapped by intellectuals whose visceral loyalties and social scientific guideposts were framed in terms of the histories of these immigrant groups. For these writers there exists an intense will to pound the square peg of race into the round hole of ethnicity.

For practitioners of class theory, the terrain upon which race may best be encountered is that of *inequality*: racial dynamics are understood primarily in terms of the social allocation of advantage and disadvantage, winners and losers, and the origins and structure of discrimination. Racial inequality is an outcome, not a cause; its roots lie elsewhere: in market imperfections, political power structures, or the search for secure means of labor control. From the perspective of the class paradigm, racial dynamics manifest these more fundamental processes; only secondarily may they take on "a life of their own," or a "relative autonomy."

For nation-based writers, the terrain upon which race may best be analyzed is *territorial*, geographical, in a particularly epochal sense.

52

The European powers divided up the world in the heyday of colonialism, assigning power and privileges to the planet's North, and misery and exploitation to its South. With the rule of Europeans and their descendants over the "natives" of the rest of the globe and their descendants went a highly flexible and adaptive, but nevertheless inexorable "color code," a system of racial distinctions that was (usually) effective in reinforcing colonial domination. The "real" issues, though, weren't racial, but *national* oppression and liberation, or (at a minimum) cultural autonomy and the right to self-determination. Thus race was assigned epiphenomenal status once again, this time as a manifestation of deeper "national" conflicts.

None of these paradigms can stand alone. There is necessarily overlap among them. Certain class approaches, as we have noted, reinforce the ethnicity school's conservative individualist model of equality. Certain nation-based analyses adopt a version of Marxism. Each paradigm has perforce to cope with the great historical and sociological weight of the others' central foci: ethnicity theory and class theory must address the issue of colonialism, for example. In our ideal-typical approach, we have necessarily given greater weight to the uniqueness of each paradigm than to continuity among the paradigms. Each does stand on its own particular ground, each does adopt a specific frame of reference which distinguishes it from the others, but each paradigm must also address a unitary social and historical problematic – that of race in the US. Hence the phenomenon of partial encounters and partial "misses" among the competing paradigms.

Though none of the three paradigms can grasp the nettle of race, each is able to develop certain fascinating insights into racial phenomena. The ethnicity school can document in rich detail the contingency and adaptability of racial identities (considered of course in ethnic group terms), basing its work on the transformations which European immigrants underwent. Thus certain apparent anomalies – the "success," for example, of Japanese Americans – can to some extent be addressed within the ethnicity framework. Ethnicity theory, especially in its post-1965 incarnation, comes closest to our concept of "racial formation," though of course this term does not appear in the ethnicity framework. Writers working within this paradigm note the frequent shifts of ethnic identity and the political significance of its contingency, but still fail to recognize at all adequately, either historically or in the present, the qualitative differences between white and non-white groups' encounters with US society. Or to put it another way, they fail to grasp the extent to which US society is racially structured from top to bottom.

In similar fashion, various class theories of race have been able to explain shifts in patterns of exploitation, mobility and social control with great insight. Yet these same approaches generally fail to notice the political and cultural dimensions of these shifts – often their most salient features. Thus William J. Wilson, probably the most incisive class theorist of race, accepts the existence of an egalitarian racial state after 1965, and Harold Baron links his conception of a new racial order to advanced capitalist reproduction imperatives in functionalist fashion.[1]

The great insight of nation-based approaches has always been their ability to connect US conditions with global patterns based in the legacy of colonialism. Yet this link has often proved tenuous. A sort of "exceptionalism" turns out to be necessary if one is to address racial dynamics in the US (and probably in respect to any particular nation's racial dynamics); this is what we seek to provide with our "racial formation" perspective.

No new theory can be proposed simply to dispense with these paradigms; there is too much of value within them. Nor is this our aim in suggesting a perspective based on the concept of "racial formation" in order to understand US racial dynamics, especially in recent decades. Rather we wish to detach racial theory from epiphenomenalism, from entanglements which in our view are superfluous and stifling, in order to grasp the complexities of racial identity, politics and social structure in the United States. We believe that much new insight is to be gained in that process, to which, in Part II, we now turn.

Part Two

Part Two

4
Racial formation

In 1982–83, Susie Guillory Phipps unsuccessfully sued the Louisiana Bureau of Vital Records to change her racial classification from black to white. The descendant of an eighteenth-century white planter and a black slave, Phipps was designated "black" in her birth certificate in accordance with a 1970 state law which declared anyone with at least one-thirty-second "Negro blood" to be black. The legal battle raised intriguing questions about the concept of race, its meaning in contemporary society, and its use (and abuse) in public policy. Assistant Attorney General Ron Davis defended the law by pointing out that some type of racial classification was necessary to comply with federal record-keeping requirements and to facilitate programs for the prevention of genetic diseases. Phipps's attorney, Brian Begue, argued that the assignment of racial categories on birth certificates was unconstitutional and that the one-thirty-second designation was inaccurate. He called on a retired Tulane University professor who cited research indicating that most whites have one-twentieth "Negro" ancestry. In the end, Phipps lost. The court upheld a state law which quantified racial identity, and in so doing affirmed the legality of assigning individuals to specific racial groupings.[1]

The Phipps case illustrates the continuing dilemma of defining race and establishing its meaning in institutional life. Today, to assert that variations in human physiognomy are racially based is to enter a constant and intense debate. *Scientific* interpretations of race have not been alone in sparking heated controversy; *religious* perspectives have done so as well.[2] Most centrally, of course, race has been a matter of *political* contention. This has been particularly true in the United States, where the concept of race has varied enormously over time without ever leaving the center stage of US history.

57

What is race?

Race consciousness, and its articulation in theories of race, is largely a modern phenomenon. When European explorers in the New World "discovered" people who looked different than themselves, these "natives" challenged then existing conceptions of the origins of the human species, and raised disturbing questions as to whether *all* could be considered in the same "family of man."[3] Religious debates flared over the attempt to reconcile the Bible with the existence of "racially distinct" people. Arguments took place over creation itself, as theories of polygenesis questioned whether God had made only one species of humanity ("monogenesis"). Europeans wondered if the natives of the New World were indeed human beings with redeemable souls. At stake were not only the prospects for conversion, but the types of treatment to be accorded them. The expropriation of property, the denial of political rights, the introduction of slavery and other forms of coercive labor, as well as outright extermination, all presupposed a worldview which distinguished Europeans – children of God, human beings, etc. – from "others." Such a worldview was needed to explain why some should be "free" and others enslaved, why some had rights to land and property while others did not. Race, and the interpretation of racial differences, was a central factor in that worldview.

In the colonial epoch science was no less a field of controversy than religion in attempts to comprehend the concept of race and its meaning. Spurred on by the classificatory scheme of living organisms devised by Linnaeus in *Systema Naturae,* many scholars in the eighteenth and nineteenth centuries dedicated themselves to the identification and ranking of variations in humankind. Race was thought of as a *biological* concept, yet its precise definition was the subject of debates which, as we have noted, continue to rage today. Despite efforts ranging from Dr Samuel Morton's studies of cranial capacity[4] to contemporary attempts to base racial classification on shared gene pools,[5] the concept of race has defied biological definition.

None of the ostensibly "objective" measures to determine and define racial categories were free from the invidious elements of racial ideology. The eighteenth century saw the popular acceptance of a concept with roots in classical Greek thought – the "Great

Chain of Being." Posing a grand hierarchy starting with inanimate objects, up through the lowliest forms of life, through "man," and culminating with God the Creator, the "Great Chain of Being" framed discussion about the gradations which existed among humankind. Which races were closer to God and which to apes? In a period where hierarchical arrangements in society were being questioned, the notion of a "Great Chain of Being" legitimated status differences and inequality with appeals to the "naturalness" of distinctions between human beings. To challenge this order would be tantamount to challenging God him/herself.[6]

In the nineteenth century, Count Arthur de Gobineau drew upon the most respected scientific studies of his day to compose his four-volume *Essay on the Inequality of Races* (1853–55). He not only greatly influenced the racial thinking of the period, but his themes were to be echoed in the racist ideologies of the next hundred years: beliefs that superior races produce superior cultures and that racial intermixtures result in the degradation of the superior racial stock. These themes found expression, for instance, in the eugenics movement inspired by Darwin's cousin, Frances Galton, which had an immense impact on scientific and sociopolitical thought in Europe and the United States.[7]

Attempts to discern the *scientific meaning* of race continue to the present day. Although most physical anthropologists and biologists have abandoned the quest for a scientific basis to determine racial categories, controversies have recently flared in the area of genetics and educational psychology. For instance, an essay by Arthur Jensen which argued that hereditary factors shape intelligence not only revived the "nature or nurture" controversy, but raised highly volatile questions about racial equality itself.[8] Clearly the attempt to establish a *biological* basis of race has not been swept into the dustbin of history, but is being resurrected in various scientific arenas. All such attempts seek to remove the concept of race from fundamental social, political, or economic determination. They suggest instead that the truth of race lies in the terrain of innate characteristics, of which skin color and other physical attributes provide only the most obvious, and in some respects most superficial, indicators.

Racial formation

Race as a social concept

The social sciences have come to reject biologistic notions of race in favor of an approach which regards race as a *social* concept. Beginning in the eighteenth century, this trend has been slow and uneven, but its direction clear. In the nineteenth century Max Weber discounted biological explanations for racial conflict and instead highlighted the social and political factors which engendered such conflict.[9] The work of pioneering cultural anthropologist Franz Boas was crucial in refuting the scientific racism of the early twentieth century by rejecting the connection between race and culture, and the assumption of a continuum of "higher" and "lower" cultural groups. Within the contemporary social science literature, race is assumed to be a variable which is shaped by broader societal forces.

Race is indeed a pre-eminently *sociohistorical* concept. Racial categories and the meaning of race are given concrete expression by the specific social relations and historical context in which they are embedded. Racial meanings have varied tremendously over time and between different societies.

In the United States, the black/white color line has historically been rigidly defined and enforced. White is seen as a "pure" category. Any racial intermixture makes one "nonwhite." In the movie *Raintree County*, Elizabeth Taylor describes the worst of fates to befall whites as "havin' a little Negra blood in ya' – just one little teeny drop and a person's all Negra."[10] This thinking flows from what Marvin Harris has characterized as the principle of *hypo-descent:*

> By what ingenious computation is the genetic tracery of a million years of evolution unraveled and each man [sic] assigned his proper social box? In the United States, the mechanism employed is the rule of hypo-descent. This descent rule requires Americans to believe that anyone who is known to have had a Negro ancestor is a Negro. We admit nothing in between. . . . "Hypo-descent" means affiliation with the subordinate rather than the superordinate group in order to avoid the ambiguity of intermediate identity. . . . The rule of hypo-descent is, therefore, an invention, which we in the United States have made in order to keep biological facts from intruding into our collective racist fantasies.[11]

The Susie Guillory Phipps case merely represents the contemporary expression of this racial logic.

By contrast, a striking feature of race relations in the lowland areas of Latin America since the abolition of slavery has been the relative absence of sharply defined racial groupings. No such rigid descent rule characterizes racial identity in many Latin American societies. Brazil, for example, has historically had less rigid conceptions of race, and thus a variety of "intermediate" racial categories exist. Indeed, as Harris notes, "One of the most striking consequences of the Brazilian system of racial identification is that parents and children and even brothers and sisters are frequently accepted as representatives of quite opposite racial types."[12] Such a possibility is incomprehensible within the logic of racial categories in the US.

To suggest another example: the notion of "passing" takes on new meaning if we compare various American cultures' means of assigning racial identity. In the United States, individuals who are actually "black" by the logic of hypo-descent have attempted to skirt the discriminatory barriers imposed by law and custom by attempting to "pass" for white.[13] Ironically, these same individuals would not be able to pass for "black" in many Latin American societies.

Consideration of the term "black" illustrates the diversity of racial meanings which can be found among different societies and historically within a given society. In contemporary British politics the term "black" is used to refer to all nonwhites. Interestingly this designation has not arisen through the racist discourse of groups such as the National Front. Rather, in political and cultural movements, Asian as well as Afro-Caribbean youth are adopting the term as an expression of self-identity.[14] The wide-ranging meanings of "black" illustrate the manner in which racial categories are shaped politically.[15]

The meaning of race is defined and contested throughout society, in both collective action and personal practice. In the process, racial categories themselves are formed, transformed, destroyed and re-formed. We use the term *racial formation* to refer to the process by which social, economic and political forces determine the content and importance of racial categories, and by which they are in turn shaped by racial meanings. Crucial to this formulation is the treatment of race as a *central axis* of social relations which cannot be subsumed under or reduced to some broader category or conception.

Racial ideology and racial identity

The seemingly obvious, "natural" and "common sense" qualities which the existing racial order exhibits themselves testify to the effectiveness of the racial formation process in constructing racial meanings and racial identities.

One of the first things we notice about people when we meet them (along with their sex) is their race. We utilize race to provide clues about *who* a person is. This fact is made painfully obvious when we encounter someone whom we cannot conveniently racially catego- rize – someone who is, for example, racially "mixed" or of an ethnic/racial group with which we are not familiar. Such an encoun- ter becomes a source of discomfort and momentarily a crisis of racial meaning. Without a racial identity, one is in danger of having no identity.

Our compass for navigating race relations depends on precon- ceived notions of what each specific racial group looks like. Com- ments such as, "Funny, you don't look black," betray an underlying image of what black should be. We also become disoriented when people do not act "black," "Latino," or indeed "white." The content of such stereotypes reveals a series of unsubstantiated beliefs about who these groups are and what "they" are like.[16]

In US society, then, a kind of "racial etiquette" exists, a set of interpretative codes and racial meanings which operate in the interactions of daily life. Rules shaped by our perception of race in a comprehensively racial society determine the "presentation of self,"[17] distinctions of status, and appropriate modes of conduct. "Etiquette" is not mere universal adherence to the dominant group's rules, but a more dynamic combination of these rules with the values and beliefs of subordinated groupings. This racial "sub- jection" is quintessentially ideological. Everybody learns some combination, some version, of the rules of racial classification, and of their own racial identity, often without obvious teaching or conscious inculcation. Race becomes "common sense" – a way of comprehending, explaining and acting in the world.

Racial beliefs operate as an "amateur biology," a way of explaining the variations in "human nature."[18] Differences in skin color and other obvious physical characteristics supposedly provide visible clues to differences lurking underneath. Temperament, sexuality, intelligence, athletic ability, aesthetic preferences and so on are presumed to be fixed and discernible from the palpable mark of race. Such diverse questions as our confidence and trust in others (for example, clerks or salespeople, media figures, neighbors), our sexual preferences and romantic images, our tastes in music, films, dance, or sports, and our very ways of talking, walking, eating and dreaming are ineluctably shaped by notions of race. Skin color "differences" are thought to explain perceived differences in intellectual, physical and artistic temperaments, and to justify distinct treatment of racially identified individuals and groups.

The continuing persistence of racial ideology suggests that these racial myths and stereotypes cannot be exposed as such in the popular imagination. They are, we think, too essential, too integral, to the maintenance of the US social order. Of course, particular meanings, stereotypes and myths can change, but the presence of a *system* of racial meanings and stereotypes, of racial ideology, seems to be a permanent feature of US culture.

Film and television, for example, have been notorious in disseminating images of racial minorities which establish for audiences what people from these groups look like, how they behave, and "who they are."[19] The power of the media lies not only in their ability to reflect the dominant racial ideology, but in their capacity to shape that ideology in the first place. D. W. Griffith's epic *Birth of a Nation*, a sympathetic treatment of the rise of the Ku Klux Klan during Reconstruction, helped to generate, consolidate and "nationalize" images of blacks which had been more disparate (more regionally specific, for example) prior to the film's appearance.[20] In US television, the necessity to define characters in the briefest and most condensed manner has led to the perpetuation of racial caricatures, as racial stereotypes serve as shorthand for scriptwriters, directors and actors, in commercials, etc. Television's tendency to address the "lowest common denominator" in order to render programs "familiar" to an enormous and diverse audience leads it regularly to assign and reassign racial characteristics to particular groups, both minority and majority.

These and innumerable other examples show that we tend to view race as something fixed and immutable – something rooted in "nature." Thus we mask the historical construction of racial categories, the shifting meaning of race, and the crucial role of politics and ideology in shaping race relations. Races do not emerge full-blown. They are the results of diverse historical practices and are continually subject to challenge over their definition and meaning.

Racialization: the historical development of race

In the United States, the racial category of "black" evolved with the consolidation of racial slavery. By the end of the seventeenth century, Africans whose specific identity was Ibo, Yoruba, Fulani, etc., were rendered "black" by an ideology of exploitation based on racial logic – the establishment and maintenance of a "color line." This of course did not occur overnight. A period of indentured servitude which was not rooted in racial logic preceded the consolidation of racial slavery. With slavery, however, a racially based understanding of society was set in motion which resulted in the shaping of a specific *racial* identity not only for the slaves but for the European settlers as well. Winthrop Jordan has observed: "From the initially common term *Christian*, at mid-century there was a marked shift toward the terms *English* and *free*. After about 1680, taking the colonies as a whole, a new term of self-identification appeared – *white*."[21]

We employ the term *racialization* to signify the extension of racial meaning to a previously racially unclassified relationship, social practice or group. Racialization is an ideological process, an historically specific one. Racial ideology is constructed from pre-existing conceptual (or, if one prefers, "discursive") elements and emerges from the struggles of competing political projects and ideas seeking to articulate similar elements differently. An account of racialization processes that avoids the pitfalls of US ethnic history[22] remains to be written.

Particularly during the nineteenth century, the category of "white" was subject to challenges brought about by the influx of diverse groups who were not of the same Anglo-Saxon stock as the founding immigrants. In the nineteenth century, political and ideological struggles emerged over the classification of Southern Europeans, the Irish and Jews, among other "non-white"

categories.[23] Nativism was only effectively curbed by the institutionalization of a racial order that drew the color line *around*,
rather than *within*, Europe.

By stopping short of racializing immigrants from Europe after the
Civil War, and by subsequently allowing their assimilation, the
American racial order was reconsolidated in the wake of the
tremendous challenge placed before it by the abolition of racial
slavery.[24] With the end of Reconstruction in 1877, an effective
program for limiting the emergent class struggles of the later
nineteenth century was forged: the definition of the working class *in
racial terms* – as "white." This was not accomplished by any
legislative decree or capitalist maneuvering to divide the working
class, but rather by white workers themselves. Many of them were
recent immigrants, who organized on racial lines as much as on
traditionally defined class lines.[25] The Irish on the West Coast, for
example, engaged in vicious anti-Chinese race-baiting and committed many pogrom-type assaults on Chinese in the course of consolidating the trade union movement in California.

Thus the very political organization of the working class was in
important ways a racial project. The legacy of racial conflicts and
arrangements shaped the definition of interests and in turn led to
the consolidation of institutional patterns (e.g. segregated unions,
dual labor markets, exclusionary legislation) which perpetuated the
color line *within* the working class. Selig Perlman, whose study of
the development of the labor movement is fairly sympathetic to this
process, notes that:

> The political issue after 1877 was racial, not financial, and the
> weapon was not merely the ballot, but also "direct action" –
> violence. The anti-Chinese agitation in California, culminating
> as it did in the Exclusion Law passed by Congress in 1882, was
> doubtless the most important single factor in the history of
> American labor, for without it the entire country might have
> been overrun by Mongolian [sic] labor and *the labor movement
> might have become a conflict of races instead of one of classes.*[26]

More recent economic transformations in the US have also
altered interpretations of racial identities and meanings. The auto-
mation of southern agriculture and the augmented labor demand of
the postwar boom transformed blacks from a largely rural, impoverished labor force to a largely urban, working-class group by

1970.[27] When boom became bust and liberal welfare statism moved rightwards, the majority of blacks came to be seen, increasingly, as part of the "underclass," as state "dependents." Thus the particularly deleterious effects on blacks of global and national economic shifts (generally rising unemployment rates, changes in the employment structure away from reliance on labor intensive work, etc.) were explained once again in the late 1970s and 1980s (as they had been in the 1940s and mid-1960s) as the result of defective black cultural norms, of familial disorganization, etc.[28] In this way new racial attributions, new racial myths, are affixed to "blacks."[29] Similar changes in racial identity are presently affecting Asians and Latinos, as such economic forces as increasing Third World impoverishment and indebtedness fuel immigration and high interest rates, Japanese competition spurs resentments, and US jobs seem to fly away to Korea and Singapore.[30]

Racial formation: the creation of racial meanings

Much racial theory, we have argued, treats race as a manifestation or epiphenomenon of other supposedly more fundamental categories of sociopolitical identity, notably those of ethnicity, class and nation. In such accounts, race is not regarded as a continually evolving category in its own right; in fact, these approaches have often imagined that race would decline in importance, even disappear, as economic or political "progress" rendered "race-thinking" obsolete.[31]

We hope to alter this situation by presenting the outlines of a theory of *racial formation*. In our view, racial meanings pervade US society, extending from the shaping of individual racial identities to the structuring of collective political action on the terrain of the state.

An approach based on the concept of racial formation should treat race in the United States as a fundamental *organizing principle* of social relationships. To give this notion some concreteness, let us distinguish between the *micro-level* and *macro-level* of social relations.

At the micro-level, race is a matter of individuality, of the formation of *identity*. The ways in which we understand ourselves and interact with others, the structuring of our practical activity – in work and family, as citizens and as thinkers (or "philosophers")[32] – these are all shaped by racial meanings and racial awareness.

At the macro-level, race is a matter of *collectivity*, of the formation of social structures: economic, political and cultural/ideological. Social structure may be understood as a series of "sites:"

> We conceive of a site as a region of social life with a coherent set of constitutive social relations – the *structure* of the site. Thus in the advanced capitalist social formation, the liberal democratic state, the capitalist economy, and the patriarchal family may be considered sites in that each may be characterized by a distinct set of "rules of the game" for participation in practices.[33]

In the space available, it is only possible to outline very briefly some racial dimensions of these sites as they exist in the United States. At the level of the economy, for example, the definition of labor ("slave versus "free"), the allocation of workers of distinct places in dual/segmented/split labor markets, and the composition of the "underclass" have all been dependent on race as organizing principles or "rules of the game." The state, as we shall demonstrate in the following chapter, is structured by such factors as racially based citizenship and naturalization laws, by racially oriented social policies of all types, and in response to political movements which, from the Workingmen's Party to the Mississippi Freedom Democratic Party, have organized political life along racial lines. The family is racial terrain *par excellence*, and has been extensively analyzed as the site of racial socialization.[34] In the cultural realm, dress, music, art, language and indeed the very concept of "taste" has been shaped by racial consciousness and racial dynamics, for instance in the absorption of black musical forms into the white "mainstream."

The racial order is organized and enforced by the continuity and reciprocity between these two "levels" of social relations. The micro- and macro-levels, however, are only analytically distinct. In our lived experience, in politics, in culture, in economic life, they are continuous and reciprocal. Racial discrimination, for example – considered as a "macro-level" set of economic, political and ideological/cultural practices – has obvious consequences for the experience and identities of individuals. It affects racial meanings, intervenes in "personal life," is interpreted politically, etc.[35] Another example: racial identity – considered as a "micro-level" complex of individual practices and "consciousness" – shapes the universe of collective action. The panoply of individual attributes – from one's patterns of speech or tastes in food or music to the economic, spatial, familial, or citizenship "role" one occupies – provides the essential themes for political organization, the elements of economic self-reliance, etc.[36]

The theory of racial formation, then, suggests that racial phenomena penetrate and link these two "levels" of social relationships. But this is only part of the story; the concept of race as an organizing principle of social relations provides a description, a *classification* of racial phenomena in the US, and also explains the continuity of these phenomena,[37] but it does not yet offer a conception of the *process* of racial formation. To grasp this process we must understand the way in which the meaning of these phenomena is politically contested.

Contesting the social meaning of race

Once we understand that race overflows the boundaries of skin color, superexploitation, social stratification, discrimination and prejudice, cultural domination and cultural resistance, state policy (or of any other particular social relationship we list), once we recognize the racial dimension present to some degree in *every* identity, institution and social practice in the United States – once we have done this, it becomes possible to speak of *racial formation*. This recognition is hard-won; there is a continuous temptation to think of race as an *essence*, as something fixed, concrete and objective, as (for example) one of the categories just enumerated. And there is also an opposite temptation: to see it as a mere illusion, which an ideal social order would eliminate.

In our view it is crucial to break with these habits of thought. The effort must be made to understand race as *an unstable and "decentered" complex of social meanings constantly being transformed by political struggle*. It is imperative that we achieve this understanding for two reasons. First, because today as in the past racial minorities pay a heavy price in human suffering as a result of their categorization as "other" by the dominant racial ideology; this is true not only in the United States, but across the world. Second, because racial politics are emblematic, we believe, of a new stage of

US politics as a whole, a new *socially based* politics.[38]

The crucial task, then, is to suggest how the widely disparate circumstances of individual and group racial identities, and of the racial institutions and social practices with which these identities are intertwined, are formed and transformed over time. This takes place, we argue, through *political contestation over racial meanings*. Such contestation occurs today throughout American society: it takes place at the level of "personal" relationships (indeed it arises *within* individuals whose very identities and racial "beliefs" are necessarily contradictory); it exists in "objective" relationships such as work or political activity; and it occurs in cultural representation.

The racial dimensions of a particular relationship or social practice are never given automatically. If they appear obvious, this only means that they are already contextualized in racial ideologies familiar to their subjects. Of course, it is often the case that the racial dynamics of a given relationship go unnoticed: far from being sources of conflict or of difficult decisions, they are "nonevents," giving rise to "nondecisions."[39]

Frequently, though, especially in recent decades, racial dynamics are quite visible in social life. They cause uncertainty in the minds of individuals subject to them ("Is this 'fair'?" "Am 'I' being recognized?" "How do I 'work' this?"). They confront institutions, local communities and families with deep-seated conflicts and agonizing dilemmas. They structure large-scale policy debates. They inspire movements. These individuals, groups, institutions and movements are moved – in our view by the efforts of "intellectuals" – to make new interpretations of racial meanings, to understand the meaning of race and racial identity in new ways. Once reinterpreted, *rearticulated*, racial meanings are disrupted and space for political contestation is opened.

Racial debate, the interpretation of race – which in previous periods of US history was relatively less problematic, often a matter of "common sense" or "human nature" – has taken up what seems to be long-term residence on the social terrain of everyday life, where people must reconcile the conflicts in their lives, or live with their inability to reconcile them. It is to this terrain that, since World War II, racial theory and racial ideology – both mainstream and radical – have been addressed. In the postwar United States, racial meanings have been most centrally (re)interpreted by social movements and most definitively institutionalized by the state.

5
The racial state

Introduction: The trajectory of racial politics

Three incidents from recent racial politics:

In 1973 a desegregation suit against the Atlanta school system
was settled. The suit had originally been filed in 1958 by black
parents with the support of the local chapter of the NAACP. In
the settlement, the plaintiffs agreed to drop the suit, and the
school board agreed to certain reforms such as the hiring of
more black teachers and administrators. According to one
commentator, the plaintiffs "decided that an Atlanta busing
plan would not serve their interests," since while the suit was
being litigated such changes as "white flight" to the Atlanta
suburbs and black immigration to the city had rendered the
school system more than 80% black. The national NAACP then
objected to the settlement on the grounds that it ". . . was a bad
outcome for blacks nationally, even if correct for the Atlanta
circumstances"; the national office, however, failed to persuade
either local chapter members or the presiding judge to overturn
the decision.[1]

In 1978 an initiative in the US Senate sought to abolish the
Bureau of Indian Affairs, which for a century had been the state
agency most central to Indian life, responsible for administering
such diverse programs as health care, education, local electoral
processes, and the allocation of mineral and water rights. The
legislative proposal would have distributed these responsibilities
among a variety of other government agencies. Indian leaders
and activists, despite their long antagonism to many BIA
practices and policies (many had in fact characterized the agency

as a colonial apparatus enforcing external control over Indian matters), mobilized *in support* of the BIA's continued existence.[2]

In 1983, after extensive maneuver, the Reagan administration completed its reorganization of the US Commission on Civil Rights, a state "watchdog" organization which had been established in the 1950s to monitor and report on progress and problems in the achievement of racial (and later, women's) equality. Under its new leadership, the Commission defined "reverse discrimination" (i.e. discrimination against whites resulting from affirmative action and other similar programs) as its first priority.[3]

Such stories reveal some of the incongruities of the relationship between racial minorities and the state. The advocacy groups and movement organizations which seek to represent minority interests, mobilize minority group members politically, and artic- ulate minority viewpoints are frequently faced with bitterly ironic political choices.

No sooner did egalitarian and anti-discrimination policies emerge from the political tempests of the 1960s than they began to "decay." As our three examples reveal, from the early 1970s of Richard Nixon to the early 1980s of Ronald Reagan, the state has sought to absorb, to marginalize and to transform (or "rearticulate") the meaning of the reforms won in the earlier decade. But as our stories also show, not only the state, but also sociopolitical developments *outside* the state, such as demographic changes and movement disagreements, have themselves played a role in these changes.

How have these transformations occurred? What are the dyna- mics of the relationships between the state and racial minorities? Why does a pattern of alternating activism and quiescence character- ize both state racial activities and movement ebbs and flows? In this chapter we consider these questions in an effort to understand the *trajectory* which contemporary racial politics – and thus racial formation processes – follow in the contemporary United States.

By "trajectory" we mean the pattern of conflict and accommodation which takes shape over time between racially based social move- ments and the policies and programs of the state. We consider the central elements of this trajectory to be the state and social move- ments, linked in a single historical framework of racial formation.

Social movements and the state are interrelated in a complex way. Racial movements arise, and race becomes a political issue, when state institutions are thought to structure and enforce a racially unjust social order.[4] State institutions acquire their racial orientations from the processes of conflict with and accommodation to racially based movements. Thus "reform," "reaction," "radical change," or "backlash" – indeed every transformation of the racial order – is constructed through a process of clash and compromise between racial movements and the state.

These are the dynamics of present-day racial politics in the US. Yet there is nothing permanent or sacred about this pattern. Indeed, the existence of political channels for the expression of racial conflict is a relatively recent phenomenon. The broad sweep of US history is characterized not by racial democracy but by racial despotism, not by trajectories of reform but by implacable denial of political rights, dehumanization, extreme exploitation and policies of minority extirpation. Democracy has never been in abundant supply where race is concerned. The very emergence of political channels through which reform can at times be achieved is an immense political victory for minorities, and for democracy itself.[5]

In order to understand the interaction of today's racial state and minority movements, we must examine the origins of racial politics in the US. In the next two sections of this chapter, we survey the historical context from which modern racial politics emerged, and the role of the state in the process of racial formation. We then proceed to a theoretical sketch of the contemporary political dynamics of race.

Historical change in the US racial order

Since the earliest days of colonialism in North America, an identifiable racial order has linked the system of political rule to the racial classification of individuals and groups. The major institutions and social relationships of US society – law, political organization, economic relationships, religion, cultural life, residential patterns, etc. – have been structured from the beginning by the racial order.

Clearly the system of racial subjection has been more monolithic, more absolute, at some historical periods than others.[6] Where political opposition was banned or useless, as it was for slaves in the

South and for Native Americans during much of the course of US history, transformation of the racial order, or resistance to it, was perforce military (or perhaps took such economic forms as sabotage). An oppositional racial ideology requires some political space, a certain minimal conceptual flexibility about race, upon which to fasten in order to recast racial meanings and constitute alternative racial institutions. During much of US history, this political and ideological space was extremely limited.

But even at its most oppressive, the racial order was unable to arrogate to itself the entire capacity for the production of racial meanings, of racial subjects. Racial minorities were always able to counterpose their own cultural traditions, their own forms of organization and identity, to the dehumanizing and enforced "invisibility" imposed by the majority society.

As the voluminous literature on black culture under slavery shows, black slaves developed cultures of resistance based on music, religion, African traditions and family ties, through which they sustained their own ideological project: the development of a "free" black identity and a collectivity dedicated to emancipation.[7] The examples of Geronimo, Sitting Bull and other Native American leaders were passed down from generation to generation as examples of resistance, and the Ghost Dance and the Native American Church were employed by particular generations of Indians to maintain a resistance culture.[8] Rodolfo Acuna has pointed out how the same "bandits" against whom Anglo vigilantes mounted expeditions after the Treaty of Guadalupe Hidalgo – Tiburcio Vasquez, Joaquin Murieta – became heroes in the Mexicano communities of the Southwest, remembered in folktales and celebrated in *corridos*.[9] We do not offer these examples to romanticize brutal repression or to give the air of revolutionary struggle to what were often grim defeats; we simply seek to affirm that even in the most uncontested periods of American racism, oppositional cultures were able, often at very great cost, to maintain themselves.

Without reviewing the vast history of racial conflict, it is still possible to make some general comments about the manner in which the racial order was historically consolidated. Gramsci's distinction between "war of maneuver" and "war of position" will prove useful here.

For much of American history, no political legitimacy was conceded to alternative or oppositional racial ideologies, to competing racially defined political projects. The absence of democratic rights, of property, of political and ideological terrain upon which to challenge the monolithic character of the racial order, forced racially defined opposition both *outward*, to the margins of society, and *inward* to the relative safety of homogeneous minority communities.

Slaves who escaped, forming communities in woods and swamps; Indians who made war on the United States in defense of their peoples and lands; Chinese and Filipinos who drew together in Chinatowns and Manilatowns in order to gain some measure of collective control over their existence – these are some examples of the movement of racial opposition *outward*, away from political engagement with the hegemonic racial state.

These same slaves, Indians, Asians (and many others), banned from the political system and relegated to what was supposed to be a permanently inferior sociocultural status, were forced *inward* upon themselves as individuals, families and communities. Tremendous cultural resources were nurtured among such communities; enormous labors were required to survive and to develop elements of an autonomy and opposition under such conditions. These circumstances can best be understood as combining with the violent clashes and necessity of resistance (to white-led race riots, military assaults, etc.) which characterized these periods, to constitute a racial *war of maneuver*.

However democratic the United States may have been in other respects (and it is clear that democracy has always been in relatively short supply), in its treatment of racial minorities it has been to varying degrees *despotic* for much of its history. "War of maneuver" describes a situation in which subordinate groups seek to preserve and extend a definite territory, to ward off violent assault, and to develop an internal society as an alternative to the repressive social system they confront.

More recent history suggests that war of maneuver is being replaced by *war of position* as racially defined minorities achieve political gains.[10] A strategy of *war of position* can only be predicated on political struggle – on the existence of diverse institutional and cultural terrains upon which oppositional political projects can be mounted, and upon which the racial state can be confronted. Prepared in large measure by the practices undertaken under conditions of war of maneuver, minorities were able to make sustained strategic incursions into the mainstream political process beginning with World War II. "Opening up" the state was a process of democratization which had effects both on state structures and on racial meanings. The postwar black movement, later joined by other racially based minority movements, sought to transform dominant racial ideology in the US, to locate its elements in a more egalitarian and democratic framework, and thereby to reconstruct the social meaning of race. The state was the logical target for this effort.

Historical development of the racial state

The state from its very inception has been concerned with the politics of race. For most of US history, state racial policy's main objective was repression and exclusion. Congress's first attempt to define American citizenship, the Naturalization Law of 1790, declared that only free "white" immigrants could qualify. The extension of eligibility to all racial groups has been slow indeed. Japanese, for example, could become naturalized citizens only after the passage of the Walter-McCarran Act of 1952.[11]

Historically, a variety of previously racially undefined groups have required categorization to situate them within the prevailing racial order. Throughout the nineteenth century, many state and federal legal arrangements recognized only three racial categories: "white," "Negro," and "Indian." In California, the influx of Chinese and the debates surrounding the legal status of Mexicans provoked a brief juridical crisis of racial definition. California attempted to resolve this dilemma by assigning Mexicans and Chinese to categories within the already existing framework of "legally defined" racial groups. In the wake of the Treaty of Guadalupe Hidalgo (1848), Mexicans were defined as a "white" population and accorded the political-legal status of "free white persons." By contrast, the California Supreme Court ruled in *People v. Hall* (1854) that Chinese should be considered "Indian" [!] and denied the political rights accorded to whites.[12]

The state's shifting racial perspective is also revealed by the census. Latinos surfaced as an ethnic category, "Persons of Spanish Mother Tongue," in 1950 and 1960. In 1970 they appeared as "Persons of Both Spanish Surname and Spanish Mother Tongue," and in 1980 the "Hispanic" category was created.[13] Such changes suggest the state's inability to "racialize" a particular group – to institutionalize it in a politically organized racial system. They also reflect the struggles through which racial minorities press their demands for recognition and equality, and dramatize the state's uncertain efforts to manage and manipulate those demands.[14]

The state is the focus of collective demands both for egalitarian and democratic reforms and for the enforcement of existing privileges. The state "intervenes" in racial conflicts, but it does not do so in a coherent or unified manner. Distinct state institutions often act in a contradictory fashion.[15]

Does the state, however clumsily, actually capture, steer, or organize the realities of racial identity and racial conflict? There is some validity to the idea of a racially "interventionist" state. With this theoretical concept, it is possible to investigate certain racial dimensions of state policy. The 1960s civil rights reforms, for example, can be interpreted as federal intervention in the area of racial discrimination.

Yet this approach does not reveal how the state itself is racially structured; it depicts the state as intervening, but not *intervened*, structuring, but not *structured*. Such a state is not basically shaped by race since it intervenes in race relations from *outside* them. The treatment afforded to racial politics is thus confined to "normal" political arenas.

In contrast to this, we suggest that the state *is* inherently racial. Far from *intervening* in racial conflicts, the state is itself increasingly the pre-eminent site of racial conflict. In the following sections of this chapter, we examine this expanding involvement of the state in the racial formation process. We first present a model of the racial state, and then consider contemporary patterns of change in the racial order, focusing on the interaction between state and social movements.

A model of the racial state

The state is composed of *institutions*, the *policies* they carry out, the *conditions and rules* which support and justify them, and the *social relations* in which they are imbedded.[16]

Every state *institution* is a racial institution, but not every institution operates in the same way. In fact, the various state institutions do not serve one coordinated racial objective; they may work at cross-purposes.[17] Therefore, race must be understood as occupying varying degrees of centrality in different state institutions and at different historical moments.

To illustrate this point, let us contrast two agencies of the federal state, the Department of Housing and Urban Development (HUD) and the National Science Foundation (NSF). HUD must deal directly with questions of residential segregation, urban development pressures, housing subsidization programs and the like; it is staffed by numerous minority-group members, and is subject to constant pressures from lobbies, community groups and local and state governments (many of which address racial issues or are organized along racial lines). Thus it can be expected to be more racially oriented than the National Science Foundation, where staffing along professional/academic lines, a technical mandate, and a politically more limited range of constituents limit the racial agenda. Nevertheless, in certain areas (e.g. hiring policies, funding priorities, positions taken in respect to racially oriented scientific disputes – does Shockley get a grant?) the NSF too is a racial institution.

Through *policies* which are explicitly or implicitly racial, state institutions organize and enforce the racial politics of everyday life. For example, they enforce racial (non)discrimination policies, which they administer, arbitrate, and encode in law. They organize racial identities by means of education, family law, and the procedures for punishment, treatment and surveillance of the criminal, deviant and ill.[18]

State institutions and their policies taken shape under a series of *conditions and rules*. These "rules of the game" integrate the disparate racial policies of different state agencies, define the scope of state activity, establish "normal" procedures for influencing policy, and set the limits of political legitimacy in general. To speak, for example, of an agency's "mandate," of a policy's "constituency," or of an epochal political "project" (the "Keynesian welfare state," the "conservative opportunity society")[19] is to accept a set of political rules about who is a political actor, what is a political interest, and how the broad state/society relationship is to be organized.[20]

The specific *social relations* through which state activity is structured constitute the materiality of politics. Examples include the complex linkages of agencies and constituencies,[21] the dynamics of coalitions and governing or oppositional blocs, and the varieties of administrative control exercised by state agencies throughout civil society.[22] Racial politics are not exceptional in this respect. For example, civil rights organizations, lobbying groups and "social programs" with significant constituency bases, legal mandates, etc., may engage the state in the "normal" politics of interest-group liberalism,[23] adopt movement tactics of direct action and confrontation "from without," or – as is most likely – combine these tactics.

The state is also imbedded in another kind of social relations: the cultural and technical norms which characterize society overall. These affect the organizational capacities of state agencies, their coordination, both with "external" social actors and with each other, and the practices of their own personnel.[24] In racial terms, these relationships are structured by "difference" in certain ways: for example, minority officials may establish caucuses or maintain informal networks with which to combat the isolation frequently encountered in bureaucratic settings.

Despite all the forces working at cross-purposes within the state – disparate demands of constituents, distinct agency mandates and prerogatives, unintended and cross-cutting consequences of policy, etc. – the state still preserves an overall unity. This is maintained in two ways. First, strategic unity is sought at the apex of the apparatus by key policy-makers, and in legislative and judicial agencies by established decision rules.[25] Second, unity is imposed on the state by its thorough interpenetration with society. In advanced capitalist societies *hegemony* is secured by a complex system of compromises, legitimating ideologies (e.g. "the rule of law"), by adherence to established political rules and bureaucratic regularities, etc.[26] Under all but the most severe conditions (economic collapse, war), this severely limits the range and legitimacy of both dominant and oppositional political initiatives, no matter how heavy the conflicts among contemporary US political institutions and their constituents may appear to be.[27]

The trajectory of racial politics

It is useful to think of the US racial order as an "unstable equilibrium."[28] The idea of politics as "the continuous process of formation and superseding of unstable equilibria" has particular resonance, we think, in describing the operation of the racial state.[29] The racial order is equilibrated by the state – encoded in law, organized through policy-making, and enforced by a repressive apparatus. But the equilibrium thus achieved is unstable, for the great variety of conflicting interests encapsulated in racial meanings and identities can be no more than pacified – at best – by the state. Racial conflict persists at every level of society, varying over time and in respect to different groups, but ubiquitous. Indeed, the state is itself penetrated and structured by the very interests whose conflicts it seeks to stabilize and control.[30]

This unstable equilibrium has at times in US history gone undisturbed for decades and even centuries, but in our epoch its degree of "stability" has lessened. Under "normal" conditions, state institutions have effectively routinized the enforcement and organization of the prevailing racial order. Constituency relationships and established political organizations are at least implicitly and frequently explicitly racial.[31] Challenges to the racial order are limited to legal and political marginality. The system of racial meanings, of racial identities and ideology, seems "natural." Such conditions seemed generally to prevail from the end of Reconstruction to the New Deal, for example.

Now let us imagine a situation in which this unstable equilibrium is disrupted. There can be many reasons for this, and the disruption may take many shapes, for example the emergence of a mass-based racial movement such as took place in the 1960s, or of a powerful counter-egalitarian thrust such as appeared in the 1870s (with the beginnings of Asian exclusion and Jim Crow), or in the 1980s (with the institutionalization of new right and neoconservative interpretations of race). We shall be concerned with movement phenomena presently. Here we are interested chiefly in the effects on the state of racial disequilibrium.

Under conditions of disrupted equilibrium, inter-institutional competition and conflict within the state is augmented, as some agencies move toward accommodation of challenging forces while others "dig in their heels." Recomposition of constituencies and political alliances takes place. Opposition groups may resort to "direct action," and explicitly seek to politicize racial identities further; challenge will also take the route of "normal politics" (legislation, legal action, electoral activity, etc.), assuming this possibility is open to racially identified minorities. Strategic unity will therefore become more necessary for the governing forces or bloc.

The establishment or restoration of conditions of unstable equilibrium – let us say by means of reform policies – suggests an opposite cyclical phase. Such a situation guarantees the relative unity of the racial state by reducing the stakes of intra-state, or inter-institutional, conflict. It poses formidable obstacles to the fomenting of oppositional political projects. It minimizes the government's need to strategize and promises the automatic reproduction of the prevailing order, obviously an optimum situation from the standpoint of the dominant racial groups.

Disruption and restoration of the racial order suggests the type of cyclical movement or pattern we designate by the term *trajectory*. Both racial movements and the racial state experience such transformations, passing through periods of rapid change and virtual stasis, through moments of massive mobilization and others of relative passivity. While the movement and state versions of the overall trajectory are independently observable, they could not exist independently of each other. Racially based political movements as we know them are inconceivable without the racial state, which provides a focus for political demands and structures the racial order. The racial state, in its turn, has been historically constructed by racial movements; it consists of agencies and programs which are the institutionalized responses to racial movements of the past.

The point at which we begin to examine the trajectory of racial politics, then, is arbitrary. Let us assume, then, a beginning point of *unstable equilibrium$_1$.* At this historical point, the racial order is (relatively) undisturbed by conflict and mobilization. The racial state is able to function (again, relatively) automatically in its organization and enforcement of the racial order. We first address the racial movement version of the trajectory, and then that of the racial state.

Racial movements come into being as the result of political projects, political interventions led by "intellectuals."[32] These projects seek to transform (or "rearticulate" – see below) the dominant racial ideology. They thereby summarize and explain problems – economic inequality, absence of political rights, cultural repression, etc. – in racial terms. The result of this ideological challenge is a disparity, a conflict, between the pre-existing racial order, organized and enforced by the state, and an oppositional ideology whose subjects are the real and potential adherents of a racially defined movement. When this conflict reaches a certain level of intensity, a phase of *crisis* is initiated.

During a period of crisis, racial movements experiment with different strategies and tactics (electoral politics, "spontaneity," cultural revitalization efforts and alternative institution-building, lobbying, direct action, etc.). We assume that at least some of these are successful in mobilizing political pressure, either through "normal" political channels or through disruption of those channels.[33] Indeed the success of a racial movement probably depends on its ability to generate a wide and flexible variety of strategies, ideological themes and political tactics, as both the minority movements of the 1960s and the new right/neoconservative movements of the present have demonstrated.

In response to political pressure, state institutions adopt policies of absorption and insulation.[34] *Absorption* reflects the realization that many demands are greater threats to the racial order before they are accepted than after they have been adopted in suitably moderate form. *Insulation* is a related process in which the state confines demands to terrains that are, if not entirely symbolic, at least not crucial to the operation of the racial order. These policies then become ideological elements which are employed both by movements and state institutions. State agencies might argue, for example, that they have already met reasonable movement demands, while movement groups might claim that reforms don't address the problem, don't go far enough, etc.

Once the general contours of state reformism are clear, movements undergo internal divisions. A certain segment of the movement is absorbed ("coopted," in 1960s parlance) along with its demands, into the state, and there constitutes the core staff and agenda of the new state programs or agencies with which reform policies are to be implemented. The remaining active segment of the movement is "radicalized," while its more passive membership drops away to take up the roles and practices defined by a rearticulated racial ideology in the newly restabilized racial order (*unstable equilibrium$_2$*).

Considering the trajectory of racial politics from the standpoint of the state, *unstable equilibrium$_1$* at first coexists with a series of effectively marginalized political projects located outside the "normal" terrain of state activity. In racial terms the state's trajectory of reform is initiated when movements challenge the pre-existent racial order. Crisis ensues when this opposition upsets the pre-existing *unstable equilibrium$_1$*. The terms of challenge can vary enormously, depending on the movement involved. Opposition can be democratic or authoritarian, primarily based in "normal" politics or in disruption; opposition can even reject explicit political definition, as in the case of cultural movements.

Crisis generates a series of conflicts within and among state agencies as particular demands are confronted and the terms of the state response (repression, concessions, symbolic responses, etc.) are debated. Agency and constituent groups, confronted by racial opposition, explore the range of potential accommodations, the possibilities for reconsolidating the racial order, and their possible roles in a racial ideology "rearticulated" in light of oppositional themes. "Hard-liners" and "moderates" appear, and compromises are sought both with the opposition and within the state itself.

Ultimately a series of reforms is enacted which partially meets oppositional demands. Reform policies are initiated and deemed potentially effective in establishing a new *unstable equilibrium$_2$*. These policies are then regularized in the form of agencies and programs whose constituency bases, like those of other state apparatuses, will consist of former adherents and sympathizers of the movement (as well as "free riders," of course). A new racial ideology is articulated, often employing themes initially framed by the oppositional movements.

The concept of the trajectory of racial politics links the two central actors in the drama of contemporary racial politics – the racial state and racially based social movements – and suggests a general pattern of interaction between them. Change in the racial order, in the social meaning and political role played by race, is achieved only when the state has initiated reforms, when it has generated new programs and agencies in response to movement demands. Movements capable of achieving such reforms only arise when there is significant "decay" in the capacities of pre-existing state programs and institutions to organize and enforce racial ideology. Contemporary patterns of change in the racial order illustrate this point clearly.

Contemporary change in the US racial order

In the period with which we are concerned, the "rules of the game" by which racial politics are organized have become tremendously complex. In the pre-World War II period change in the racial order was epochal in scope, shaped by the conditions of "war of maneuver" in which minorities had very little access to the political system, and understood in a context of assumed racial inequalities (i.e. comprehensive and generally unexamined racism). Today all of this has been swept away.

In the present day, racial change is the product of the interaction of racially based social movements and the racial state. In the postwar period, minority-based movements, led by the black movement, radically challenged the dominant racial ideology. As a result of this challenge, the racial order anchored by the state was itself destabilized, and a comprehensive process of reform was initiated. Later still, the reformed racial state became the target for further challenge, this time from the right. Racial politics now take place under conditions of "war of position," in which minorities have achieved significant (though by no means equal) representation in the political system, and in an ideological climate in which the *meaning* of racial equality can be debated, but the desirability of some form of equality is assumed. The new "rules of the game" thus contain *both* the legacy of movement efforts to rearticulate the meaning of race and to mobilize minorities politically on the basis of the new racial ideologies thus achieved, *and* the heritage of deep-seated racism and inequality.

As we have argued, social movements create collective identity, collective subjectivity, by offering their adherents a different view of themselves and their world; different, that is, from the characteristic worldviews and self-concepts of the social order which the movements are challenging. Based upon that newly forged collective identity, they address the state politically, demanding change. This is particularly true of contemporary racial movements. In fact these movements largely established the parameters within which popular and radical democratic movements (so-called "new social movements") operate in the US.

Racial movement mobilization and "normal" politics (the state, electoral activity, constituency formation, administrative and judicial systems, etc.) are now linked in a reciprocal process. Demands for state reform – for the transformation of racial society as a whole – are the consequences of transformations in collective identity, indeed in the meaning of race itself, "translated" from the cultural /ideological terrain of everyday life into the terms of political discourse. Such "translations" may come from movements themselves, or they may originate in "normal" political processes as electoral bases are sought, judicial decisions handed down, administrative procedures contested, etc. Our conception of the "trajectory" of racial movements and state reform policies suggests that the transformation of the racial order comes about by means of an alternately equilibrated and disrupted relationship between the formation of racial ideology and the elaboration of state policy.

Today racial movements not only pose new demands originating outside state institutions, but may also frame their "common identity" in response to state-based racial initiatives. The concept of "Asian American," for example, arose as a political label in the 1960s. This reflected the similarity of treatment that various groups such as Chinese Americans, Japanese Americans, Korean Americans, etc. (groups which had not previously considered themselves as having a common political agenda) received at the hands of state institutions. The census, the legislatures, the courts, the educational system, the military, the welfare state apparatus – each in its own way a racial institution – are all sources of such radical change.

At the same time racial movements (both radical and conservative) continue to present the state with political demands. We understand this process as the *rearticulation* of racial ideology. Racially based movements begin as political projects which both build upon and break away from their cultural and political predecessors. Movement projects take shape in the interaction of civil society and the racial state. Movements set out to question the meaning of race and the nature of racial identity (e.g. "blackness," "Chicanismo," "minority" status; or for that matter, "majority" status, "whiteness"), while state initiatives seek to reinforce or transform the "unstable equilibrium" of racial politics in response to movement demands. Such "projects" challenge pre-existing racial ideology. They are efforts to *rearticulate* the meaning of race, and responses to such efforts.

The rearticulation of pre-existing racial ideology is a dual process of *disorganization* of the dominant ideology and of *construction* of an alternative, oppositional framework.

The dominant ideology can be disorganized in various ways. An insurgent movement, led by "intellectuals," may question whether the dominant racial ideology properly applies to the collective experience of its members. Examples of this interrogation of the pre-existing system of racial categories and beliefs may be found not only in militant movement rhetoric[35] but also in popular and intellectual discourse. During the 1960s, for instance, minority economists, political scientists, sociologists and psychologists rejected dominant social science perspectives on racial grounds:

> For years, traditional (white) social science research – especially on political life and organizations – told us how politically workable and healthy the society was, how all the groups in society were getting pretty much their fair share, or moving certainly in that direction. There was a social scientific myth of consensus and progress developed.[36]

Similarly, during the 1970s, conservative, whites-oriented racial movements, such as those of the "new right" or the "unmeltable" ethnics, developed counter-egalitarian challenges to the reforms which minority movements had achieved in the previous decade.[37] In this way the overarching racial ideology – in which racial minorities and the white majority alike recognize themselves – is called into question.

Insurgent racial minority movements also try to redefine the essential aspects of group identity. Demands for "self-determination" (which of course are linked to important democratic traditions in the US) attain currency, while past organizational efforts are criticized. For example, militants of the 1960s attacked the political accommodations and compromises into which pre-existing community organizations and leaderships had entered. The NAACP and Urban League, the GI Forum and LULAC were criticized as "Uncle Toms" and "Tio Tacos" who had succumbed to "cooptation."[38] Militants also denounced various cultural practices in minority communities which were judged to reinforce submission and dependence. Malcolm X, for instance, excoriated the black practice of "conking" (i.e. straightening) the hair with lye.[39]

The construction of an oppositional movement employs a wide variety of ideological themes. Racially based movements have as their most fundamental task the creation of new identities, new racial meanings, new collective subjectivity. Not only does the articulation of a new racial ideology involve the recombination of pre-existent meanings and identities, but it also draws on quite hetérodox and unexpected sources.[40]

The disorganization of the dominant racial ideology, the construction of a new set of racial meanings and identities, the transition from political project to oppositional movement, is a complex, uneven process, marked by considerable instability and tension. Change is being demanded, but any change in the system of racial meanings will affect all groups, all identities. Challenging the dominant racial ideology inherently involves not only reconceptualizing one's own racial identity, but a reformulation of the meaning of race in general. To challenge the position of blacks in society is to challenge the position of whites.[41]

Racial movements, built on the terrain of civil society, necessarily confront the state as they begin to upset the unstable equilibrium of the racial order. Once an oppositional racial ideology has been articulated, once the dominant racial ideology has been confronted, it becomes possible to demand reform of state racial policies and institutions. There has been a change in the "rules of the game." A new political terrain has been opened up.

By the same token, once such challenges have been posed and become part of the established political discourse, they in turn become subject to rearticulation. The state reforms won by minority movements in the 1960s, and the racial definitions and meanings embodied in these reforms, provided a formidable range of targets for "counter-reformers" in the 1970s. "New right" and neoconservative currents, armed with the still-dominant social scientific paradigm of ethnicity theory, were able to carry on their own political "project." They were able to rearticulate racial ideology and restructure racial politics once again.

In the next chapters, we consider in detail the process by which the particular trajectory of racial politics – which involved both democratizing and authoritarian movements, both state reform and state reaction – developed in the postwar United States.

Part Three

6
The great transformation

Introduction

The racial upsurges of the 1950s and 1960s were among the most
tempestuous events in postwar American history. The struggles for
voting rights, the sit-ins and boycotts to desegregate public facilities, the ghetto rebellions of the mid-1960s, and the political
mobilizations of Latinos, Indians and Asian Americans, dramatically transformed the political and cultural landscape of the US.
The postwar period has indeed been a racial crucible. During these
decades, new conceptions of racial identity and its meaning, new
modes of political organization and confrontation, and new definitions of the state's role in promoting and achieving "equality" were
explored, debated, and fought out on the battlegrounds of politics.

The racial minority movements responsible for these developments achieved limited but very real reforms in their struggle for
racial justice and equality. By the 1970s, however, through repression, cooptation and fragmentation, the racial minority movements
experienced a sharp decline, losing their vitality and coherence. In
the ensuing context of the economic, political and cultural crises of
the period, even the moderate gains they had achieved came under
attack by an alliance of right-wing and conservative forces.

In this chapter, we examine the minority movement upsurge of
the 1950s and 1960s. We do not seek to reprise the history of these
decades, but to employ our theory of *racial formation* to interpret
the events of the period. We suggest that two important changes
characterize the racial politics of the 1950s and 1960s: the first of
these was a *paradigm shift:* the established system of racial meanings and identities, based in the ethnicity paradigm of race, experienced increasing strain and opposition. This opposition gradually

took shape within the civil rights movement, as the challenge it had launched against segregation in the South was transformed into a national movement against racism.[1] The second change was the mobilization of *new social movements*, led by the black movement, as the primary means for contesting the nature of racial politics. These movements irreversibly expanded the terrain of political contest, and set the stage for the general reorganization of US politics.

Paradigm shift The modern civil rights movement was initially organized *within* the dominant paradigm of ethnicity. The ethnicity perspective provided an analytic framework by which to assess the situation of blacks, and correspondingly shaped the movement's political agenda. The early movement leaders were racial moderates who sought to end "race-thinking" and assure "equality" to each individual. The movement initially focused its energies on the South, where the ethnicity paradigm remained a challenging ideology to the racist logic of segregation. Later, when demands for racial reforms attained national scope and expanded beyond the black movement to other racially defined minorities, the limited explanatory abilities and programmatic usefulness of the ethnicity paradigm were revealed. The "eclipse" of this perspective led to a period where competing paradigms – the class- and nation-based views – flourished and contested for hegemony.

New social movements The upsurge of racially based movements which began in the 1950s was a contest over the *social meaning* of race. It was this process which created what we call "the great transformation"[2] of racial awareness, racial meaning, racial subjectivity. Race is not only a matter of politics, economics, or culture, but of all these "levels" of lived experience simultaneously. It is a pre-eminently *social* phenomenon, something which suffuses each individual identity, each family and community, yet equally penetrates state institutions and market relationships. The racial minority movements of the period were the first *new social movements* – the first to expand the concerns of politics to the social, to the terrain of everyday life. New social movement politics would later prove "contagious," leading to the mobilization of other racial minorities, as well as other groups whose concerns were principally social. As playwright David Edgar has noted, most of the new social movements of the 1960s – student, feminist and gay – drew upon the black struggle "as a central organizational fact or as a defining political metaphor and inspiration."[3]

Taken together, these two interrelated dimensions – the eclipse of the ethnicity paradigm and the emergence of new social movement politics – constitute an alternative framework by which to assess the racial politics of the period. Our account suggests that racial identity, the racial state, and the very nature of racial politics as a whole were radically transformed during the 1960s – transformed so profoundly that the racial meanings established during this period continue to shape politics, even in the current period of reaction.

While the 1960s witnessed the "demise" of the ethnicity paradigm and the flourishing of perspectives within the class-based and nation-based paradigms of race, none of the challenging viewpoints could achieve hegemonic status. They suffered from serious deficiencies, in part because (as we have argued in Part I) of their reduction of race to another phenomenon and the "partial" nature of their analysis. The subsequent waning of the movements and specific organizations operating within these challenging paradigms left a vacuum in racial theory and politics. This created the political space for the resurgence of the ethnicity paradigm in the 1980s.

Despite this, the depth and breadth of "the great transformation" can hardly be exaggerated. The forging of new collective racial identities during the 1950s and 1960s has been the enduring legacy of the racial minority movements. Today, as gains won in the past are rolled back and most organizations prove unable to rally a mass constituency in racial minority communities, the persistence of the new racial identities developed during this period stands out as the single truly formidable obstacle to the consolidation of a newly repressive racial order. Apparently, the movements themselves could disintegrate, the policies for which they fought could be reversed, their leaders could be coopted or destroyed, but the racial subjectivity and self-awareness which they developed had taken permanent hold, and no amount of repression or cooptation could change that. The genie was out of the bottle.

The emergence of the civil rights movement

The moderate goals of the early civil rights movement did not challenge the nationally dominant paradigm of racial theory, the ethnicity perspective. Indeed, early movement rhetoric often explicitly appealed to the ideal of a "race-free" society, the centerpiece of the liberal ethnicity vision.[4] This was consistent with the call for integration framed by Gunnar Myrdal in 1944, or with Nathan Glazer's description of the "national consensus" which abolished Jim Crow in the mid-1960s.[5]

Although its political goals were moderate, the black movement had to adopt the radical tactics of disruption and "direct action" due to the "massive resistance" strategy of the South, a region which clung to the racist assumption of an earlier paradigm. The modern civil rights movement came into being when southern black organizations, frustrated by Southern intransigence and drawing on both national and indigenous support bases, moved to mobilize a *mass* constituency in the South. They thus augmented the tactics of judicial/legislative activism – used in the elite politics which had previously characterized the civil rights struggle[6] – with those of direct action, which required an active "grass-roots" constituency. This was the key shift of the mid-1950s.

What made this change possible? Traditionally studies of social movements have developed models of "collective behavior" or "resource mobilization" to explain the emergence of significant struggles for change. Analyses of the formation of the modern civil rights movement in the mid-1950s are often based on one of these models.[7] Clearly both these approaches have their merits: the essential conditions for each – inadequacy of "normal" political channels to process demands (collective behavior model), and availability of material and political resources for the mobilization of movement constituencies (resource mobilization model) – were both present. The monolithic southern resistance to desegregation is an instance of the failure of "normal" politics to respond to demands for change. The role of such organizations as the local NAACP chapters, and particularly the black churches, recently documented by Aldon Morris,[8] exemplifies the centrality of resource mobilization issues.

Although both the resistance to change and the availability of economic and political resources in the black community were essential components of the civil rights movement's shift to a direct action strategy, neither of these conditions were sufficient to spark the transition. A third factor, perhaps the most central, was required. This was an ideological or cultural intervention, the politicization of black identity, the *rearticulation of black collective subjectivity*. It was this change which would eventually place radical objectives on the agenda of racial minority movements, facilitate the diffusion of racially based movement activity to other groups, and become anathema to the moderate advocates of civil rights operating within the ethnicity paradigm of race.

Origins of new social movement politics: identity, rearticulation and political opposition

Before the black movement's appearance on the political stage, the US political system had not significantly changed since the New Deal. The Democratic Party had served as a repository of consensus ever since Roosevelt led it to power in the 1930s. Compromise and pragmatic coalition-building among disparate interests, constituencies and loyalties ("interest-group liberalism")[9] shaped national politics. "Interests" themselves were largely defined economically. Such a system had obvious limitations in its ability to respond to challenges which cut across "class" (or "status") lines. It was limited by an inability to confront an unjust *social* system which had not only economic but also political and cultural causes and consequences.[10]

In its efforts to transform precisely that social system, the black movement sought to *expand* the concerns of politics, without abandoning the earlier economically centered logic. This expansion of "normal" politics to include racial issues – this "common sense" recognition of the political elements at the heart of racial identities and meanings – made possible the movement's greatest triumphs, its most permanent successes. These did not lie in its legislative accomplishments, but rather in its ability to create new racial "subjects." The black movement *redefined the meaning of racial identity*, and consequently of race *itself*, in American society.

Social movements create collective identity by offering their adherents a different view of themselves and their world; different, that is, from the worldview and self-concepts offered by the established social order. They do this by the process of *rearticulation*,[11] which produces new subjectivity by making use of information and knowledge already present in the subject's mind. They take elements and themes of her/his culture and traditions and infuse them with new meaning.

The civil rights movement linked traditional black cultural and religious themes with the ideas and strategies of social movements around the world. On this basis it could rearticulate black collective subjectivity – it could forge a new black politics.

The movement's "intellectuals" were largely preachers. They infused their activism with a well-known set of symbols and rhetorical tools.[12] The centuries-long black interrogation of biblical images of bondage and liberation – as embodied in the Exodus, for instance, or the theology of Christian redemption – had traditionally furnished a familiar vocabulary and textual reference point for freedom struggle, a home-grown "liberation theology."[13]

The civil rights movement augmented this imagery with ideas, lessons and strategies developed in India, Africa, Europe (in the experience of anti-Nazi resistance[14]) and in the US (in the sit-down strikes of the 1930s). Martin Luther King's application of the Gandhian philosophy of *satyagraha*, the adoption of the "sit-in" as a tactic for forcing integration, and the parallels drawn to African liberation movements, were examples of this borrowing from the repertoire of other political struggles.

The formation of the modern civil rights movement is a classical illustration of rearticulation processes. In order to win mass black support for the tactics of direct action, it was necessary to replace the established cultural norms through which ordinary blacks, particularly in the South, had previously sought to ameliorate the impact of racial oppression: "shuckin and jivin," "putting on Whitey," feigning ignorance and humility, etc. These strategies had served in the past to limit the extent of white control, to insulate the black community and black institutions from white intrusion and surveillance, and to protect individual blacks who ran afoul of white authority. But they had also limited the extent and depth of black organization, organization that would be necessary to challenge the system of segregation. They had been pre-political responses, survival efforts carried out by blacks as *individuals* in the absence of a movement. They were, in effect, adaptations to powerlessness.[15]

The modern civil rights movement sought not to survive racial oppression, but to overthrow it. Thus the traditional ideological themes of liberation and redemption, and the political tactics of protest derived from movements around the world, were incorporated in the heat of political struggle as elements of a new *identity*, one of *collective* opposition. According to Robert Moses or Martin

Luther King Jr, blacks were, collectively, the moral, spiritual and political leadership of American society. They represented not only their own centuries-long struggle for freedom, but the highest and noblest aspirations of white America as well.

Far from having to passively accept the " 'bukes and scorns" of segregation and perhaps trying to outmaneuver "Whitey," blacks were now called upon to oppose the system with righteous and disciplined action: "To accept passively an unjust system is to cooperate with that system; thereby the oppressed become as evil as the oppressor. Noncooperation with evil is as much a moral obligation as cooperation with good."[16]

The old linkages of religious and cultural themes – of the Christian virtues of humility, of "turning the other cheek" – were thus not negated, but dramatically captured by the movement. The "culture of resistance" with which these virtues had previously been identified was displaced from an emphasis on individual survival to one of collective action. This process of rearticulation made the movement's political agenda possible, especially its challenge to the existing racial state.

The radicalization of the black movement: black power

In subsequent stages of the movement's history, rearticulation processes continued to function as radical perspectives filled the void created by the eclipse of the ethnicity paradigm. This is particularly true of the emergence of *black power*. After the moderate demands of the civil rights movement were met in 1964 with the passage of the Civil Rights Act, and in 1965 with the enactment of voting rights legislation, many black activists saw their underlying ideals as unfulfilled. Not only had they failed to create a "beloved community" (which they now admitted had been a utopian vision[17]), but they had failed to achieve significant change in the social conditions faced by blacks. Kenneth Clark echoed these sentiments in 1967: "The masses of Negroes are now starkly aware that recent civil rights victories benefited a very small number of middle-class Negroes while their predicament remained the same or worsened."[18]

The radicalization of an important segment of the black

movement took shape in the myriad disappointments and disillusionments that afflicted civil rights activists: the acrimonious division between SNCC (Student Nonviolent Coordinating Committee) and civil rights moderates at the August 1963 March on Washinton;[19] the ferocity of the Birmingham campaign of April-May 1963, combined with the limited victory won there;[20] the experience of the Mississippi Freedom Democratic Party, a SNCC-organized project to unseat the segregationist "regular" delegation at the 1964 Democratic Party convention in Atlantic City;[21] the onset of rioting in many northern cities during the summer of 1964, followed by hundreds of riots during the next four years;[22] and the development of a new "backlash" politics in the middle 1960s, after the "massive resistance" strategy of the South had been broken.[23]

By the time of the Selma campaign (February-March 1965), no more than limited tactical cooperation existed between the radicals, led by SNCC, and the moderate SCLC (Southern Christian Leadership Conference). Militants from SNCC were infuriated when King, maneuvering between Washington, the federal courts, and the marchers themselves, halted an attempt to march from Selma to Montgomery on 10 March 1965.[24] By June 1966, when diverse civil rights groups came together to complete a march through Mississippi begun by James Meredith (who had been shot by a sniper), there was open competition between advocates of "black power" and supporters of integration.

Beginning with the Meredith march,[25] the more radical wing of the movement signalled its disillusionment with past emphases on civil rights and the transformative power of nonviolence. SNCC and CORE (Congress of Racial Equality), in particular, adopted the more militant positions associated with the slogan *black power*.

Black power was a flexible, even amorphous concept, but it was frequently interpreted to mean separatism. It was this connotation which the moderates, operating within the ethnicity paradigm, despised and strenuously denounced: "We of the NAACP [National Association for the Advancement of Colored People] will have none of this. It is the father of hatred and the mother of violence. Black power can mean in the end only black death."[26]

Ironically, the cry of "black power" was no more a complete break with the civil rights movement than that movement had been a break with the older "establishment" of civil rights organizations such as the NAACP and National Urban League. The concept of black power embraced a wide spectrum of political tendencies, extending from moderate "self-help" groups through reform-oriented advocates of "community control" to cultural and revolutionary nationalists. The concept's emergence as a rallying cry was an effort once more to rearticulate traditional themes of the black movement. An effort which, interestingly, drew upon the themes of the dominant ethnicity paradigm and the civil rights movement, while simultaneously rejecting their integrationist and assimilationist goals.

In the early 1960s, ethnicity theorists, mindful of their model's origins in the experiences of white ethnic groups of previous generations, suggested that blacks in the North should be organized as an interest group.[27] Much of the black power current could be understood as following this advice. The idea that the black community should patronize businesses owned by blacks, that it should adopt cooperative forms of organization, that it should mobilize politically at the local level ("community control") were concepts which borrowed as much from the tradition of Booker T. Washington as they did from those of Cyril Briggs, Marcus Garvey, or Malcolm X. Robert Allen notes that in many respects black power was "only another form of traditional ethnic group politics."[28]

Despite its many "moderate" elements, black power drew an important line of demarcation within the black movement and deeply disturbed the dominant (i.e. white) political culture. White liberals reacted in horror when their ethnic prescriptions were put into practice by black militants and quickly retreated into a fundamentalist individualism which would have embarrassed Adam Smith.[29]

While embracing aspects of the ethnicity paradigm, black power theorists also initiated a rupture with that perspective by drawing upon colonial analogies to analyze the plight of blacks in America, and by focusing attention on racially based intra-class conflict. The political implications of this paradigmatic shift represented a distinct departure from the "interest group" politics of the ethnicity paradigm. Some examples were Stokely Carmichael and Charles V. Hamilton's *Black Power: The Politics of Liberation in America*,[30] which addressed black conditions in the US within a nationalist paradigm, and James Boggs's essays,[31] which focused on the role of black industrial workers and urban struggles from a perspective based in Marxism-Leninism.

A key figure in the transition from civil rights to black power was Malcolm X, who placed a radical nationalist position on the political agenda and attracted mass black support for that view. First as organizer and chief spokesperson for the Nation of Islam, and then, briefly, as founder of the Organization of Afro-American Unity, Malcolm played a role unparalleled in the black community since Garvey's time. Although he often derided the civil rights movement, referring to its organizations and leaders as "Uncle Toms," Malcolm also recognized the importance of raising civil rights demands, even while arguing that the US could not meet them.[32] After his 1963 break with the Nation of Islam, Malcolm moved closer to the radical wing of the movement and influenced SNCC thinking. In late 1964 he met with SNCC leaders in Nairobi, Kenya, at which time he stressed the importance of Pan-Africanism for US blacks. He also approached socialist positions in a number of respects.[33] Malcolm formulated a radical challenge to the moderate agenda of the civil rights movement and prefigured the themes of black power. In February 1965 he was assassinated at the Audubon Ballroom in Harlem, under circumstances that remain mysterious.[34]

Black power advocates and adherents broke away from the earlier black movement's struggle for a "raceless society." Integration, they argued, could only be a *result* of political power and equality, never its cause. The radicalization of the black movement appropriated the legacy of civil rights, much as the earlier movement had appropriated the legacy of the southern "culture of resistance" which had been nourished in the black church, in black music, in folklore and literature, even in food.[35]

In addition to the demand for social justice, the question of "self-determination" was raised. The prospect of having not only "rights" but also "power" once again rearticulated black cultural and political traditions, reviving themes from black political history. The cultural nationalism and black Marxism of the late 1960s were restatements of positions which harked back to the 1920s and 1930s, the days of the Harlem Renaissance, the African Blood Brotherhood, the Garvey movement, and the "black nation" thesis of the Communist Party.[36] The nation-based paradigm was not, however, synonymous with radical politics. Less "progressive" – or, as Huey P. Newton once called them, "pork chop" – nationalists tended to dilute their vision of black power by ignoring its racial dimensions for a more limited, "ethnic" view of its meaning. These groups often adopted reformist orientations, embracing "black capitalism," for example.[37] Here the distinction between the two paradigms became muted.

Encountering and reforming the racial state

There were two phases to the minority encounter with the state in the 1950s and 1960s.[38] The first phase was shaped by the civil rights movement's mass mobilization in the South, a "direct action" political strategy which, as we have seen, already depended upon new social movement politics, on the "politics of identity." This first phase resulted in the civil rights reforms of the mid-1960s. Through desegregation campaigns the black movement set in motion a reform-oriented democratization process. The resulting concessions were limited but real: policy shifts through executive order and legislation, judicial action against specific racist practices, establishment of new state programs and agencies with "equal opportunity" mandates, and the hiring of many black activists by state institutions. These victories ended the exceptional situation in the South by forcing that region to accept the nationally dominant racial ideology, as defined by the ethnicity paradigm. The reforms of the 1960s also signalled the fulfillment of that paradigm's vision of racial equality.

The second phase of the movement/state encounter was marked by the fragmentation of the minority movements into competing currents during the institutionalization of the racial reforms of the mid-1960s. This took place as the new reforms took hold, gradually and partially transforming the movement into a constituency for the new programs its efforts had won.

The state was the chief movement target for several reasons. First, the state, as the "factor of cohesion in society,"[39] had historically maintained and organized racial practices. In the present, too, it gave shape to the racial order. Second, the state was traversed by the same antagonisms which penetrated the entire society, antagonisms that were themselves the results of past cycles of racial struggle. The lukewarm commitments to desegregation of public employment and the armed forces extracted by A. Philip Randolph from Roosevelt and Truman, the use of the 14th

Amendment by NAACP lawyer Thurgood Marshall to challenge school segregation, the freedom rides of the 1940s and 1960s (which probed the federal commitment to integration of interstate travel), and the voting rights drives in the South were all examples of the small but significant "openings" through which the existing racial state was susceptible to challenge. Movement tactics often sought to make use of the state's internal racial contradictions. For example, the voting rights drives sought to induce confrontations between different branches of the state: the courts vs. state legislatures, federal police vs. local or state police. The idea was to force the federal government to defend civil rights from infringement by racist local and state agencies.

By the latter stages of this process – the late 1960s – the reform-oriented program of the black movement had acquired a foothold in state institutions such as social service agencies, and in electorally based positions. At the same time, splits and divisions had surfaced in the movement, and in minority communities as well. These included inter-group rivalries, class divisions, controversies over strategy, and disputes over the meaning of race within the minority movements themselves (e.g. integration vs. black power).[40] Class polarization was deepening within minority communities as those who were able to do so took advantage of new jobs and educational opportunities, while the majority of ghetto and barrio dwellers remained locked in poverty. The war on poverty was lost, as King had warned, on the battlefields of Vietnam.[41] Some formerly integrated movement organizations now became all black (e.g. SNCC); others that formed in the mid-1960s were organized from the beginning as exclusively black, Mexican American, Asian American, etc.

In the racial minority movements of the period, the state confronted a new type of opposition. Racial minority movements challenged established racial practices simultaneously through direct action, through penetration of the mainstream political arena (electoral/institutional projects from voter registration to community organization), and through "ethical/political" tactics (taking the "moral initiative," developing "resistance cultures," etc.).[42] These movements were able to link spontaneity and mass participation, on the one hand, with electoral/institutional politics, on the other. The unifying element in this opposition was at first the burgeoning collective subjectivity of blacks – and later that of other minorities –

which connected demands for access to the state with more radical demands for freedom, "self-determination," cultural and organizational autonomy, "community control," and a host of other issues.

By combining these different oppositional tactics, the racial minority movements of the 1960s initiated the reforms which eventually created a new racial state. This new state, however, was not the institutional fulfillment of the movements' ideals. Rather it held a cloudy mirror up to its antagonists, reflecting their demands (and indeed their rearticulated racial identities) in a distorted fashion.

The state responded to movement demands with tactics of *absorption* and *insulation*.[43] Absorption (or cooptation) reflected the recognition that movement demands were often greater threats as rallying cries for minority opposition than they were after they had been adopted in suitably moderate form. Furthermore, absorption resulted in a certain "ghettoization" within state institutions that transformed militancy into constituency.[44] A pluralist interest-group framework replaces "grass-roots" opposition as the main organizational dynamic.

For example, civil rights workers in the South during the 1960s were continually frustrated in their efforts to obtain Justice Department protection for their efforts, frequently asking why the US government was so willing to "defend democracy" in Vietnam but so slow to do so in Mississippi.[45] In such a form the demand for federal protection was ominous, for it linked issues which state policy-makers preferred to keep separate and thus "insulated" (see below) from movement demands. US foreign and domestic policy, interventionism abroad and racial despotism at home, and the domestic and international "third worlds" were all articulated in a single oppositional demand for *state guarantees of democratic rights*. But once the demand for protection was absorbed, appearing in the creation of the Community Relations Service in the Justice Department under the Civil Rights Act of 1964, its challenge to the state was largely blunted.[46]

Insulation is a related process in which the state confines democratizing demands to areas that are, if not entirely symbolic, at least not crucial to its operation as a "factor of cohesion" in society. The federal system in the United States permits a degree of insulation of key state institutions from popular demands that is unequalled elsewhere in the capitalist democracies.[47] Thus whole areas of potential conflict, such as the operation of the Federal Reserve

Board or the framing of tax policy, were defined as nonracial issues during the 1960s.

Challenging paradigms and strategic divisions

By the late 1960s, the fragmentation within the racial minority movements was clearly visible and consolidated into discernible currents. New social movement politics had galvanized activists in their respective communities, but the lack of theoretical clarity about racial dynamics in the US splintered political action. Although the ethnicity paradigm had been seriously challenged, it remained an important explanatory model, not only for academics but also for movement activists. The challenging paradigms – the class- and nation-based views – gave rise to counterposed strategic orientations. Strategic divisions also flowed from class cleavages internal to minority communities, from state repression which marginalized radical tendencies, and from the very effectiveness of state strategies of reform, which tended to replace movement perspectives with the constituency-based viewpoints of "normal" politics.

Three broad political currents can be recognized within the racial minority movement of this period.[48] These were *electoral/institutional "entrism," socialism*, and *nationalism*.

Advocates of *electoral/institutional entrism* argued for greater movement participation in existing political organizations and processes, such as party politics, local government agencies, welfare state and poverty programs, etc. While this tendency was perhaps most closely associated with the reform orientation of moderate movement factions, more militant currents also adopted "entrist" perspectives, for example the La Raza Unida Party[49] or the Georgia legislative campaigns of SNCC activist Julian Bond.[50] The necessity of "entering the mainstream" was advocated for the following reasons: to avoid marginalization, since no other historically continuous political terrain was available to minority activists; to achieve reforms that would allow for further movement-building, redistribution of income, goods and services, and increased access to the racial state; and to educate and "raise consciousness," since electoral office and bureaucratic position confer opportunities to publicize one's views and to initiate policy.

A second tendency was the *socialist* tradition. Marxist-Leninist and internal colonialist perspectives were the main representatives of this current. Marxist-Leninist approaches pointed out the class dimensions of anti-racist struggles. They argued that racism is an indispensable support to advanced capitalism; that class cleavages exist within minority communities (this served to curb excessive nationalism and point out the dangers of multi-class alliances); and that it was essential to base organizational efforts on the (traditionally defined) working class. Somewhat paradoxically, Marxist-Leninist groups often successfully recruited minority memberships, particularly among students, even as they became increasingly marginal on the US political landscape.[51]

Internal colonialist perspectives saw racism as an ongoing historical process which contained *both* class- and nationally based elements. Racially defined communities within the US were analogized to colonies, and said to face the same types of economic exploitation and cultural domination which the developed nations had visited on the underdeveloped ones. The internal colonialism rubric included a strategic spectrum running all the way from moderate reform initiatives to revolution and "national liberation." Demands for increases in the number of "natives" occupying key posts in businesses or state institutions (police, schools, social agencies), plans to achieve "community control" of the ghetto and barrio economies, and schemes for a two-stage revolutionary process[52] analogous to the Angolan or Vietnamese experiences, were all put forward based on the internal colonialism analysis.

Nationalism was a diverse current whose main strategic unity lay in rejection of the assimilationist and integrationist tendencies associated with the movement moderates. A tremendous diversity of political tendencies were understood in different minority communities under the "nationalist" label.

In the black community, for example, the term referred not only to a legacy of radical opposition to integration, but also to the "separate development" strategy associated with Booker T. Washington, and to various Pan-Africanist currents which passed through Garvey and DuBois. It also encompassed black Marxism-Leninism and anti-colonialist orientations (which straddle the nationalist and socialist categories), and even included a cultural nationalist current which was largely anti-political.

In the Mexican American community, nationalism had its roots in Mexican revolutionary traditions, notably those of land struggles,[53] and in the proximity of the border. In the pre-1960s period, political activity aimed at improving conditions for Mexican Americans in the US had been linked to an "entrist" perspective of civil rights/integration, such as that advocated by LULAC or the GI Forum. Nationalism in this context focused on Mexico, not the US and was fuelled by immigration, geographical proximity, and the regional particularities of the border area, on both the Mexican and US sides.[54]

With the 1960s, though, an alternative *Chicano* nationalism appeared, which rearticulated many traditionally Mexican elements within a US-based perspective, usually focused on the Southwest. In Chicano communities, new "anti-colonial" struggles erupted, taking the form of land seizures as well as the community control struggles of the urban barrio.

The struggle for land was necessarily premised on the existence of substantial Mexican American populations which could constitute local majoritarian constituencies for radical political action. Such concentrations in turn reflected the long-standing semi-colonial conditions which existed in many rural areas of the Southwest. In these areas Mexican Americans were an impoverished agricultural labor force, exploited by agribusiness interests, victimized by immigration policies, and heir to a "colonial labor system."[55]

The urban manifestations of this new *Chicanismo* largely took shape among student and youth organizations, which flourished in the Mexican American community during the middle and late 1960s, often adopting cultural nationalist orientations.[56] Many groups rejected the Mexican American identity, which they saw as assimilationist, in favor of a specifically Chicano identity which in their view reflected commitment to a new and higher level of political struggle.[57]

Asian American nationalism, for the most part, centered on community control issues. In many cities Asian Americans fought to prevent commercial transformation or obliteration of their communities. In many urban areas, such as San Francisco, Manilatowns and Japantowns have been destroyed by urban renewal schemes which have dispersed residents. Always a popular tourist attraction, Chinatowns have been the site of continual political battles over low-cost housing versus commercial development.[58] Within this context, Asian Americans sought to build alternative institutions which would more adequately address the needs of community residents than could the state or the existing conservative community leadership.

Cultural nationalism found expression in every minority community. This was an explicit critique of the dominant Eurocentric (i.e. white) culture, understood to pervade both everyday life and "high culture." Cultural nationalists sought to redefine and recapture the specificity of their minority cultures, an objective which they identified as "nationalist." Painting, theatre, dance, music, language, even cars and clothes, all became media through which a new style could be developed, and through which "genuine" oppositional culture could be distinguished from assimilationist practices.

In the Chicano student movement, a variety of organizations sought to educate their members and communities about their heritage and the lost "nation" of *Aztlan*, to set up schools and cultural clubs (for folk dancing, mural painting, etc.), and to found journals and newspapers.[59] In Native American communities there was a return to traditional religious and spiritual concerns. Cultural nationalism helped to link distinct groups who were racialized as one monolithic entity. The very term "Asian American" arose to express the similarity of experiences and treatment at the hands of various institutions which the specific "ethnicities" of Japanese, Chinese, Korean and Filipino, among others, encountered in the US. Cultural and historical antagonisms which existed between these groups were muted among college students who became radicalized during the Vietnam War. The war was seen as a racist one in which Asian life as a whole was regarded as "cheap."[60]

Each of these tendencies – "entrism," socialism, and nationalism – rearticulated racial ideology and each responded to existing racial practices while initiating new ones.

The electoral/institutional "*entrists*" built political organizations that could win elections, penetrate and influence state bureaucracies, and either exercise power in the Democratic Party[61] or openly compete with it. By the 1970s forces such as the Congressional Black Caucus and the Joint Center for Political Studies had achieved real influence on the national political scene, while local political machines developed under victorious black and Chicano mayors in such cities as Atlanta, Birmingham, Denver, Detroit, Philadelphia and San Antonio.[62] These instrumentalities were in turn linked to the many civil rights, lobbying, and local political groups, including those at the neighborhood, social agency, union, or church level. Thus as a result of the 1960s movement victories, social programs and policies – with all their limitations – addressed the needs of minority communities as never before. The nascent influence of "entrist" minority activists made innovations not only in the obvious areas of policy, in employment, housing, education and health, but also established the less obvious racial content of such policy areas as foreign affairs, taxation, environment, science and arts support, etc. The network of "entrists" as a whole played a key long-term role in maintaining minority viewpoints and positions – for example the Congressional Black Caucus's annual alternative budget proposals – in the mainstream political process.

Among the *socialists*, Marxist-Leninists confronted the substantial class cleavages that exist in minority communities, as well as the conflicts that exist *among* minority groups (such as black/Asian American competition for housing or Chicano/black rivalries for electoral office), precisely by stressing the supposedly "fundamental" class conflict. This pointed to an alternative perspective which could allow people to understand that the sources of racial oppression lay in the broader society. The focus on class, it was felt, could permit communication across the chasms and gulfs that separate minority communities and racial minorities as a whole from the white working class.

Socialists or nationalists who adopted the internal colonialist approach offered a synthesis of cultural nationalism and the Marxist-Leninist analysis of class, arguing that cultural domination reinforced and shaped class domination, and that racial logic characterized the system as a whole. Strategies based on the internal colonialism perspective frequently focused on community control struggles, and on efforts to develop autonomous racial minority organizations.[63]

Nationalists called on minority communities to develop their unique histories, distinct collective identities and separate political agendas. They opposed both integrationist political currents and the homogenizing, culturally dominant thematics of "mainstream" America. This generated the range of particularist racial movements we have described above – focused on Africa, *Aztlan*, or the ghetto/barrio as a locus of "community control."[64] Cultural nationalists in every minority community challenged the ubiquitous and at times forcible imposition of the dominant white culture.[65] They often formulated this challenge in terms which were explicitly anti-political, focusing on the recreation (and creation!) of the cultural framework by which their group recognized and understood itself.

Considered critically, none of these political projects succeeded even remotely in forging an oppositional racial ideology or movement capable of radically transforming the US racial order. The electoral/institutional "entrists" succumbed to illusions about the malleability of the racial state and were forced into a new version of ethnic group pluralism – the idea that racial minorities, like the white ethnics of the past, could claim their rights through "normal" political channels. The Marxist-Leninists could fight racism only by recourse to a futile dogma, and moreover one which consigned race to the terrain of "false consciousness." The internal colonialists, like an earlier generation of black (and other minority) nationalists, refused to recognize the particularities of the US racial order and the limits of all analogies with revolutionary movements abroad.[66] The cultural nationalists ignored the political sphere, and indeed heaped scorn upon both reform-oriented "entrists" and minority socialists.[67]

All these tendencies were but partial assaults on the US racial order; all failed to grasp the comprehensive manner by which race is structured into the US social fabric. All *reduced* race: to interest group, class fraction, nationality, or cultural identity. Perhaps most importantly, all these approaches lacked adequate conceptions of the racial state. In their radical as much as in their moderate phases, minority movements neglected the state's role in the organization and enforcement of the US racial order, not to mention its capacity for adaptation under political pressure.

The movement's limits also arose from the strategic divisions that befell it as a result of its own successes. Here the black movement's fate is illustrative. Only in the South, while fighting against a backward political structure and overt cultural oppression, had the black movement been able to maintain a *de*-centered unity, even when internal debates were fierce. Once it moved north, the black movement began to split, because competing political projects, linked to different segments of the community, sought either integration in the (reformed) mainstream, or more radical transformation of the dominant racial order.

After initial victories against segregation were won, one sector of the movement was thus reconstituted as an interest group, seeking an end to racism understood as discrimination and prejudice, and turning its back on the oppositional "politics of identity." Once the organized black movement became a mere constituency, though, it found itself locked in a bear hug with the state institutions whose programs it had itself demanded, while simultaneously isolated from the core institutions of the modern state.

The radical sectors of the movement were marginalized in cultural arenas or on the left. Cultural nationalists disdained engagement with the racial state. Those who confronted the state from radical positions (SNCC, the Black Panther Party, the League of Revolutionary Black Workers, and others) were met with intense repression.

Beyond this, organizationally, the minority movements of the 1950s and 1960s nearly ceased to exist. Yet, as we have argued, the complex of racial meanings had been irrevocably altered by years of political activity, by intense campaigns for racial equality and democracy, by the transformed character of "blackness," "whiteness," and all other racial identities that the movements had initiated. The specter of racial equality and, beyond that, of an end to racial oppression itself, continued to haunt American dreams and nightmares.

7
Race and reaction

Introduction

In March 1985, some 2500 people gathered in Alabama to com-
memorate a dramatic chapter in the history of the civil rights
movement. Twenty years before, Martin Luther King Jr had led
more than 4000 demonstrators on a fifty-mile march from Selma to
Montgomery, a major turning point in the struggle for black voting
rights. Twenty years later, Rev. Joseph E. Lowery, president of the
Southern Christian Leadership Conference, told the crowd
gathered at the commemoration, "We have kept the faith but the
nation has not kept its promise." Political forces, including the
Reagan administration itself, were trying to "turn back the clock of
racial history."[1]

Lowery's comments were painfully accurate. The state of black
America is worsening when measured by indicators such as unemployment rates, number of families falling below the poverty line,
and the widening gap between white and black infant mortality
rates.[2] Yet despite these continuing problems, the American populace remains callous about the situation of blacks and other racial
minorities. A new mood of "social meanness" pervades the US, and
many Americans resent having to provide for the "under-
privileged." Indeed many feel that far from being the victims of
deprivation, racial minorities are unfairly receiving "preferential
treatment" with respect to jobs and educational opportunities.

How, after several decades of attempts to eliminate racial inequality, did we get to this point? What political and ideological
shifts have occurred to bring about such a tragic reversal?

Although much has been written about racial minority movements, little attention has been given to the way racial issues have

109

shaped political movements on the right in the 1980s. Certainly there has been an explicit revitalization of the racist ideologies of the past, but there are also new currents which seek to reinterpret the meaning of race in the US, to *rearticulate* racial ideology once more, this time in a conservative direction. These currents have incubated and developed in the political space created by the racial minority movements of the past several decades. They include a wide range of perceptions about racial politics and the meaning of race in American life.

Among the welter of reactionary and conservative tendencies, we focus our attention on three main currents: the *far right*, the *new right*, and *neoconservatism*. While varying widely in perspective, these currents share a similar ambition, to discredit the key ideas and objectives of the 1960s minority movements. In attempting to do so by advancing their own vision of race, they are transforming the terrain of racial politics once again.

In this chapter, we first examine the historical context for racially based reaction; we then survey these three currents with an analytic focus on the processes of rearticulation they employ; we conclude with an examination of the Reagan administration's role in consolidating and abetting the racial reaction which these currents advocate.

The context for reaction

The seemingly quiescent 1970s, a decade without a firm identity, constituted a period of profound social transformation and dislocation in American life. During these years, many of the themes of racial reaction, of opposition to the egalitarian ideals of the 1960s, were developed and disseminated. For the first time in a sustained and programmatic way, setbacks in the domestic economy and US reversals on the international level were "explained" by attacking the liberal interventionist state. Many of these criticisms had racial subtexts.

The decade was shaped by profound sectoral and regional economic dislocations. Jobs and industry fled the "frostbelt" (formerly the industrial center of US prosperity and progress) for the conservative "sunbelt" of the South and West. The "sunset" industries of steel, rubber and auto production of the Northeast gave way to the "sunrise" electronic and emergent technologies of the sunbelt. The issue of "deindustrialization" gradually moved to the center of economic debates, as workers faced plant shut-downs, redundancy, and limited hi-tech occupational opportunities.[3]

Inflation also surged to unprecedented levels, eroding consumer purchasing power and curtailing investment. The problem of "stagflation," which Keynesian policies were helpless to overcome, came to seem a permanent feature of US economic life.[4]

The state was the obvious target of criticism for the poor performance of the economy. The state was apparently unable to act, as its New Deal lineage obliged it to do, to solve or at least ameliorate economic problems. Indeed, the state was blamed for obstructing the economy's "natural" tendencies toward recovery. Once state programs had been seen as treatments for the disease of economic crisis; now they began to appear as the disease itself. Meanwhile, economic sluggishness persisted, state revenues remained low, and demands for state intervention were heard from every social and economic quarter.

Thus arose the "fiscal crisis of the state," which manifested itself on local, state and national levels.[5] The near bankruptcy of major cities, the property tax revolt (exemplified by California's Prop. 13 tax-cutting initiative), and the soaring federal deficit provided further fuel both for the crisis and for growing anti-statist sentiment.

In the international arena, the country suffered the humiliating "losses" of Vietnam, Nicaragua and Iran in the 1970s. The formerly uncontested hegemony of the US was slowly being eroded, not only on the world stage, but also in the American popular imagination. The Bretton Woods system, the structure which formerly dominated postwar international finance, had collapsed by 1973.[6] With it went the unique advantages which the US had previously enjoyed in international trade. Suddenly, it seemed, the US was being "held for ransom" by the OPEC nations, which controlled "our" vital energy resources – a thought not taken lightly by Americans waiting in endless lines for gas. The Iranian revolution also came to typify this fall from grace. America was more literally "held hostage" by politico-religious forces far beyond popular comprehension.

As the decade ended, no relief was in sight. US manufacturers were losing their markets to foreign competitors and the trade deficit grew alarmingly. People in the US painfully contemplated the idea that perhaps we were not "No. 1" anymore.

Many of these changes which began during the 1970s – and which have continued and deepened in the 1980s – have been discussed by other observers, but few have appreciated their implicit racial dimensions. Popular ideology often makes use of racial themes as a framework by which to comprehend major problems, be they the declining US dominance in the world, dislocations in the workforce, or the fiscal crisis of state. Some examples:

Domestic economic woes are attributed to unfair foreign competition – with Japan receiving an inordinate amount of blame.[7] National polls show an increase in unfavorable attitudes toward Japan, while labor leaders and politicians employ racist cliches redolent of World War II propaganda in their demands for restrictions on Japanese imports.[8] Asian Americans are particularly sensitive to, and affected by, this shift in climate.[9]

The current influx of immigrants and refugees from Mexico, Cambodia, Vietnam, Haiti, and Cuba (among other countries) has been met in a climate of scarcity with "fear and loathing." Many blame job loss and dislocation on the seemingly endless stream of "illegal aliens."[10] Rising unemployment, scarce housing, and social program cutbacks have contributed to demands for restriction, if not outright exclusion.[11] A restrictive new immigration law, based on last session's Simpson-Mazzoli bill, will probably be passed in 1986 with bipartisan and administrative support.[12]

The reversals of the 1970s called into question the scope and capacities of the so-called "welfare state." During the pre-crisis era, the Great Society had promised the elimination of poverty and of the invidious effects of racial discrimination. Yet the problems remained – indeed some had intensified throughout the 1970s. It was time, conservatives argued with increasing popular support, to stop "throwing good money after bad." In attempting to remedy problems of poverty and inequality, the state, they charged, only made them worse and instilled a parasitic dependency in its clients.[13] The tax revolt was but one popular indication of this sentiment. Taxes, it was argued, replenished and expanded the welfare state, and its stereotypically minority clientele, at the expense of "productive" (i.e. white) taxpayers.[14] Another target was affirmative action policies. Through its reckless intervention, conservatives alleged, the state committed "reverse discrimination" – *whites* were now the victims of racial discrimination in education and the job market. The dislocations which began in the 1970s, then, were often understood *racially*. This racial connection has various implications; for example, it has fed into random acts of racial violence. But perhaps more importantly, "racial" issues have become central to the agenda of those forces and projects seeking a rightward realignment in US politics. The far right, the new right, and neoconservatism have reopened the 1960s debates about racial identity and racial equality, and have questioned once more the role of racial issues in the democratic political process. The effectiveness of a right-wing challenge to ideals promoted by the racial minority movements of the 1960s hinges on its ability to rearticulate the meaning of race in contemporary American society.

The rearticulation of racial ideology

As we have noted in the preceding chapter, the racial minority movements of the postwar period dramatically reshaped the political and cultural landscape of the nation. They imparted new meaning to established traditions and ideas. Equality, group and individual rights, and the legitimate scope of state activity, were reinterpreted, *rearticulated*, by these movements in a radical democratic discourse. Ironically, by challenging the racial verities of the past and revamping the old political terrain, the racial minority movements set the stage for the racial reaction which first appeared in the late-1960s, grew and developed in the 1970s, and reached maturity in the 1980s.

There were clear limits to any attempt to undo the effects of the "great transformation." In the aftermath of the 1960s, any effective challenge to the egalitarian ideals framed by the minority movements could not longer rely on the racism of the past. Racial equality had to be acknowledged as a desirable goal. But the *meaning* of equality, and the proper means for achieving it, remained matters of considerable debate.

With the exception of some on the far right, the racial reaction which has developed in the last two decades claims to favor racial equality. Its vision is that of a "colorblind" society where racial considerations are never entertained in the selection of leaders, in

113

hiring decisions, and the distribution of goods and services in general. As the right sees it, racial problems today center on the new forms of racial "injustice" which originated in the "great transformation." This new injustice confers group rights on racial minority groups, thus granting a new form of privilege – that of "preferential treatment."

The culprit behind this new form of "racism" is seen as the state itself. In attempting to eliminate racial discrimination, the state went too far. It legitimated group rights, established affirmative action mandates, and spent money on a range of social programs which, according to the right, debilitated, rather than uplifted, its target populations. In this scenario, the victims of racial discrimination have dramatically shifted from racial minorities to whites, particularly white males.

The forces of racial reaction have seized on the notion of racial equality advanced by the racial minority movements and *rearticulated* its meaning for the contemporary period. Racial reaction has repackaged the earlier themes – infusing them with new political meaning and linking them to other key elements of conservative ideology.

The different currents of reaction have not all been equally successful in shifting the terms of racial politics. The far right for the most part has revived the racist ideologies of previous periods. Yet even this current has employed processes of rearticulation in its attempt to attack the liberal state as the perpetrator of a racially unjust society. The new right's use of "code words" (nonracial rhetoric used to disguise racial issues) is a classic example of rearticulation, geared to mobilize a mass base threatened by minority gains, but disinclined to embrace overtly racist politics. Neoconservatism represents the most sophisticated effort to rearticulate racial ideology. It has developed a limited but real coherence in challenging the underpinnings of the 1960s quest for social justice. It has sketched out a vision of an "egalitarian" society where racial considerations are no longer the concern of state policy. We now turn our attention to each of these three currents.

The far right

In 1980, Tom Metzger, a television repairman from San Diego

County, California, won nomination as the Democratic candidate for Congress in the 43rd Congressional District. His bid received national attention when it was revealed that Metzger, among other posts on the far right, was once Grand Dragon of the California branch of the Ku Klux Klan. An embarrassed state central committee subsequently stripped him of his Democratic Party membership.[15]

Metzger was always civic-minded. He first garnered public attention when he offered to help the US Border Patrol hunt down "illegal aliens." He also offered Klan members as a "goon squad" against the organizing efforts of the United Farm Workers union in the fields of California. He later dropped the Klan affiliation to found the White American Resistance (WAR) and he currently appears on "Race and Reason," a "white man's talk show" which is broadcast on public access cable television in San Francisco, San Diego, Orange County in California, and in Austin, Texas.

Metzger is not alone in his efforts. A range of white supremacist groups exists – Aryan Nations, the Silent Brotherhood, the Order, and of course, various sects of the Ku Klux Klan. Most are interconnected and constitute an underground network which embraces neo-Nazis, survivalists, and militant tax resisters, among others. They have come to public attention through a series of dramatic crimes such as the killing of Jewish radio talk show host Alan Berg in Denver, a Brinks armored car robbery in Ukiah, California, and numerous shoot-outs with federal police.

Since the Civil War, white supremacist groups have periodically appeared on the American political scene. As D.W. Griffith's epic *Birth of a Nation* (1915) effectively conveyed, there was a "populist" impulse in such politics which resonated with whites who felt dislocated by the changes around them. In the view of such groups, racial "justice" (i.e. white supremacy) is perpetually threatened and the legitimate authorities are always too weak, naive, or corrupt to maintain America's "true" identity. Such logic has often inspired vigilante action as white supremacist groups sought to restore "white honor" and a "just" racial order.

In the past, the targets of such actions were racial minority groups themselves – groups which had to be terrorized into "knowing their place." In the 1980s, however, the target has shifted to the federal government. For example, to the neofascists of the shadowy Order, the "Zionist Occupied Government" (ZOG) is now the problem.

115

To the Posse Comitatus, the federal income tax represents the opening wedge in the government's assault on white rights. Klansman Thomas Robb, publisher of *The Torch* newsletter, summarizes the historic difference between previous and current far right thinking:

> The Klan in the '20s made a mistake thinking that evil resided in men who came home drunk or in Negroes who walked on the wrong side of the street. Today we see the evil is coming out of the government. To go out and shoot a Negro is foolish. It's not the Negro in the alley who's responsible for what's wrong with this country. It's the traitors in Washington.[16]

Targeting the federal government is a direct response to the racial activism of the state in the 1960s. Busing, affirmative action, and other egalitarian measures have created, in the white supremacist view, a racially unjust society. The society has become "polluted"[17] and the federal government, and liberalism in particular, are responsible. Pastor Richard G. Butler of the Aryan Nations preaches such a view at his "Church of Jesus Christ Christian"[18] in Idaho:

> When the Declaration of Independence talks about "one people," it's not talking about a nation made for Asia, Africa, India [or] the Soviet Union. That's a document based on a Christian people. We have watched like frightened sheep as do-gooders sniveling about the underprivileged gleefully grabbed our children by the nape of the neck and rubbed their faces in filth to create equality.[19]

As some commentators have noted, the economic dislocations of the current period have much to do with the revitalized presence of the far right.[20] In the midst of massive farm foreclosures and the crisis of the American farmer as a whole, the far right has fed on rural despair and formed such groups as the Farmers Liberation Army, the Christian-Patriots Defense League, and the new Populist Party.[21]

But economic arguments are insufficient to explain the growth and popularity of far right and white supremacist organizations. The revitalized presence of such groups is also a political response to the liberal state and reflects a crisis of identity engendered by the 1960s. The far right attempts to develop a new white identity, to reassert the very meaning of *whiteness*, which has been rendered unstable and unclear by the minority challenges of the 1960s.[22] Nor is it clear what "rights" white people have in the wake of challenges to their formerly privileged status.

The appeal of the far right project extends, therefore, to people who would normally disagree with extreme racist views. More moderate sympathizers can naively view such politics as merely the expression of "white interest group" politics. As a supporter of Metzger's congressional bid told a television interviewer:

> It's nice to have someone that represents the white people. It seems like nobody cares what the white people say anymore and all the candidates seem to run around and go out to all the minorities and never even once ask the white people how they feel so I guess we're turned around: the whites are now the minority and the minorities are the majority.[23]

Even as the far right gains a certain legitimacy with those more "mainstream" white conservatives who do not share its violence, the rightward drift of American politics as a whole has also drawn far-right sympathizers into the newly emerging conservative consensus.[24] The dominant trend is almost certainly away from the far right and towards the new right.[25] As "moderate" right-wing demands against busing and affirmative action achieve success through legitimate political channels, hard-core extremists may find themselves increasingly politically isolated. Observers fear that this isolation will push far right groups to adopt terrorist tactics.[26]

We think it will be difficult, if not impossible, to revive past white supremacist notions of race in the current period, or to attract a mass base to such an explicitly racist political project. The tenor of national debates about race – what we have called the *context for reaction* – precludes such a possibility.

The right-wing initiatives which seek to overturn the minority achievements of the 1960s, will, therefore, need to advance a new racial politics. Once again they must try to *rearticulate*, and not merely reverse, the meaning of race and the fundamental issues arising from racial inequality. The far right is not able to do this and therefore represents a "failed" attempt at rearticulation. The far right has tried to reassert white identity and reaffirm the nation as "the white man's country." It has shifted the blame for racial injustice from individual racial minorities to the state. But it continues to cling to biological notions of race and racial purity which render it fairly similar to the racism prevalent at the turn of the century. Its inability to part with these basic racist assumptions doom the far right to political marginality.

Though incapable of rearticulating the radical democratic racial ideologies of the 1960s, the far right is hardly vanishing. The far right can act as a "conscience" for other parts of the American right, or serve as their "shock troops."[27] If our analysis is correct, its inability to establish a broad political base may force its degeneration into terrorism.[28] Its numbers may be small and its political impact minor, but the far right may remain a frightening and highly visible reminder of the violence which has often characterized the enforcement of the racial order.

The new right: origins

Walter Dean Burnham has noted that the political culture of the US is highly influenced by the values of seventeenth-century dissenting Protestantism and that this has frequently become manifest in periods of transition and crisis:

> Whenever and wherever the pressures of "modernization" – secularity, urbanization, the growing importance of science – have become unusually intense, episodes of revivalism and culture-issue politics have swept over the American social landscape. In all such cases since at least the end of the Civil War, such movements have been more or less explicitly reactionary, and have frequently been linked with other kinds of reaction in explicitly political ways.[29]

The new right operates in this political space. It is a contemporary attempt to create an authoritarian, right-wing populism – a populism fuelled by resentment.

The appeal of the new right is based on the way many people experienced "the great transformation" and the transformations and dislocations of the past two decades. These shocks inspired fear. They portended the collapse of the "American Dream" – the apolitical, perpetually prosperous, militarily invincible and deeply self-absorbed and self-righteous "mainstream" American culture was, we think, shaken to its foundations by developments over this period. Commonly held concepts of nation, community and family were transformed, and no new principle of cohesion, no new cultural center, emerged to replace them. New collective identities, rooted in the "new social movements," remained fragmented and politically disunited.

In short, the US was politically "balkanized" as differences of all sorts – regional, racial, sexual, religious – became more visible, while economic stability and global military supremacy seemed to vanish. A plethora of interest groups, it seemed, had suddenly emerged, invoking a bewildering array of new social and political values, creating unprecedented political fragmentation, and leaving the "mainstream" with no clear notion of the "common good."[30]

In the face of these challenges, traditional conservatism seemed to have little to offer – society and politics, and the conventional way in which they were understood, had already been radically transformed. Only the appearance of the new right in the middle 1970s gave the millions of threatened members of the "silent majority" (Richard Nixon's phrase, let it be remembered, coined to steal some of George Wallace's thunder) any relief. The new right was a well-organized alternative to the moral and existential chaos of the preceding decades: a network of conservative organizations with an aggressive political style, an outspoken religious and cultural traditionalism, and a clear populist commitment.

Gillian Peele defines the new right as "a loose movement of conservative politicians and a collection of general-purpose political organizations which have developed independently of the political parties."[31] Typical new right affiliates are the American Conservative Union, the National Conservative Political Action Committee (NCPAC), the Conservative Caucus, the Young Americans for Freedom, and a group of fundamentalist Protestant sects incorporating millions of adherents. Leading figures of the new right are fundraiser/publisher Richard A. Viguerie, Paul Weyrich (Committee for the Survival of a Free Congress), Howard Phillips (Conservative Caucus), and John T. Dolan (NCPAC), as well as activist Phyllis Schlafly (Eagle Forum, Stop-ERA) and fundamentalist evangelist Rev. Jerry Falwell (Moral Majority). Periodicals identified with the new right are the *Conservative Digest, Policy Review* and *New Guard*. The key new right think tank is the Heritage Foundation, founded by brewer Joseph Coors and Paul Weyrich in 1973. Central to the new right's growth has been the use of direct-mail solicitation: "Collecting millions of dollars in small contributions from blue-collar workers and housewives, the New Right feeds on discontent, anger, insecurity, and resentment, and flourishes on backlash politics."[32]

Much has been written about the new right's tendency to focus on controversial *social* issues as a means of rallying and organizing its constituency. Left and progressive analyses have argued that the defining project of the new right is the reassertion of "patriarchy" by attacking the limited gains of the feminist and gay movements.[33] While much of this is true, such analyses understate the crucial importance of *race* as a defining issue. Race was crucial in the initial reaction against the progressive gains of the 1960s (then known as "backlash", e.g. anti-busing movements),[34] central to the electoral perspective of the new right (the "southern strategy"), and continues to be a major, if at times disguised, issue for the new right today.

In this respect the racial politics of the new right cannot be seen as a simple "backlash" against the gains of the 1960s movements for racial equality. In the early 1970s, there was little awareness among progressive analysts that behind "backlash" was a potentially innovative political project: *authoritarian populism*.

New right populism combined such venerable American ideological themes as respect for authority, mistrust of "big government" and defense of traditional morality with resistance to minority demands for group rights. The latter concern should be hardly surprising. A striking feature of America's populist tradition, reaching back to Andrew Jackson, is that it has been fuelled by heavy doses of nativism and racism.

The new right cannot simply defend patterns of racial inequality by demanding a return to segregation, for example, or by reviving simplistic notions of biological superiority/inferiority.[35] As we have previously noted, the racial upheavals of the 1960s precluded a direct return to this form of racial logic.

The new right objective, however, was to dismantle the political gains of racial minorities. Since these gains could not be easily reversed, they had to be *rearticulated*. The key device used by the new right in its effort to limit the political gains of racial minority movements has been "code words." These are phrases and symbols which refer indirectly to racial themes, but do not directly challenge popular democratic or egalitarian ideals (e.g. justice, equal opportunity). Beginning with the Wallace campaign of 1968, we can trace the pattern of new right experimentation with these code words, and with the rearticulation of racial meanings they attempt.

The first rumblings of the present-day new right agenda were heard in George Wallace's 1968 presidential bid. Wallace's initial role on the national political stage had been that of die-hard segregationist.[36] His entry into the presidential race was first seen as a replay of the Dixiecrat strategy which had led to the candidacy of Strom Thurmond twenty years before. Few analysts expected Wallace to have mass appeal outside the South, yet in northern blue-collar strongholds like Milwaukee, Detroit and Philadelphia, he demonstrated surprising strength.

Although Wallace's image as a racist politician had originally placed him in the national spotlight, it did not make good Presidential politics, and he was forced to incorporate his racial message as a subtext, implicit but "coded," in a populist appeal. Wallace thus struck certain chords that anticipated the new right agenda – defense of traditional values, opposition to "big government," and patriotic and militaristic themes. But the centerpiece of his appeal was his racial politics. Wallace was a law-and-order candidate, an anti-statist, an inheritor of classical southern populist traditions. He called for the stepped-up use of force to repress ghetto rebellions, derided the black movement and the war on poverty, and attacked liberal politicians and intellectuals. Wallace departed from his early 1960s style, however, by avoiding direct race-baiting.

During the same campaign, political analyst Kevin Phillips submitted a lengthy and rather scholarly analysis of US voting trends to Nixon headquarters, arguing that a Republican victory and long-term electoral realignment was possible on racial grounds. Published the following year as *The Emerging Republican Majority*, Phillips's book suggested a turn to the right and the use of "coded" anti-black campaign rhetoric (e.g. law and order).[37] Wallace's success, the disarray in Democratic ranks caused by the "Negro socioeconomic revolution," and polling data from blue-collar districts around the country convinced Phillips that a strategic approach of this kind (dubbed the "southern strategy") could fundamentally shift political alignments which had been in effect since 1932.

These innovations bore rich political fruit. They coincided with the fragmentation of the New Deal coalition, the "loss" of the war on poverty, and the decline of the black movement. They represented an apparent alternative to ghetto riots and white guilt, to the integration of northern schools and the onset of stagflation. They effortlessly, if demagogically, appealed to a majority of the electorate – something which the new social movements of minorities, anti-war activists and feminists had not succeeded in doing.

Most important of all, the "coded" racial politics of the late 1960s and after did not repudiate the legacy of the minority movements; indeed, they adopted a conservative egalitarian version of their demands.[38] Nixon advocated "black capitalism" and on the advice of Daniel Patrick Moynihan drew up a welfare reform plan featuring a guaranteed annual income.[39] While not a new rightist himself, Nixon set the stage for the later new right ascendance by simultaneously coopting *both* Wallace and suitably moderate blacks (and other minorities), by espousing *both* law and order and a negative income tax, neighborhood schools *and* black capitalism.

Cultural politics, anti-statism, and the "new class"

Today the new right agenda is far more advanced. There is no flirtation with the sort of centrism Nixon represented. The new right dream is to consolidate a "new majority" which can dismantle the welfare state, legislate a return to "traditional morality," and stem the tide of political and cultural dislocation which the 1960s and 1970s represented.[40] This project links the assault on liberalism and "secular humanism,"[41] the obsession with individual guilt and responsibility where social questions are concerned (crime, sex, education, poverty), with a fierce *anti-statism*. The political strategy involved is populist: use of the .initiative process, for example, serves as an "end-run" around the courts, the bureaucracy, the Congress and state legislatures. Traditional conservatives such as Alan Crawford label this channeling of popular rage through direct democratic channels "antipolitical":

> A near-constant theme of conservative thought, from Edmund
> Burke to William Buckley, has been that unrestrained
> expressions of popular will militate against the orderly processes
> of government on which stable societies depend. . . . The New
> Right, impatient for short-run results, has rejected this
> dominant theme of conservatism in favor of direct democracy,

threatening to shatter the safeguards against political centralization and, therefore, freedom itself.[42]

Crawford believes that "the New Right exploits social protest and encourages class hostility by trying to fuel the hostilities of lower-middle-class Americans against those above and below them on the economic ladder."[43] Some analysts see the new right as a status revolt[44] by those who, according to Ben Wattenberg, are "unyoung, unpoor and unblack"[45] – those whose identities and interests were articulated *negatively* by the social movements of the 1960s and the crises of the 1970s. They resent any mobility on the part of lower-status groups, and demand that the political process recognize the traditional values to which they subscribe. Their anger is directed at those who are "not like themselves;" this involves a racial dimension which is experienced as a *cultural* threat as much as an economic one:

> [T]he fear of black power, "reverse discrimination," at the community level – associated with fear of crime, property devaluation, dirtiness and noisiness – reflects not only the direct economic crunch on white working-class people but also a less tangible sense of cultural disintegration.[46]

The failure of the Great Society and other liberal experiments has also focused attention on members of the *new class* (educators, administrators, planners, consultants, network journalists, etc.) and revived traditional themes of *anti-statism*. The new right believes that "pointy-heads" control the state and are responsible for the current political, economic and cultural malaise. During the 1960s and 1970s the state was recklessly allowed to expand and intervene in every aspect of social life; it now dictates policy with disastrous results. In particular, it has acceded to racial minority demands and now gives minorities privileged access to jobs and social services. Ed Davis, a new right cult figure and former Chief of the Los Angeles Police Department, put it this way: "I always felt that the government really was out to force me to hire 4-foot-11 transvestite morons."[47]

Critiques of liberal statism abound on the new right. The Supreme Court is criticized for liberal bias in matters of race relations. The electoral college system is opposed for restricting third-party efforts and, as Kevin Phillips has suggested, maximizing the influence of a "Third World state"[48] such as California. While constantly calling for a return to the basics of the Constitution, new right activists also seem intent on revising it through amendments to stop busing, prohibit abortions, or encourage school prayer.

New right figures appeal to white racial anxieties. Spiro Agnew's acceptance by the new right was based on the way he "talked back" to black leaders. Sen. Jesse Helms built his reputation by refusing to pursue black votes in North Carolina and by his highly publicized smears of Martin Luther King, Jr as a communist.[49] New right columnist Patrick J. Buchanan has argued, as a headline put it, that the "GOP Vote Search Should Bypass Ghetto" since blacks have been ungrateful for Republican efforts to help and assist them.[50]

As we have argued, race and class politics interface and overlap in the United States. Individuals and groups interpret their conditions of existence and their subjective experiences in ways which draw upon both racially based and class-based meanings:

> On one side, threatening traditional values, are the feminists,
> the liberals, the university communities, minorities, residents of
> urban centers, and the media. On the other – the side of the
> angels – are the "pro-family" forces, the leadership of the New
> Right and its disgruntled constituents, plus a growing political
> movement of fundamentalist evangelical ministers. . . . Both
> sides are competing for the soul of America.[51]

Thus the new right grafts together issues of race and issues of class. New right publisher William Rusher provides an apt illustration of the racial dimension "hidden" in much of the "new class" analysis on the right:

> A new economic division, pits the producers – businessmen,
> manufacturers, hard-hats, blue-collar workers, and farmers –
> against a new and powerful class of non-producers comprised of
> a liberal verbalist elite (the dominant media, the major
> foundations and research institutions, the educational
> establishment, the federal and state bureaucracies) and a
> semipermanent welfare constituency, all coexisting happily in a
> state of mutually sustaining symbiosis.[52]

The "semipermanent welfare constituency" is implicitly non-white in the popular political imagination.[53] Rusher's approach conjures up anti-big government sentiments by blaming unemployment among minorities for parasitism at the expense of "productive" workers. His *ressentiment* is racial, even though his vocabulary is that of class. This rearticulation of racial ideology is, we believe, crucial to recent new right advances.

The new right generally does not display *overt* racism. It has gained political currency by rearticulating racial ideology. As we have argued, rearticulation does not require an explicitly racial discourse, and would in fact be severely limited by any direct advocacy of racial inequality. Here are some examples of this process.

Busing The new right has opposed busing not as an overt effort to maintain residential or school segregation, but as an assault on "the community" and "the family." School integration, new right activists have argued, means that the state usurps the decision-making powers which should be vested in parents: deciding in what kind of communities their children will be raised and what kind of education their children will receive. A similar argument is made against busing on "pro-family" grounds. As Gordon and Hunter suggest,

> The anti-busing movement is nourished by . . . fears for the loss
> of the family. The loss of neighborhood schools is perceived as a
> threat to community, and therefore family stability by many
> people, particularly in cities where ethnically homogenous
> communities remain.[54]

The formerly progressive theme of "community control" and "parental involvement" are thus harnessed to prevent race mixing in the schools, while charges of racism are blunted or avoided altogether. One measure of the success of this anti-integration strategy was the confusion it sewed even on the left during the Boston busing controversy of the 1970s.[55]

Textbook censorship The monitoring of books for public school adoption is another issue where a "hidden" racial dimension informs new right politics. In 1975 the Heritage Foundation formed the National Congress for Educational Excellence to coordinate the activities of roughly 200 textbook-protester organizations nationwide. This effort capitalized on the feelings of many whites that their values and lifestyles were being neglected by "multicultural" texts.[56] The new right, in this instance, can push a racial agenda merely by arguing for "traditional" lifestyles and families, for the return to a more homogeneous image of everyday life, purged of "secular humanism" and the rest of the unsettling ambiguities of the 1960s and 1970s. Textbooks focusing on Dick and Jane and Spot, and avoiding any mention of Ahmad or Chabrika, Fernando or Nguyen, effectively *re*-marginalize minority cultures without ever having to invoke issues of race.

"Reverse discrimination" On the issue of affirmative action, the right has made significant advances in rearticulating the meaning of racial equality. The strength of this argument is its specific appeal to equality and "fairness." What has become unfair, the right argues, is the state's accommodation to the demands of racial minorities and other "special interests" at the expense of whites. The new right's ability to mobilize resentment against the "group rights" demands of racial minorities dovetails with the neoconservative argument that only "equality of opportunity" can be a valid objective of state policy. The ability of the new right to mobilize "grass roots" opposition to residential and school desegregation, to preferential hiring and school admissions schemes, and to minority "set-asides" in government contracting provides a populist counterpoint to the more abstract and theoretically developed critique developed by ethnicity theorists such as Nathan Glazer and Michael Novak. It is to this current that we now turn our attention.

Neoconservatism

Neoconservatism and affirmative action

Perhaps worst of all from the ethnicity theory point of view, blacks and other racial minorities questioned the legitimacy of reforms based on the principle of equality of *individuals*, seeking instead a radical *collective* equality ("group rights") which ethnicity theory viewed as anathema to a democracy. Such a policy would break faith with the generations who had come before, break faith with the civic ideals which were the soul of American society. True, the ethnicity theorists had flirted briefly with the idea of "equality of result" during the early heady days of the Great Society. Moynihan, for example, was co-author of an important 1965 speech by Lyndon Johnson which contained these famous lines:

[F]reedom is not enough. You do not wipe away the scars of

centuries by saying: Now you are free to go where you want, do as you desire, and choose the leaders you please.

You do not take a person who, for years, has been hobbled by chains and liberate him [sic], bring him up to the starting line of a race and then say, "you are free to compete with all the others," and still justly believe that you have been completely fair.

Thus it is not enough just to open the gates of opportunity. All our citizens must have the ability to walk through those gates.

This is the next and more profound stage of the battle for civil rights. We seek not just freedom but opportunity – not just legal equity but human ability – not just equality as a right and a theory but equality as a fact and as a result.[57]

Very quickly, though, they drew back from the larger implications of this position. Glazer wrote during the same year that "a new national interest" in "the final liquidation of Negro separation" was being defined, and that blacks themselves had best not oppose it, for "When an ethnic group interest has clashed with a national interest, we have been quite ruthless and even extreme in overriding the group interest."[58]

By the 1970s, opposition to minority demands for "group rights" had become a centerpiece of the neoconservative perspective. The ethnicity theorists associated with the current did not ground their arguments, as some in the new right did, on "white rights." They minimized references to "reverse discrimination" or "reverse racism," preferring to center their critique on the illegitimacy of state policies which engaged in "race-thinking." Thus Glazer's objections to affirmative action policies centered on their ineffectiveness and their challenge to the fundamental civil ideals which had made the "American ethnic pattern" possible: individualism, market-based opportunity, and the curtailment of excessive state interventionism. Affirmative action, he wrote,

[H]as meant that we abandon the first principle of a liberal society, that the individual's interests and good and welfare are the test of a good society, for we now attach benefits and penalties to individuals simply on the basis of their race, color, and national origins. The implications of this new course are increasing consciousness of the significance of group membership, an increasing divisiveness on the basis of race, color, and national origin, and a spreading resentment among the disfavored groups against the favored ones. If the individual is the measure, however, our public concern is with the individual's capacity to work out an individual fate by means of education, work, and self-realization in the various spheres of life. Then how the figures add up on the basis of whatever measure of group we use may be interesting, but should be of no concern to public policy.[59]

He did not argue that white resentment against such programs was justified – in the manner of a William Rusher or a George Wallace – only that it was inevitable.[60] This distinguishes the neoconservative and new right oppositions to such policies: the neoconservatives fear the politics of *ressentiment* as an unwanted consequence of state over-involvement, while the new right mobilizes precisely such sentiments.

The power of the neoconservative critique of affirmative action is based on the ability of such authors as Glazer to present themselves as simultaneously opposed both to discrimination and to anti-discrimination measures based on "group rights" principles. The neoconservatives thus refocus the debate on the question of what *means* are best for achieving equality. Such an approach is attractive but misleading.

In the neoconservative view opposition to affirmative action is consistent with the goals of the civil rights movement; it is a challenge to "race-thinking."[61] According to this logic, only individual rights exist, only individual opportunity can be guaranteed by law, and only "merit" justifies the granting of privilege. Yet even the most cursory examination of such arguments reveals their deeper political subtexts. Glazer's concern about the resentments and heightened racial polarization any *abandonment* of traditional liberalism would inspire, for example, does not extend to the resentments and polarization which *adherence* to liberalism entails. Morris Abram, a former liberal partisan of civil rights serving on the US Civil Rights Commission in its present "Reaganite" form, proposes the extension of unionization as a better remedy than affirmative action for alleviating minority poverty and powerlessness.[62] Thereby he merely indicates which groups he considers acceptable vehicles for political demands. Workers are apparently free to have collective interests, but racial minorities are not. Concepts of "individual merit," as Philip Green has shown, have the same shallowness. "Merit" is a political construct, by which employers, schools, state agencies, etc. legitimate the allocation of benefits to favored (i.e. organized) constituencies, and deny the validity of competing claims.[63]

Once we recognize that the attack on affirmative action is not simply about "fairness," but also about the maintenance of existing social positions and political stability, it becomes easier to explain its enormous appeal. The unpopularity of affirmative action by now extends far beyond the new right and the neoconservatives who originally authored the "reverse discrimination" critique. In our view the defeat of affirmative action testifies to two things: the subtlety and pervasiveness of the right's rearticulation of the meaning of racial equality as a matter of individual rather than group or collective concern, and the increasing convergence of the neoconservative and new right tendencies.

Rearticulating the meaning of racial equality The concept of "reverse discrimination" appropriates the demand for equality presented by the minority movements of the 1960s and stands it on its head. The neoconservative argument redefines racial meanings in such a way as to contain the more radical implications of the 1960s upsurge. Racial discrimination and racial equality – in the neoconservative model – are problems to be confronted *only* at an individual level, once legal systems of discrimination such as *de jure* segregation have been eliminated. Thus discrimination may be an illegitimate infringement on individual rights, but it can no longer be a legitimate source for group demands. What the neoconservatives oppose is thus not racial equality but racial collectivity.

By limiting themselves to considering discrimination against *individuals*, though, the neoconservatives have trivialized the problem of racial equality, and of equality in general. Discrimination never derived its main strength from individual actions or prejudices, however great these might have been or might still be. Its most fundamental characteristic was always its roots in the racially organized *social* order. The minority movements of the 1950s and 1960s, even in their early, "moderate" incarnations, definitively questioned this social assignment of identities and racial meanings. It is this questioning, this challenge, that the neoconservatives seek to confine and reorganize in their assault on affirmative action.

They do this by limiting the meaning of racial discrimination to the curtailment of individual rights, a distinction that could apply to whites and nonwhites alike. The social logic of race is thus rendered opaque without any necessary recourse to explicit prejudice or institutionalized inequality as in the segregation laws of the past.

Convergence of neoconservatism and the new right Neoconservatism incubated in the ever-widening division between liberals and radicals of the late 1960s and early 1970s, and drew further strength from the rise of the new right. In the eyes of the ethnicity theorists, not only were the black radicals and other new social movements upsetting the pluralist consensus of tolerance, individualism, accommodation of conflicting interests through established political processes, etc., but they were inspiring a right-wing intolerance equal to their own, and threatening to open a second breach in the body politic, this time to the liberals' right. As the 1960s drew to a close and the 1970s began, many ethnicity theorists felt they had to choose an alliance with the right in order to stem the tide of radical collectivism which the black movement had set in motion. They embraced neoconservatism in the pages of *Commentary* and *The Public Interest*, and in editorials in *The Wall Street Journal*. In a series of publications emerging from Harvard, they spelled out the tragic implications of affirmative action.[64]

The neoconservatives originally polemicized against the politics of *ressentiment*, but by the 1980s they had made their peace with its chief practitioners, the forces of the new right. This was, in our view, largely a matter of political expedience. It must be remembered that the radical democratic demands (of "equality of result," etc.) typified by affirmative action particularly threatened certain vulnerable groups. Unionized workers benefiting from *de facto* segregated seniority systems, for example, or white ethnic residents of urban enclaves who felt themselves to be an "endangered species" – hemmed in by ghettos or barrios, fearful of crime – became potential conservative constituencies. These groups were certainly harmed by the implementation of affirmative action in employment, busing, and minority "set-asides," though the extent of the threat such programs represented is a matter of debate.[65] By formulating a sophisticated counter-argument to minority calls for "equality of result," neoconservative scholars rationalized existing systems of racial inequality. They helped the beneficiaries of *de facto* occupational segregation, for example, to avoid confronting the disquieting implication of racism.[66] Thus the neoconservative scholars of ethnicity tacitly provided ammunition to the new right in its racially based mobilization of (ethnic, working-class, etc.) whites.

Having seen the radical challengers at home throw their support to communist revolutionaries fighting the US in Vietnam and elsewhere, having experienced a series of threats to traditional values of family, the work ethic and sexual discipline (in such new social movements as feminism, welfare rights and gay liberation), the neoconservatives ultimately came to share many points of agreement with the new right. True, some divergent elements remained – for example some neoconservatives who had been associated with Hubert Humphrey and Henry "Scoop" Jackson continued to support certain welfare state programs and trade unionism, however much they detested affirmative action and were cold war hawks – but in all the main points a new intellectual and policy-oriented realignment had occurred. Once more, the issue of race had played a crucial role in restructuring the central dynamics – political, cultural and, perhaps most important, intellectual – of US society.

The Reagan "revolution"

During the Vice-Presidential debate in October 1984, George Bush was clearly overwhelmed by questions on minorities and racial discrimination. As Jack White of *Time Magazine* reminded Bush,

> Many critics of your administration say that it is the most hostile to minorities in recent memory. Have you perhaps inadvertently encouraged that view by supporting tuition tax credits, the anti-busing amendment and siding with Bob Jones University in a case before the Supreme Court, your original opposition to the Voting Rights extension and so forth?[67]

Bush sidestepped some issues and made vague statements about others, but was clearly at a loss to justify the Reagan administration record.

Reagan's record on racial policy is not a particularly enlightened one. Since his emergence as a Republican leader, Reagan has opposed every major civil rights measure considered by Congress.

131

He opposed the Civil Rights Act of 1964, denouncing it as a "bad piece of legislation," and the Voting Rights Act of 1965, opining that "The Constitution very specifically reserves control of voting to local governments. Additional legislation is unnecessary."[68] His consistency on racial issues extended through the 1980 and 1984 Presidential campaigns. On the campaign trail in 1980, Reagan told the South that he favored "state's rights" in the same Mississippi town where civil rights workers James Chaney, Andrew Goodman and Michael Schwerner had been murdered by Klansmen in 1964.

During that same campaign, speaking by telephone from a Chicago political dinner to her husband in New Hampshire, Nancy Reagan said she wished he could be with her to "see all these beautiful white people."[69] It was a revealing *faux pas*. President Reagan, more than any other President in recent memory, has cultivated an image as "the white people's President." In the 1984 election, Reagan took 74 percent of the white male vote in the South, 68 percent in the West, and 66 percent in the nation as a whole: "Reagan won every category of white males except white Jewish males. . . . He won rich and poor, Catholic and Protestant, young and old, North and South, Yuppie and blue collar. Generally he won them by overwhelming margins."[70]

The impact of Reagan's 1984 success among white men will resonate not only in the Republican but also in the Democratic Party for years to come. As Democratic pollster William Hamilton warned, the Democrats "can't very well lose [the white male vote] by 2 to 1 and expect to be serious players in a two-party system."[71] Many Democrats argue that the Party has lost touch with a majoritarian constituency and needs to shed its image as the vehicle of "special interests." In such a context, racial minority demands are bound to be submerged. In February 1985, newly elected Democratic National Committee Chair Paul Kirk said that caucuses within the DNC (representing such groups as blacks, Hispanics, Asian/Pacific Islanders, women and gays) were "political nonsense" and promised to abolish them.[72]

On the policy level, the Reagan administration has taken its cue from both the new right and neoconservatives, arguing that the important forms of racial discrimination have been eliminated. Thus most civil rights remedies and mechanisms for achieving racial equality are now considered to discriminate *against whites*. In January 1985, Reagan remarked that some civil rights organizations are no longer needed because they have accomplished their goals.[73] School busing plans and affirmative action policies have come under attack by the Reagan "revolutionaries." Former Attorney General William French Smith dropped desegregation appeals in cities such as Kansas City and Houston and slowed integration efforts in Chicago, Phoenix, Albuquerque and Rochester. Then Secretary of Labor Raymond Donovan issued new regulations in 1981 which substantially weakened the affirmative action requirements attached to federal contracts.

In an important 1985 Supreme Court case, the Justice Department opposed the city of Indianapolis's efforts to use hiring quotas to help minorities get jobs in local government.[74] In the same year, the Department urged over fifty states, counties and cities to voluntarily modify their affirmative action plans to remove numerical goals and quotas. It was hinted that failure to comply "voluntarily" might result in court action.

The Reagan administration is also trying to alter the perception of racial discrimination by eliminating record-keeping. In March 1985, the Office of Management and Budget ordered the Department of Housing and Urban Development and the Veterans Administration to stop tracking the racial and ethnic characteristics of Americans who receive benefits from these two agencies. This will severely hamper the administration of civil rights and fair housing programs. George D. Moerman, assistant director for loan policy for the VA, said that the lack of information "will put us in the position where, if abuse exists, we will not be able to find it."[75] During the same period, the administration opposed a bill (HR 1171) which would have required the FBI's uniform crime reports to include categories of offenses "involving the expression of racial, ethnic or religious prejudice." Reagan administration officials felt that it would be too difficult to include "hate crime" categories in national crime statistics.

The clearest example of the administration's flagrant disregard for civil rights is its maneuvers to reshape the composition and philosophy of the US Civil Rights Commission.[76]

While President Reagan has departed from significant aspects of the new right agenda, he seems in firm agreement with new right racial positions. The welfare state is being drastically reduced with the rationale that such spending not only fails to ameliorate the problems of poverty but actually exacerbates them.[77] These cuts have disproportionately affected racial minorities.[78] Schemes such as urban "free enterprise zones" coupled with the attempt to deal with unemployment in the inner cities by instituting a subminimum wage echo new right anti-statism and arguments that only the "free market" can alleviate minority poverty.

Perhaps the biggest reversals have taken place in the affirmative action policies. As we have argued, under the guise of creating a truly "colorblind" society, administration officials seem intent on defining and eliminating the "new racism." As Reagan's US Civil Rights Commission Chairman Clarence Pendleton Jr characterizes it, "the new racists, many of them black, exhibit the classical behavior system of racism. They treat blacks differently than whites because of their race."[79] The tables have turned. It is the liberals who are now guilty of racism. Blacks, and other minorities, need to be saved from liberal efforts to help them.

While actively initiating and promoting policies which have a devastating effect on racial minorities, the "Teflon President" has managed to avoid seeming like a mean-spirited racist. Roger Wilkins has commented on the numerous "photo opportunities" which Reagan has provided the press, in order to display his "enlightened" racial attitudes. He helicoptered out to a black family's house in suburban Maryland to condemn the burning of a cross on their lawn. He dined with the family of a black second-grade student with whom he corresponded. How, asked Wilkins, can a man who shows such concern and consorts so easily with blacks be a racist? "It was," he surmised, "a shrewd way of sending the message that unremitting opposition to the true interests of black people doesn't make one a mean racist."[80] Robby Cohen suggests that Reagan's attitudes and policies represent "neo-segregationism:"

> Neo-segregation is segregation with the overt racism taken out,
> a type of sugarcoated Jim Crow in which "big government"
> rather than racial integration is the public target. But, of course,
> it is the civil rights activism of this "big government" which has
> served as the chief vehicle for desegregating American society
> from the 1950s to the day Reagan took office.[81]

While Reagan has incurred the wrath of some quarters of the right for his abandonment of, or slow-moving posture towards, some social issues (e.g. anti-abortion laws and prayer in public schools), his scorecard on racial issues remains nearly impeccable. Reagan has harnessed the discontent which has been simmering among the large numbers of whites who have felt threatened by the racial politics of the past two decades. He has opposed racial equality and civil rights for minorities in a manner which seems on the surface "color blind." After commenting on studies which suggest that racism motivates some people to become Republicans, political scientist Merle Black noted that:

> Reagan's kind of civilized the racial issue. He's taken what
> Wallace never could do and made it acceptable. It fits in with
> their [white students'] sense of perceived injustice, with what
> they see as the status of being a white person not being as high as
> it was 15, 20 or 30 years ago.[82]

Reagan has "civilized" the race issue by being quite adept at rearticulating the issues of race and racial equality. Drawing on themes derived from both new right and neoconservative currents, Reagan has successfully assaulted the racial policies initiated in response to "the great transformation." Under his leadership, the federal government has reversed itself and switched sides on racial policy. This was accomplished by reworking recent history to suggest that discrimination against racial minorities had been drastically curbed and by radically transforming the state institutions which were previously mandated to "protect" racial minority interests.

The racial reaction initiated in the late 1960s and early 1970s has developed into a pervasive ideological effort to reinterpret once again the meaning of race in the US. As the Reagan administration adopted its major themes, it has achieved legitimate, if not hegemonic, status in "normal" politics. Racial reaction has attained maturity and power, operating behind a subtle and seductive veneer of opposition to "race-thinking."

Conclusion

At the end of World War II, Henry Luce's designation of the coming period as "the American century" hardly seemed an exaggerated vision of things to come. The United States seemingly had limitless opportunities: to develop and extend its unparalleled economic and commercial position, to project its political and military power globally, and to institutionalize its vision of political democracy and social justice as a model for the world to emulate. Americans delighted in their country's unprecedented pre-eminence; they viewed themselves as the world's saviors.

The American century was short-lived. In the 1980s Americans are painfully contemplating the possibility that the dream is over. The United States does not appear to dominate world affairs, but instead to cope with a prevalent climate of disruption in the global arena. Once the world's creditor, it is today its chief debtor; once the chief exporter of manufactured goods, it is today their main importer. Once the model of democracy for the underdeveloped world, the US is now racked with doubt about the proper level of support for "authoritarian" regimes there. Once able to guarantee a prosperous and secure future to its citizens, the US now contemplates a minimum unemployment rate (in periods of economic expansion, to say nothing of contraction) of 7 per cent, and a national debt in the $200 billion per annum range. Since 1970 the US has experienced defeat in war, the impeachment and resignation of a President, an inflationary peak of 22 percent, peacetime shortages of oil and gas, and the fall of Keynesianism and the political alignment which it sustained. It has also witnessed the election of a President whose chief commitment is to stem the tide of deterioration these events suggest. Yet despite that President's most devout wishes, America is *not* "back," and it is hardly "standing tall."

137

Conclusion

Although no one factor, no single causative principle, can adequately account for the contemporary crisis, there is an aspect of recent US history whose political importance in structuring the present situation has been systematically overlooked. We refer, of course, to the *racial* dimension of American life. In contrast to much of existing political and racial theory, the present work has emphasized the *centrality of race* in American society. We have sought to explain the process by which race has shaped, and been shaped by, US politics.

We have approached race as a phenomenon whose meaning is contested throughout social life. Race is a constituent of the individual psyche and of relationships among individuals; it is also an irreducible component of collective identities and social structures. In American history, racial dynamics have been a traditional source both of conflict and division and of renewal and cultural awareness. Race has been a key determinant of mass movements, state policy, and even foreign policy in the United States. Racial meaning systems are contested and racial ideologies mobilized in *political* relationships.

Beginning in the 1950s and more intensively in the 1960s, racially based social movements initiated a "great transformation" of the American political universe, creating new organizations, new collective identities and new political norms; challenging past racial practices and stereotypes; and ushering in a wave of democratizing social reform. The ability of racially based movements to *rearticulate* traditional political and cultural themes – first among blacks, and later among Latinos, Asian Americans and Indians – permitted the entry of millions of racial minority group members into the political process. They initiated a trajectory of reform which exposed the limits of all previously existing political orientations – conservative, liberal and radical. In transforming the meaning of race and the contours of racial politics, the racially based movements transformed the meaning and contours of American politics itself.

Political mobilization along racial lines resulted in the enactment of reforms which dramatically restructured the racial order, reorganized state institutions, and initiated whole new realms of state activity. In processing racial demands, the state demonstrated a tremendous flexibility and resilience. Using strategies of *absorption* and *insulation*, the state was able to put forth moderate reforms

138

while simultaneously containing the more radical potentialities of the minority upsurge.

In the effort to adapt to the new racial politics they themselves had created, racial movements lost their decentered political unity. Working within the newly reformed racial state was more possible, and confronting it more difficult, than during the preceding period. Opposition to the backward and coercive racial order of the South had permitted a tenuous alliance between moderate and radical currents of the movement, an alliance which the winning of civil rights reforms ruptured. The "triumph" of liberal democracy failed to placate radicals who sought not only *rights*, but power and resources as well. The conferring of rights did not appreciably change the circumstances of a black youth in Harlem or a *vato loco* in East Los Angeles. What was heralded as a great victory by liberals appeared to the radicals as merely a more streamlined version of racial oppression.

The dominant paradigm of ethnicity, the centerpiece of liberal racial politics, fell into disrepute among radicals. Radical theories of race – the class-based and nation-based paradigms – challenged the explanatory power and political efficacy of the ethnicity perspective. Embracing these new paradigmatic conceptions, radical movement tendencies advanced their demands for a more throughgoing restructuring of the social order – one which would recognize the pervasiveness of racial oppression not only in "normal" politics, but in the organization of the labor market, in the geography of living space, and in the forms of cultural life.

Yet these challengers failed to consolidate a new political project of "radical democracy" which could expand beyond the issue of race and aspire to majoritarian status. This failure was due to factors both "internal" and "external" to the movement itself. Internally, the radical currents were increasingly racked by fragmentation along class and political lines. Tensions developed between (and among) those engaged in electoral work, workplace organizing, "anti-poverty" projects and the "long march through the institutions"; activists politicized on the university and college campuses; and those, like the Black Panther Party, who sought to mobilize the "lumpenproletariat".[1] Some organizations became romantically fascinated by Third World revolutionary movements whose "lessons" were largely irrelevant to US conditions. This fragmentation resulted in the absence of a unified politics and the inability to define a coherent political subject. Externally, the racially based movements were, by the 1970s, largely outmaneuvered by the new racial state which had responded to moderate demands and marginalized radical ones.

The 1980s bear ironic witness to the impact of the racial minority upsurge on the overall political terrain in the United States. While failing to consolidate a new radical democratic politics with majoritarian aspirations, "the great transformation" provided the political space in which a right-wing reaction could incubate and develop its political agenda.

The new social movements inspired a profound reaction, even revulsion, in those whose political and cultural reference points they challenged. Intellectuals decried a "crisis of democracy"[2] in which the political system was becoming "overloaded." The self-identification of the majority of Americans as "conservative" (as opposed to "liberal") emerged as people came to perceive the racial minority, women's and peace movements as opposed to the "traditional" values they upheld. The new social movements were held responsible for the decline and dislocations Americans had experienced in the late 1960s and after. According to Jonathan Rieder, liberalism is now associated with "profligacy, spinelessness, malevolence, masochism, elitism, fantasy, idealism, softness, irresponsibility, and sanctimoniousness," while conservatism has "connotations of pragmatism, character, reciprocity, truthfulness, stoicism, manliness, realism, hardness, vengeance, strictness, and responsibility."[3] Liberalism is seen as beholden to minorities, for whom it provides "handouts," while conservatism is thought to embrace traditional individualist (and thus "colorblind") values of hard work and sacrifice.

Amid a general decline of US economic and political hegemony around the globe, the resurgent right has adopted an "authoritarian populist"[4] character which sharply contrasts with traditional conservatism. The primary objectives of the right wing are the containment of the demands and political vision of the new social movements, the restoration of "governability" to democracy, and the reassertion of traditional cultural and social values.

For the present, the right-wing reaction has captured the popular political imagination – its analysis of the ills which beset the nation and its prescription for reclaiming the "American century" have resonated with large parts of the American public. Popular support for the Reagan administration, reflected in Reagan's "landslide" electoral victory in 1984, testifies to the eclipse of New Deal liberalism and provides political justification for the rightward trend in social policy. Racial policy has been dramatically affected. The Reagan administration has demonstrated its opposition to affirmative action, reconstituted the US Civil Rights Commission in order to fight "reverse discrimination," relaxed or eliminated government action against racist practices and institutions, and in general attempted to reverse the political consequences of the "great transformation."

Yet right-wing initiatives cannot really dismiss racial history. The accomplishments of the 1960s cannot simply be reversed. Since 1965, for example, it has been impossible to argue *for* segregation or *against* racial equality. Any "legitimate" politics must claim to favor racial equality *in the abstract*, even if specific egalitarian measures are condemned. To argue for a return to the explicitly racist ideology of pre-civil rights movement days is to move to the proto-fascist fringes of the far right. An unabashedly "white man's government" would face severe opposition and would bring about an immediate crisis of legitimacy – at the very least it would have to be presented as a state of emergency requiring the suspension of democratic rights.[5]

Racial reaction, therefore, encounters clear limits in the wake of the political and ideological transformations of the 1960s. Both because of the successes of "the great transformation" and because the minority movements could not be consolidated as a permanent radical democratic political force, the right has been able to re-articulate racial meanings once again. This time, it is not the justice but the very *meaning* of racial equality which is at stake. The right, especially the neoconservatives, have fought hard to institutionalize their interpretation – focused on "equality of opportunity" and explicitly oblivious to "equality of result" – as the national "common sense."

From the standpoint of racial theory, we are witnessing the resurrection of the ethnicity paradigm in a new form. The theory which once justified state racial interventionism is now presented in far more market-oriented terms.[6] The theory which once encouraged racial minorities (see, of course, as "ethnic groups") to organize along interest-group lines, in pursuit of greater political power and distributional equity in the allocation of public

141

resources, now shrinks from such prospects.

Of course, neoconservatism is but one of several tendencies on the right. If the far right may be generally characterized by an explicit racism, the new right lies somewhere between these two tendencies. Unlike the far right, the new right is adroit enough to avoid overt appeals to white supremacy. Unlike the neoconservatives, though, the new right has not renounced the use of racial "code words," and continues political mobilization on the basis of an implicit racial agenda. This is not conscious manipulation for the most part, but rather a consequence of the "great transformation," which brought to light the ubiquity of race. Given that racial meaning inheres in every social relationship, given the "threat" to "traditional" values posed by the new social movements, and given the correspondence between the racial upsurge of the 1960s and America's seeming fall from divine grace, is it all that surprising that a "racial reaction" can be found on the new right? Our study suggests that no post-1960s political initiative can avoid being interpreted, to some degree, through the lens of racial ideology.

In the current period of overall economic, political and cultural crisis, then, the options for racial policy are rather bleak. Clearly, in the current climate of anti-statism, the expansion of state activity to deal with impoverishment and the invidious effects of racism in housing, education and welfare is unlikely. On the other hand, a "proto-fascist" solution[7] is equally untenable since it would have to contend with the enormous disruptive powers of racial minorities, particularly those of the underclass.

Jesse Jackson's 1984 Presidential bid, and his efforts to build a "Rainbow Coalition," suggest some possible features of the rearticulation of racial politics by the left. The Jackson campaign displayed a refreshingly explicit racial awareness by emphasizing the "multicultural" nature of US society. Yet the Rainbow Coalition also faced the necessity of submerging overt racial appeals. The legacy of the "great transformation," which as we have seen limits the racial logic of the right, also limits the possibilities for the left. Jackson's campaign would have been less "credible" in the national spotlight if he had appeared as "the black candidate" who sought only to win votes and express the interests of a black constituency. Jackson's success in escaping such a label was limited. His campaign sought to weld together groups traditionally marginalized in electoral politics (such as racial minorities, the poor, women, environmentalists, and even the organized left) to consolidate a new political bloc. Thus the Rainbow Coalition recognized that any politics which aspires to majoritarian status in the current period needs to move *beyond* a purely racially based agenda.

What does the immediate future hold? It is unlikely that we shall experience a period of racially based mobilization such as "the great transformation." The conjuncture in which the 1960s racial upsurge occurred was almost certainly unique. The sophistication of the contemporary racial state and the transformed political landscape as a whole seem to thwart any short-term radical political initiative based in opposition to the racial order.

Racial minority communities have undergone huge changes in the past two decades. There have been enormous debates about the dramatic class cleavages which have arisen *within* these communities, and about their consequences for political action.[8] For Asian American and Latino communities, the liberalization of immigration laws in the mid-1960s has led to a vast influx of both "old" and "new" groups. Koreans, Vietnamese, Laotians and Filipinos are distinct in ethnic and class composition from each other and from more "established" groups such as Japanese Americans. An increasingly variegated "community" makes it difficult to speak of a shared experience, common sensibility, or unified political outlook. In the face of these realities, political mobilization along presumed "racial" lines becomes an ambiguous project, even though state policy, and the majority of the American public, continues to identify the groups mentioned along racial lines (i.e. as "Asians").[9]

While racially based mobilization is not likely to arise on a large scale in the present period, it seems equally unlikely that the right-wing reaction will consolidate itself on racial grounds. The Reagan administration's attempt to create a "colorblind society" will instead initiate a vicious cycle of economic and political inequality. The neoconservative theorists who endorse the Reagan strategy (and indeed have helped to fashion it) cling, in our view, to a deterministic model of race which vastly overemphasizes America's capacity for incorporating "difference." While such trends do exist, very powerful counter-tendencies toward permanent racial division simply cannot be ignored. The central argument of this work, the central issue in racial policy – that US racial dynamics are the subject of permanent political contestation – cannot be addressed by "colorblind" theory or policy.

Conclusion

For now, racial dynamics are adrift in the unsettling waters of an overall crisis in US politics and culture. From the 1960s to the 1980s, racial politics profoundly transformed personal identity, collective action, the state and American society as a whole. The nature of racial contest the next time around remains open.

Notes and references

Introduction

1 *San Francisco Chronicle*, 30 January 1985 and the *New York Times*, 30 January 1985. See also J.K. Yamamoto, "Civil Rights Commission Under Fire," *Pacific Citizen*, 5 April 1985.

2 By racism we mean those social practices which (explicitly or implicitly) attribute merits or allocate values to members of racially categorized groups solely because of their "race."

3 This is an introductory formulation. We shall have more to say later about the numerous variations (ethnic, national, class-based, etc.) possible within racial identity. Among Latinos, for example, the Puerto Rican, Central American and Cuban cases all retain certain distinct aspects; among Asians, Chinese, Vietnamese and other Southeast Asians, and Filipinos all have particular histories in the US. There are those whose racial category is ambiguous at present (e.g. Arabs). Further still, racial classification, as we shall argue below, is always flexible, a process without an end point or finality of any kind.

4 Concepts such as "internal colonialism" might offer important insights into US racial conditions, but because they ultimately reason by analogy, they cannot range over the uniqueness and complexities of American racial ideology or politics.

5 In a letter to the *New York Times*, Mr Ko Yung Tung made these comments on the 1980 census:

> "I was somewhat puzzled and disturbed by the question relating to race/national origin on my census form. The categories were 'white, black, Japanese, Chinese, Korean,' etc.
>
> "If the question is intended to get statistics on race, why is there a distinction between, say, Chinese and Japanese? They are both of the same race. If it is intended to elicit answers as to national origin, why are all whites undifferentiated? Why not German, French, Irish, etc.? Moreover, if this is to be an accurate study, it should allow for 'mixed' people. I myself am half Manchu and half Chinese (Han). My wife is 'white' (part Dutch, English, German, and Irish). What does that make my children?

"I had hoped that by 1980 the US government was more enlightened. The question reflects at best ignorance, at worst racism." (Cited in Lewis M. Killian, "Black Power and White Reactions: The Revitalization of Race-Thinking in the United States," *Annals of The American Academy of Social and Political Sciences* no. 454 (March, 1981) p.50.)

6 The inclusion of the categories of "Hispanic" and "Asian and Pacific Islanders" in the 1980 US census, for example, was the result of lobbying efforts and Congressional debate.

7 We employ this term with reservations to distinguish the popular movements of the postwar period from their earlier antecedents (where applicable), and from movements of class- or status-based groups understood in the traditional Marxian or Weberian sense.

The black movement was hardly "new." It was the oldest and probably the most vital popular movement in US history. Why, then, do we characterize it as the founding "new" social movement in the postwar period? The postwar black movement was different from its predecessors in *its ability to confront racial oppression simultaneously as an individually experienced and as a collectively organized phenomenon.* This is what it imparted to other new social movements. They have all interpreted politically the "immediate experience" of their members, adding the range of issues this engendered to the older grievances their predecessors had lodged, such as (in the case of the black movement) discrimination and prejudice. This "politics of identity" which spilled over into arenas not traditionally defined as "political" is what made the new social movements "new."

8 Rearticulation is the process of redefinition of political interests and identities, through a process of recombination of familiar ideas and values in hitherto unrecognized ways. This concept is more fully elaborated in Chapters 5 and 6.

9 It should be noted that while many of the class- and nation-based studies of race challenged the ethnicity perspective from a radical position, by no means all of these analyses entertained such views.

Part I

Introduction: Paradigms of race: ethnicity, class and nation

1 Blauner writes: ". . .[T]he general conceptual frame of European theory implicitly assumed the decline and disappearance of ethnicity in the modern world; it offered no hints in the other direction. Without significant alteration, American sociology synthesized this framework into its models of social structure and change." (Robert Blauner, *Racial Oppression in America* (New York: Harper & Row, 1972), p. 4.) See also Herman Schwendinger and Julia R. Schwendinger, *The Sociologists of the Chair: A Radical Analysis of the Formative Years of North American*

Sociology (1883–1922) (New York: Basic Books, 1974), p. 39.)

2   After a promising start in the early period, the study of race and
    ethnic relations suffered. . . . With little room for ethnic and racial
    phenomena in the macroscopic models of social structure and
    process, the field was isolated from general sociological theory and
    particularly from those leading conceptual themes that might have
    provided coherence and useful lines of inquiry: stratification, culture,
    community. The study of race relations developed in a kind of
    vacuum; no overall theoretical framework guided its research and
    development. (Blauner, op. cit., p. 5)

3   Lyman notes: "It [the race-relations cycle] was ideology too, for Park
    believed that once the racial cycle was completed, the social arena would
    be cleared of those racial impediments interfering with the inevitable
    class struggle." (Lyman, op. cit., p. 27.)

4   Blauner, op. cit., p. 2.

5   This alternative perspective rooted in a notion of institutional racism is
    elaborated in Louis L. Knowles and Kenneth Prewitt, eds, *Institutional
    Racism in America* (Englewood Cliffs, New Jersey: Prentice-Hall, 1969).

6   Van den Berghe in a section critiquing the dominant trends in the study
    of race relations notes that:
    . . . in spite of the claim of many social scientists that detachment
    and objectivity are possible and that they can dissociate their roles as
    scientists and as private citizens, much of the work done by North
    Americans in the area of race has, until the last three or four years,
    been strongly flavored with a great deal of optimism and
    complacency about the basic "goodness" of American society and
    with the cautious, slightly left-of-center, reformist, meliorative,
    gradualist approach of "liberal" intellectuals.
    He goes on to say: "The field has been dominated by a functionalist
    view of society and a definition of the race problem as one of integration
    and assimilation of minorities into the mainstream of a consensus-based
    society." (Pierre L. van den Berghe, *Race and Racism: A Comparative
    Perspective* (New York: Wiley, 1967), p. 7.)

7   The concept of a *paradigm* in scientific or scholarly investigation gained
    currency with the publication of Thomas S. Kuhn's *The Structure of
    Scientific Revolutions* (Chicago: University of Chicago Press, 1970, 2nd
    edn). Our usage of the term is slightly at variance with Kuhn's. A racial
    paradigm, in our view, is an assumed theoretical category which classifies
    racial phenomena. In our epoch there has been a strong reluctance in
    social scientific circles to indulge in "race-thinking" (undoubtedly due to
    the legacy of biologism with which pre-World War II scholarship encoun-
    tered issues of race). Thus existing theories understand race in terms of
    other, supposedly more fundamental or objective, social scientific cate-
    gories. These categories can be aggregated, ideal typically, into the three
    paradigms of ethnicity-, class- and nation-based racial theories.

1 The dominant paradigm: ethnicity-based theory

1 William Peterson, "Concepts of Ethnicity," in W. Peterson, M. Novak and P. Gleason, *Concepts of Ethnicity: Selections from the Harvard Encyclopedia of American Ethnic Groups* (Cambridge, Mass.: Harvard University Press, 1982) p. 2.

2 The biologistic view of race, of course, predated slavery's abolition. For example, in 1792 Dr Benjamin Rush, one of the "Founding Fathers," presented a paper before the American Philosophical Society which argued that the "color" and "figure" of blacks were derived from a form of leprosy. He was convinced that with proper treatment, blacks could be cured (i.e. become white) and eventually assimilated into the general population. See Ronald T. Takaki, *Iron Cages: Race and Culture in 19th-Century America* (Seattle: University of Washington Press, 1979), pp. 28–35. For present purposes, it is not terribly important whether a single dominant current of race-thinking spanned the pre- and post-Civil War period, or whether, starting in the later nineteenth century, a new biologistic paradigm emerged.

3 For the definitive intellectual history, see Thomas F. Gossett, *Race: The History of an Idea in America* (Dallas: Southern Methodist University Press, 1963); Peter I. Rose, *The Subject is Race* (New York: Oxford University Press, 1968), esp. pp. 11–66. A great deal of inflammatory "theoretical" material appeared during this time within the biologistic paradigm, e.g. Madison Grant, *The Passing of the Great Race* (New York: Scribners, 1916). Two good recent histories of eugenics are Allen Chase, *The Legacy of Malthus* (New York: Knopf, 1977), and Daniel J. Kelves, *In the Name of Eugenics: Genetics and the Uses of Human Heredity* (New York: Knopf, 1985).

4 Kallen's *Culture and Democracy in America* (New York: Boni & Liveright, 1924) first appeared in *The Nation* in 1915; for Park's contributions see Everett Hughes *et al.,* eds., *Race and Culture,* vol. 1 of *The Collected Papers of Robert E. Park* (Glencoe, Ill: The Free Press, 1950). A direct line runs through Park from the pioneering black struggles of the post-Reconstruction epoch and the modern ethnicity-based approaches of Frazier, Myrdal and Hughes. The Marxist racial theorist Oliver C. Cox was also a student of Park. A good general account of the early days of modern racial (i.e. ethnicity) theory can be found in Rose, op. cit.

5 See William Peterson, op. cit.; N. Glazer and Daniel P. Moynihan, "Introduction," in Glazer and Moynihan, eds, *Ethnicity: Theory and Experience* (Cambridge, Mass.: Harvard University Press, 1975) p. 4.

6 Nathan Glazer, "Blacks and Ethnic Groups: The Difference and the Political Difference It Makes," in *idem, Ethnic Dilemmas, 1964–1982* (Cambridge, Mass.: Harvard University Press, 1983) p. 74, offers a slightly different laundry list of the cultural determinants of ethnicity.

7 Park's "race relations cycle," for example, typifies this assumption, not because it is biologistic (Park is clear in thinking about race in social terms), but because the origins of groups which first come into "culture

contact" with one another are not theorized. See Robert E. Park, "Our Racial Frontier on the Pacific" [1926], in *Race and Culture*, op. cit.

8 See, for example, Clifford Geertz, "The Integrative Revolution: Primordial Sentiments and Civil Politics in New States," in *idem*, ed., *Old Societies and New States* (Glencoe, Ill: The Free Press, 1963); Orlando Patterson, *Ethnic Chauvinism: The Reactionary Response* (New York: Stein & Day, 1977). Gerald Berreman has argued that ethnic identities are "partial," representing a range of options in self-presentation that is essentially politically determined. See his "Bazaar Behavior: Social Identity and Social Interaction in Urban India," in G. DeVos and L. Romanucci-Ross, eds, *Ethnic Identity* (Palo Alto, Cal.: Mayfield, 1975).

9 Early work includes Park, op. cit.; see also his "Introduction" to Louis Wirth, *The Ghetto* (Chicago: University of Chicago Press, 1956 [1928]); Horace Kallen, op. cit., was the first systematic presentation of the "cultural pluralist" position and thus the first to argue from within ethnicity theory against assimilationism. Kallen's framework is explicitly Atlanticist. See also W. Lloyd Warner and Leo Srole, *The Social Systems of American Ethnic Groups* (New Haven: Yale University Press, 1945) for a caste-oriented approach which contrasts the prospects for assimilation (or "mobility") of white and nonwhite "ethnic groups"; this book thus straddles our ethnicity and class paradigms. Some representative modern work includes Milton M. Gordon, *Assimilation in American Life* (New York: Oxford University Press, 1964); Glazer and Moynihan, eds, op. cit., M. Walzer, E.T. Kantowicz, J. Higham and M. Harrington, *The Politics of Ethnicity: Selections from the Harvard Encyclopedia of American Ethnic Groups* (Cambridge, Mass.: Harvard University Press, 1982).

10 For two contrasting views of New Deal policies toward blacks, see Harvard Sitkoff, *A New Deal For Blacks: The Emergence of Civil Rights as a National Issue* (New York: Hill & Wang, 1978); Nancy J. Weiss, *Farewell to the Party of Lincoln: Black Politics in the Age of FDR* (Princeton: Princeton University Press, 1983).

11 Milton M. Gordon, op. cit., pp. 88–114.

12 Robert E. Park, "Introduction" to Louis Wirth, *The Ghetto*, op. cit., p. vii.

13 Gunnar Myrdal, *An American Dilemma: The Negro Problem and Modern Democracy*, Twentieth Anniversary Edition (New York: Harper & Row, 1962 [1944]).

14 The study's collaborators included, among many others, Arnold Rose and Richard Sterner (Myrdal's principal associates), Ralph Bunche, Doxey Wilkerson, Sterling A. Brown, St. Clair Drake, E. Franklin Frazier, Melville J. Herskovits, Otto Klineberg, Edward Shils and Louis Wirth; consultants included W.E.B. DuBois, Horace Cayton, Robert E. Park, W. I. Thomas, Hortense Powdermaker, John Dollard, Alain Locke, Walter White, Abram L. Harris, Ruth Benedict and numerous others.

15 See for example Myrdal, op. cit., p. 929. *An American Dilemma*'s

version of the ethnicity paradigm was thus not the only one possible; indeed, cultural pluralist versions were left in the ambiguous status of competing accounts within the dominant approach.

16 Ibid., pp. 1021–2; emphasis original.

17 Ibid., p. 927ff. Frazier later asserted this position as a supposed support to integration efforts:

> Since the institutions, the social stratification, and the culture of the Negro community are essentially the same as those of the larger community, it is not strange that the Negro minority belongs among the assimilationist rather than the pluralist, secessionist, or militant minorities. It is seldom that one finds Negroes who think of themselves as possessing a different culture from whites and that their culture should be preserved. (E. Franklin Frazier, *The Negro in the United States*, rev. edn (New York: Macmillan, 1957) p. 681.)

This argument, of course, is part of a larger controversy concerning black cultural heritage, the survival of African elements in slave culture, etc., with which we cannot engage here.

18 Nathan Glazer and Daniel Patrick Moynihan, *Beyond the Melting Pot*, 2nd edn (Cambridge, Mass.: MIT Press, 1970).

19 Ibid., p. 17.

20 Ibid., emphasis original.

21 Blacks are, for ethnicity theory, the great exception among racial minorities to the immigrant pattern, for they experienced the formal and legal discrimination of slavery and its aftermath. Other racially defined groups were seen as fitting more easily into the immigrant/ ethnic model. See Nathan Glazer, "The Peoples of America," in *Ethnic Dilemmas*, op. cit., pp. 25–7.

22 See for example Gordon, op. cit., p. 249:

> [Government] . . . must not use racial criteria positively in order to impose desegregation upon public facilities in an institutional area where such segregation is not a function of racial discrimination directly [i.e., there is no explicit effort to discriminate-MO/HW] but results from discrimination operating in another institutional area, or from other causes.

23 The support offered by ethnicity theory to the civil rights movement's struggle in the South was not a mere matter of some professors signing petitions or advertisements. As the dominant racial paradigm, ethnicity theory represented racial "common sense" and informed state policy. The movement's substantial moderate support was thus vouchsafed it, so long as its target remained the "backward" South. See Chapter 6 below.

24 Nathan Glazer and Daniel P. Moynihan, *Beyond the Melting Pot*, op. cit., p. x.

25 See note 20 above. Glazer's treatment of the question may be found in "Blacks and Ethnic Groups: The Difference and the Political Difference It Makes," in Glazer, *Ethnic Dilemmas*, op. cit.

26 Any attempt at a definitive marking of the split between the dominant racial theory – based on the ethnicity paradigm – and the black movement will inevitably be arbitrary.

27 The neoconservative position is reviewed in depth in Chapter 7 below. We offer only the briefest of remarks here.

28 See "The Negro Family: The Case For National Action," in L. Rainwater and W. Yancey, *The Moynihan Report and the Politics of Controversy* (Cambridge, Mass.: MIT Press, 1967), p. 49. See also, in the same volume, the speech of President Lyndon Johnson, "To Fulfill These Rights," delivered 4 June 1965 at Howard University, and drafted in part by Moynihan.

29 Glazer argued, also in 1965, that a "new national interest" in "the final liquidation of Negro separation" was being defined, and that blacks themselves had best not oppose it, for "When an ethnic group interest has clashed with a national interest, we have been quite ruthless and even extreme in overriding the group interest" ("The Peoples of America," in *Ethnic Dilemmas*, op. cit., p. 27).

30 See, for example, Robert Blauner, *Racial Oppression in America* (New York: Harper & Row, 1972), pp. 88–89n, 125; Stanley Lieberson, *A Piece of The Pie: Blacks and White Immigrants Since 1880* (Berkeley: University of California Press, 1980); Alexander Saxton, "Nathan Glazer, Daniel Moynihan, and the Cult of Ethnicity," *Amerasia Journal*, vol. 4, no. 2 (1977); William P. Ryan, *Blaming The Victim*, rev. edn (New York: Vintage, 1976).

31 Glazer and Moynihan, "Introduction," in *idem*, eds, *Ethnicity: Theory and Experience* (Cambridge, Mass.: Harvard University Press, 1975), p. 7.

32 It also brings to mind Moynihan's earlier "tangle of pathology" thesis, contained in his "The Negro Family," op. cit.

33 Milton Gordon, *Assimilation in American Life*, op. cit., p. 70.

34 See, among a welter of possible sources, Kenneth Clark, *Dark Ghetto* (New York: Harper & Row, 1965); Carol B. Stack, *All Our Kin: Strategies for Survival in a Black Community* (New York: Harper & Row, 1974); John Langston Gwaltney, *Drylongso: A Self-Portrait of Black America* (New York: Vintage, 1980).

35 We discuss the process of "racialization" in Chapter 5 below.

2 The challenging paradigms: class-based theory

1 Stuart Hall, "Race, Articulation, and Societies Structured in Dominance," in *Sociological Theories: Race and Colonialism* (Paris: UNESCO, 1980) p. 306.

2 H. Gerth and C. Wright Mills, eds, *From Max Weber: Essays in Sociology* (New York: Oxford University Press, 1958) pp. 181–3.

3 Currently, much theoretical debate has arisen over the nature of "the economic." Is there a particular kind of real relationship, for example market exchange or immediate production (the "transformation of

nature" through labor) that can be understood as purely or quintessentially "economic"? Or, to the contrary, is "the economic" a merely
analytically distinct aspect of most, if not all, social relationships, in
which various forms of "appropriation," "exchange," etc. are practiced, "power" is exercised, and "meaning" produced? This is not the
place to examine these issues in depth, although we believe that all
social relationships, including those of material production, are inherently structured politically and ideologically, as well as by "market
rationality" (a category which also has noneconomic aspects). See
Samuel Bowles and Herbert Gintis, "Structure and Practice in the
Labor Theory of Value," in *Review of Radical Political Economics,* vol.
12, no. 4 (Winter 1981); and *idem*, "On the Heterogeneity of Power,"
unpublished MS, 1983. In regard to the implications of this perspective
for Marxian theory, Ernesto Laclau's remarks are provocative:

> I think the critique of economism should have a much wider
> deconstructive effect on traditional Marxist theory. That is, we
> should no longer conceive the economy as a homogeneous milieu
> that follows its own endogenous laws of development. . . . Today
> we can see that the space which traditional Marxism designated
> "the economy" is in fact the terrain of proliferation of discourses.
> We have discourses of authority, technical discourses, discourses of
> accountancy, discourses of information. Even categories such as
> profit can no longer be accepted as unequivocal. For instance, a
> multinational corporation today develops complex political and
> economic strategies within which the search for profit certainly
> plays a fundamental role, but does so within a whole policy of
> investment which can often require sacrificing immediate profits to
> wider strategic aims. The functioning of the economy itself is a
> political functioning, and cannot be understood in terms of a single
> logic. What we need today . . . is a non-economistic understanding
> of the economy, one which introduces the primary of politics at the
> level of the "infrastructure" itself.

Cf. Ernesto Laclau and Chantal Mouffe, "Recasting Marxism: Hegemony and New Political Movements," *Socialist Review* 66 (vol. 12, no.
6) November-December 1982, p. 92. See also Chantal Mouffe,
"Working-Class Hegemony and the Struggle for Socialism," *Studies in
Political Economy* 12 (Fall 1983).

4 Therefore, in the broad terms we have employed to describe the
paradigm, these are class theories, even if the authors assume the
existence of a totally free market. An early and influential example was
Gary Becker, *The Economics of Discrimination* (Chicago: University
of Chicago Press, 1957), which analogizes race relations to international
trade! Such "institutional" economists as Lester Thurow, who have
subjected these approaches to critical readings, have understood the
"idealistic" side of the neoclassicists very well. See Lester Thurow,
Poverty and Discrimination (Washington, DC: Brookings, 1969).

5 Each approach is dealt with as an "ideal type." Just as there is no "pure"

case of a class-, ethnic group-, or nation-based theory of race, so there is no "pure" stratification approach to race.

6 Milton Friedman, *Capitalism and Freedom* (Chicago: University of Chacago Press, 1962) pp. 108–10. Assuming for the moment an orthodox and unproblematic neoclassical theory, race may only appear in two ways: there may be efforts to explain the initial appearance of racial inequality, and there may be debates about the efficiency of market forces in ending it.

7 Cf. respectively, Becker, op. cit.; Thurow, op. cit.; Walter E. Williams, *The State Against Blacks* (New York: McGraw-Hill, 1982).

8 Most market-based analyses (and many other treatments as well) think of race in black-white terms. We consider such frameworks, where not required by the study's content (e.g. in studies of slavery), to be distorted and limited accounts of the range of racial phenomena. Our practice is to indicate that an author frames discussion of race in terms of blacks and whites, making no reference to other groups, by ourselves employing this terminology. Where the full range of racial minorities is being considered, we attempt to reflect this in our terminology as well.

9 Michael Reich, *Racial Inequality* (Princeton: Princeton University Press, 1981) pp. 86–8.

10 Williams, op. cit.; Thomas Sowell, "Racism, Quotas, and the Front Door," *The Wall Street Journal*, 28 July 1979, p. 8.

11 Some Marxian theories, for example split labor market perspectives, also entertain a version of this idea. The reliance on labor market dualisms to explain racial inequality is prevalent in Marxist analysis of all sorts. See "Class conflict theory" below.

12 William Julius Wilson, *The Declining Significance of Race*, 2nd edn (Chicago: University of Chicago Press, 1978) p. 17.

13 S. Shulman, "Race, Class, and Occupational Stratification: A Critique of William Julius Wilson's *The Declining Significance of Race*," in *Review of Radical Political Economics*, vol. 13, no. 3 (Fall 1981); Paul Joseph, "An Implicit Marxist Theory of Race? A Review Essay of William Julius Wilson's *The Declining Significance of Race*" (unpublished MS, n.d.); Alfonso Pinkney, *The Myth of Black Progress* (New York: Cambridge University Press, 1984). See also Michael Omi's review in *The Insurgent Sociologist*, vol. 10, no. 2 (Fall 1980).

14 See Wilson, *The Declining Significance of Race*, op. cit., p. 161.

15 See, for example, Thomas Sowell, ed., *The Fairmont Papers* (San Francisco: Institute for Contemporary Society, 1981). There is nothing particularly new in these phenomena. It is instructive to compare the new ethos of "black conservatism" to the classical works on the subject, such as E. Franklin Frazier, *Black Bourgeoisie* (New York: The Free Press, 1957), and W.E.B. DuBois, *The Philadelphia Negro* (New York: Schocken, 1967 [1899]).

16 Many civil rights activists moved into government service during the 1960s; see Frances Fox Piven and Richard A. Cloward, *Poor People's Movements: Why They Succeed, How They Fail* (New York: Pantheon, 1977) pp. 254–5. Black attendance in college soared dramatically from

the mid-1960s onward, which derived from numerous sources: the passage of equal opportunity legislation and federal efforts to improve secondary schooling for minorities, demands made upon colleges and universities by minority students and communities, etc. This in turn affected the production of skilled black professionals; see Institute for the Study of Educational Policy, *Equal Educational Opportunity: An Assessment* (Washington, DC: Howard University Press, 1976). See also Richard B. Freeman, *Black Elite: The New Market for Highly Educated Black Americans* (New York: McGraw-Hill, 1976), pp. 290–1.

17 Neoconservative writers and new rightists have been quite clear about their abhorrence for the "new class" and its "dependents." Wilson argues that blacks continue to constitute disproportionate numbers of the latter category, but he neglects the fact that the new "privileged" black stratum is very much a "new class" phenomenon. On the relationship between the "new class" and the "underclass," see Peter Steinfels, *The Neoconservatives: The Men Who Are Changing America's Politics* (New York: Simon & Schuster, 1979), pp. 290–1.

18 The classic studies of race as a "caste" phenomenon in the US are John Dollard, *Caste and Class in a Southern Town* (New York: Harper & Row, 1937); W. Lloyd Warner and Leo Srole, *The Social Systems of American Ethnic Groups* (New Haven: Yale University Press, 1945), esp. pp. 295–6.

19 Cf. Hubert M. Blalock, *Toward a Theory of Minority-Group Relations* (New York: Wiley, 1967); Michael Banton, "Ethnic Groups and the Theory of Rational Choice," in *Sociological Theories: Race and Colonialism* (Paris: UNESCO, 1980).

20 The problems of the class-based view do not originate so much, we argue, from assertions of the "primacy" of class as from the contention that class is an "objective" relationship. See the conclusion of this chapter.

21 John Roemer, "Divide and Conquer: Microfoundations of a Marxian Theory of Wage Discrimination," *Bell Journal of Economics* (Autumn 1979), provides an interesting new version of this neo-Marxist approach. Roemer's effort is to establish a microeconomic logic for capitalists' "divide and rule" strategies within particular enterprises, thus resolving a question which has been debated between "segmentation" and "split" labor market theorists of the class conflict school. The political orientation that informs Roemer's concept of interests is thus more micro-level as well.

22 Alexander Saxton, *The Indispensable Enemy* (Berkeley: University of California Press, 1971).

23 For example, Bowles and Gintis have recently suggested that

[B]lacks and whites share a common form of exploitation *as workers*, but clearly a distinct form *as races*. Moreover, this system of racial exploitation is directly incorporated into the site of capitalist production itself. (Samuel Bowles and Herbert Gintis,

"On the Heterogeneity of Power," unpublished MS, 1983, p. 29.)

While the first sentence appears true, the second seems much more problematic. Queried on the point, Bowles has said that what is intended here is ". . . capitalist production broadly construed to mean production (narrowly construed) and distribution" (Samuel Bowles, personal communication, October 16, 1984.) This implies stratification within classes along racial lines – segmentation of the working class – which in turn can be identified with labor *market* segmentation.

There is one possible exception: the assignment of workers to different jobs on a racial basis. See Martin Oppenheimer, "The Sub-Proletariat: Dark Skins and Dirty Work," *The Insurgent Sociologist*, no.4 (1974).

24 Oliver C. Cox, *Caste, Class, and Race* (New York: Monthly Review Press, 1970 [1948]); Reich, op. cit.

25 Edna Bonacich, "A Theory of Ethnic Antagonism: the Split Labor Market," *American Sociological Review* 37 (1972); *idem*, "Advanced Capitalism and Black/White Relations in the United States: A Split Labor Market Interpretation," *American Sociological Review* 41 (1976); Jeffrey Prager, "White Racial Privilege and Social Change: An Examination of Theories of Racism," *Berkeley Journal of Sociology*, 1972–73. Prager's approach is based on "internal colonialism" categories, but overlaps significantly with "split labor market" arguments as well.

26 Since our main interest here is the class conflict perspective we have found it useful to concentrate on Reich *et al*. With respect to Piore and Doeringer's valuable contributions, though, it is important to note that as institutionalists, they are under less compulsion to insert every aspect of "segmentation" in a unified class theory. Their procedure is more "middle-range," and therefore often more convincing, than the more schematic Marxian approaches. For example, in studying so-called "internal labor markets" (within large firms) they find evidence of several different, and shifting, "class alliances" among management, elite labor and secondary labor. Indeed, they recognize significant discontinuities in the patterns of "segmentation" itself. Race is thus seen as cutting more than one way. Such an ostensibly "Weberian" analysis is in many ways more in harmony with a racial formation perspective than is the overarching segmentation theory of Reich *et al*. P. Doeringer and M. Piore, *Internal Labor Markets and Manpower Analysis* (Lexington, Mass.: Heath, 1971), p. 136; see also M. Piore, *Birds of Passage: Migrant Labor and Industrial Societies* (New York: Cambridge University Press, 1979).

27 Reich, *Racial Inequality*, op. cit.

28 David M. Gordon, Richard Edwards and Michael Reich, *Segmented Work, Divided Workers: The Historical Transformation of Labor in the United States* (New York: Cambridge University Press, 1982).

29 Reich, *Racial Inequality*, op. cit., p. 269. Another recent example of this line of argument may be found in Erik Olin Wright: ". . .[I]n spite

of the divisive character of racism and in spite of the material differences between white and black workers which racism generates, workers of all races nevertheless share a fundamental class situation and thus share fundamental class interests." ("Race, Class and Income Inequality," *American Journal of Sociology*, vol. 83, no. 6 (1978), p. 1397).

30 Gordon, Edwards and Reich, op. cit., p. 16.

31 Reich, Gordon and Edwards, "A Theory of Labor Market Segmentation," in *American Economic Review* 63 (May 1973).

32 Gordon, Edwards and Reich, *Segmented Work*, op. cit., p. 209.

33 Ibid., p. 220.

34 Bonacich, "A Theory of Ethnic Antagonism," op. cit.; "Advanced Capitalism and Black/White Relations," op. cit.; *idem,* "The Past, Present, and Future of Split Labor Market Theory," in C.B. Marrett and C. Leggon, eds, *Research in Racial and Ethnic Relations* (Greenwich, Conn.: JAI Press, 1979); *idem*, "Class Approaches to Ethnicity and Race," *The Insurgent Sociologist*, vol. X, no. 2 (Fall 1980).

35 Bonacich, "Class Approaches," op. cit., p. 14.

36 Split labor market approaches correlate well to the nation-based paradigm of race, especially in certain of its more Marxian variants which stress the "privileges" of "metropolitan" over "colonial" or "peripheral" labor forces. Cf. Prager, op. cit.

37 Bonacich, "Advanced Capitalism and Black/White Relations," op. cit., p. 44.

38 Ibid. This critique has occasioned notable silence from Reich *et al.* Roemer's reformulation is the most serious attempt to address these issues by a "segmentation" theorist; see Roemer, op. cit. Michael Burawoy has suggested that the debate confuses capitalist class with individual capitalist interests; see Burawoy, "The Capitalist State in South Africa: Marxist and Sociological Perspectives on Race and Class," in M. Zeitlin, ed., *Political Power and Social Theory*, vol.2 (Greenwich, Conn.: JAI Press, 1981) p. 283. Roemer addresses this point in part with his notion of "divide and rule in a single firm."

39 Doeringer and Piore, op. cit.

40 James O'Connor, *The Fiscal Crisis of the State* (New York: St Martin's Press, 1973).

41 For an interesting critique of dual labor market theory, particularly directed at the segmentation approach, see Constance Lever-Tracy, "The Paradigm Crisis of Dualism: Decay or Regeneration?", in *Politics and Society*, vol. 13, no. 1 (1984).

42 Ibid., p. 83.

43 The US differs in this respect from the few societies which are even more racially divided, e.g. South Africa, although even there, as class formation processes are affected by the political imperative of black *embourgeoisement*, the lines of contiguity between race and class are beginning to blur. In respect to the US case, this point should not be interpreted to mean that racial *stratification* does not exist. Our point is rather that segmentation/split models of the labor market are unable to specify with any certainty or comprehensiveness the locations and

defining characteristics of their "segments" and "splits," and that, contrary to appearances, race does not furnish an adequate guidepost to these lines of demarcation. For an excellent comparative study of racial dynamics in the US and South Africa, see George Frederickson, *White Supremacy* (New York: Oxford University Press, 1982).

44 See, for example, Adam Przeworski, "Proletariat Into a Class: The Processes of Class Formation from Karl Kautsky's *The Class Struggle* to Recent Controversies," *Politics and Society*, vol. 7, no. 4 (1977).

45 For an exemplary effort to analyze the politics of production in terms similar to these, see Michael Burawoy, "Terrains of Contest: Factory and State Under Capitalism and Socialism," *Socialist Review* 58 (July-August 1981).

46 Two useful attempts which focus on earlier historical conjunctures are David Montgomery, *Workers' Control in America* (New York: Cambridge University Press, 1979) and Herbert Gutman, "The Negro and the United Mine Workers of America: The Career and Letters of Richard L. Davis and Something of Their Meaning, 1890–1900," in *idem, Work, Culture, and Society in Industrializing America* (New York: Knopf, 1976).

3 The challenging paradigms: nation-based theory

1 In 1854, for example, a National Emigration Convention was held at Pittsburgh, with Delany in the leadership, which called for emigration ". . . towards those places where the black and colored man comprise, by population . . . the ruling element of the body politic." J.H. Bracey, Jr, A. Meier, and E. Rudwick, eds, *Black Nationalism in America* (Indianapolis and New York: Bobbs-Merrill, 1970), p. 93.

2 (Greenwich, Conn.: Fawcett, 1961 [1903]). See also Robert L. Allen, *Black Awakening in Capitalist America: An Analytic History* (Garden City, New York: Doubleday, 1969), p. 97.

3 Harold Cruse, *Rebellion or Revolution?* (New York: William Morrow, 1968); *The Crisis of the Negro Intellectual* (New York: William Morrow, 1967).

4 The phrase, of course, is Immanuel Wallerstein's. See his *The Modern World System*, vols I and II (New York: Academic Press, 1974, 1980). Other interesting observations by Wallerstein on race and colonialism, to which we cannot address ourselves here, may be found in "Social Conflict in Post-Independence Black Africa: The Concepts of Race and Status-Group Reconsidered," in Ernest Q. Campbell, ed., *Racial Tensions and National Identity* (Nashville, Tennessee: Vanderbilt University Press, 1972); "The Rise and Future Demise of the World Capitalist System: Concepts for Comparative Analysis," in Wallerstein, *The Capitalist World-Economy* (New York: Cambridge University Press, 1979); and "Class Formation in the Capitalist World-Economy," in ibid.

5 The vestiges of colonialism extend to a wide variety of contemporary global arrangements. For example: although the introduction of

high-tech satellite communications systems has allowed many Third World countries to break the monopoly of international communications traffic held by many of their former European rulers, examples of "communications colonialism" still exist. Gregory C. Staple notes that "A.T. & T. routes U.S. telephone calls to Angola via Portugal, which receives a 20 percent cut of the toll charges; U.S. calls to Benin are routed via France, which receives roughly $3 for a routine three-minute call" (Gregory C. Staple, "Satellite Politics: The Assault on Intelsat," *The Nation*, vol.239, no.21 (22 December 1984)).

6 See Alfonso Pinkney, *Red, Black, and Green: Black Nationalism in the United States* (New York: Cambridge University Press, 1976); Bracey, Meier and Rudwick, op. cit.

7 See for example E. Rudwick, "DuBois vs. Garvey: Racial Propagandists at War," *Journal of Negro Education* XXVII (Fall 1959); J.H. Clarke, ed., *Marcus Garvey and the Vision of Africa* (New York: Vintage, 1974), esp. pp. 195–255.

8 A sixth (or seventh, depending on which events are counted) Pan-African Congress was held in Tanzania in 1974.

9 Some general sources on the Garvey movement: Clarke, ed., op. cit.; T.H. Vincent, *Black Power and the Garvey Movement* (Berkeley: Ramparts Press, 1971); and the recently begun series of volumes containing Garvey's complete papers, being edited by R.A. Hill, which represents the first systematic effort to present and interpret the movement's written legacy. (The first volume has appeared as Hill, ed., *The Marcus Garvey and Universal Negro Improvement Association Papers* (Berkeley: University of California Press, 1983); additional volumes are forthcoming.)

10 See among many statements his "Speech at Royal Albert Hall," in Clarke, ed., op. cit., pp. 284–99.

11 E.U. Essien-Udom, *Black Nationalism: A Search for Identity in America* (Chicago: University of Chicago Press, 1962) p. 50.

12 Garvey visited Ku Klux Klan headquarters in June 1922, and subsequently declared his agreement with the Klan that "this is a white man's country." He also flirted with the Anglo-Saxon Clubs of America, a white supremacist group led by one John Powell. His connection with such groups was certainly ill-advised, but his motivation in making these contacts has never been sufficiently explained. He was obviously not in agreement with such groups on white supremacy itself. See Richard B. Moore, "The Critics and Opponents of Marcus Garvey," in Clarke, ed., op. cit., pp. 225, 233–4.

13 Much important work must go without mention here, and Garveyism is thus afforded a pride of place which, in scholarly terms, it perhaps does not deserve. At the least, the contributions of such Pan-Africanist writers as DuBois, Padmore, or James (all of whom fused Pan-Africanism with Marxism to greater or lesser extent, and who found Garvey politically misguided if not vulgar), should be mentioned.

14 Even oppositing tendencies of black nationalism were so influenced. For example, it is unlikely that the Communist Party would have

adopted its "black nation" approach in 1928 had not Party leaders both in the US and in Moscow become alarmed at Garvey's successes. See below.

15 Two good general sources on Pan-Africanist theory are Colin Legum, *Pan Africanism: A Short Political Guide* (New York: Praeger, 1965), and R. Chrisman and N. Hare, *Pan Africanism* (Indianapolis and New York: Bobbs-Merrill, 1974).

16 On Carmichael's 1967 meetings with Sekou Toure and Kwame Nkrumah in Guinea, see Clayborne Carson, *In Struggle: SNCC and the Black Awakening of the 1960s*, (Cambridge, Mass.: Harvard University Press, 1981) p. 276. Carmichael later founded a small Pan-Africanist party in the US, the All African People's Revolutionary Party.

17 See Manning Marable, "Black Nationalism in the 1970s: Through the Prism of Race and Class," *Socialist Review* no. 50–51 (March-June 1980) pp. 86–8. Of course, we do not argue that such issues as apartheid have no relevance for black politics in the US; we simply suggest that they cannot be *substituted* for domestic concerns. Recent successful actions undertaken in the US in opposition to apartheid suggest that it may present an important rallying point for a broader black agenda that also includes coalition-building.

18 See Alain Locke, *The New Negro* (New York: Atheneum, 1968).

19 Some examples: "low-rider" youth culture and the mural movement in the Chicano barrios of the Southwest; the re-emphasis currently being given to Native American customs and religious and spiritual traditions by Native activists. See Roxanne Dunbar Ortiz, "Land and Nationhood: The American Indian Struggle for Self-Determination and Survival," *Socialist Review*, no.63–64 (May-August 1982).

20 Cruse, op. cit.

21 *Rebellion or Revolution*, op. cit., p. 111.

22 See his "Revolutionary Nationalism and the Afro-American," *Studies on the Left*, vol.2, no.3 (1962).

23 *Rebellion or Revolution*, op. cit., pp. 111–12.

24 Ibid.

25 Ibid., p. 117.

26 Ibid., p. 112.

27 Cruse's contention that the demand for "public ownership" of the cultural apparatus formed the basis for a new revolutionary nationalist politics must be doubted. As he presented it, his program was utopian. The *integration* of the US cultural apparatus, on the other hand, proved rather easy, demonstrating, as Robert Allen has pointed out, how far the co-optation of cultural nationalism was possible. See Allen, *Black Awakening*, op. cit., p. 179.

28 Both Karenga and Baraka abandoned their cultural nationalist positions in the 1970s. Compare Baraka, *Raise, Race, Rays, Raze* (New York: Random House, 1971) and *idem*, "Needed: A Black Revolutionary Strategy," *The Black Scholar* (October 1975); Pinkney, *Red, Black, and Green*, op. cit., pp. 127–43, treats Karenga and Baraka in their

cultural nationalist periods.

29 A good example is Baraka's essay on "A Black Value System," *The Black Scholar*, November 1969, which *ascribes* to African traditions Baraka's culturally oriented agenda of the period.

30 See Gonzales's poem, *Yo Soy Joaquin/I Am Joaquin* (New York: Bantam, 1972); see also *idem*, "El Plan de Aztlan," in Richard A. Garcia, ed., *The Chicanos in America, 1540–1974* (Dobbs Ferry, New York: Oceana Press, 1977).

31 Adolph L. Reed, Jr, "Black Particularity Reconsidered," *Telos*, no.39 (Spring 1979), p. 86.

32 Karl Marx and Frederick Engels, *Manifesto of the Communist Party* (Peking: Foreign Language Press, 1968), p. 55.

33 This point is elaborated by Michael Lowy, "Marxists and the National Question," *New Left Review*, no.96 (March-April 1976). For specific references see Karl Marx and Frederick Engels, *On Colonialism: Articles from the New York Tribune and Other Writings* (New York: International Publishers, 1972) and *Ireland and the Irish Question: A Collection of Writings by Karl Marx and Frederick Engels* (New York: International Publishers, 1972).

34 V.I. Lenin, *Questions of National Policy and Proletarian Internationalism* (Moscow: Progress Publishers, 1970). Lenin sought to place these "national" conflicts in their international "class" context: the relationship between the proletariat of the "oppressor" nation and the proletariat of the "oppressed" nation (the so-called "aristocracy of labor") was also one of exploitation.

35 Horace B. Davis, ed., *The National Question: Selected Writings by Rosa Luxemburg* (New York: Monthly Review Press, 1976).

36 Joseph Stalin, *Marxism and the National-Colonial Question* (San Francisco: Proletarian Publishers, 1975), p. 22. We cannot dwell on the mechanical nature of this approach here.

37 See, for example, Revolutionary Union, *Red Papers 5: National Liberation and Proletarian Revolution in the U.S.* (Chicago: Revolutionary Union, n.d.) and October League, *The Struggle for Black Liberation and Socialist Revolution* (Chicago: October League, 1976).

38 Some of the analyses are tragically humorous. The Communist Labor Party understood the black nation in the following manner:

> Owing to the specifics of the rise of USNA [United States of North America] imperialism and the history of the Black Belt of the South, there arose a nation, oppressed by USNA [United States North American] imperialism, whose social root and base was the aforementioned Negro people. . . . Now, when referring to the nation, we use the term Negro and mean national and not color. . . . In the sense of national, Negroes are both the 'black' majority and 'white' minority. (Nelson Peery, *The Negro National Colonial Question* (Chicago: Workers' Press, 1975), p. 11.)

One can well imagine the success of efforts to organize both blacks and whites in the South on the basis of their common identity as "Negroes."

39 For a critique of this literature and an analysis of its application see Racism Research Project, *Critique of the Black Nation Thesis* (Berkeley: Racism Research Project, 1975).

40 S. Berger, *Peasants Against Politics: Rural Organization in Brittany, 1907–1967* (Cambridge, Mass.: Harvard University Press, 1972).

41 Julio Cotler, "The Mechanics of Internal Domination and Social Change in Peru," in I.L. Horowitz, ed., *Masses in Latin America* (New York: Oxford University Press, 1970).

42 Harold Wolpe, "The Theory of Internal Colonialism," in I. Oxall *et al.*, eds, *Beyond The Sociology of Development* (London: Routledge & Kegan Paul, 1975).

43 M. Hechter, *Internal Colonialism: The Celtic Fringe in British National Development* (Berkeley: University of California Press, 1975).

44 S. Carmichael and C.V. Hamilton, *Black Power* (New York: Random House, 1967); Robert L. Allen, *Black Awakening*, op. cit.

45 Joan W. Moore, *Mexican Americans* (Englewood Cliffs, New Jersey: Prentice-Hall, 1970); M. Barrera, C. Munoz and G. Ornelas, "The Barrio as Internal Colony," in H. Hahn, ed., *People and Politics in Urban Society* (Beverly Hills, Cal.: Sage, 1972); see also M. Barrera, *Race and Class in the Southwest* (Notre Dame: University of Notre Dame Press, 1979); G. Flores, "Internal Colonialism and Racial Minorities in the US: An Overview," in F. Bonilla and R. Girling, eds, *Structures of Dependency* (Stanford, Cal.: Stanford University Press, 1973).

46 Robert Blauner, *Racial Oppression in America* (New York: Harper & Row, 1972); Blauner's approach, like other "internal colonialism" analyses, can be faulted for deviating significantly from the original meaning of the term "colonialism." Burawoy, for example, offers a definition of colonialism that reasserts the criterion of territoriality in terms which no "internal" application can satisfy: "Colonialism may be defined as the conquest and administration by a 'metropolitan country' of a geographically separate territory in order to utilize available resources (usually human or natural) for the creation of surplus which is repatriated to the metropolis." Michael Burawoy, "Race, Class, and Colonialism," *Social and Economic Studies*, vol.24, no.4 (December 1974), p. 546. Blauner's version of internal colonialism may be at variance with this more traditional notion, but it does not differ substantially from other "internal" approaches in this respect and is thus useful as a typical example.

47 Compare Blauner, op. cit., pp. 88–9, and Nathan Glazer, *Ethnic Dilemmas, 1964–1982* (Cambridge, Mass.: Harvard University Press, 1983), pp. 79–88.

48 "My own developing framework," Blauner writes, "probably owes more to the social movements of the oppressed than to standard sociology." Blauner, op. cit., p. viii.

49 Ibid., p. 55. Blauner is not unaware that economic suffering and political persecution in their countries of origin impelled much immigration to the US, but he notes that these problems, however dire,

did not force their victims to come to the US *specifically*. Many European emigrants headed for South America, for example. For these and other reasons, we are in accord with Blauner's distinction here.

50 Ibid., p. 89.

51 See Piven and Cloward, *Poor Peoples' Movements*, op. cit.; P. Bachrach and M. Baratz, *Power and Poverty* (New York: Oxford University Press, 1971).

52 See M. Omi's review of William Julius Wilson's *The Declining Significance of Race*, in *Insurgent Sociologist*, vol. 10, no. 2 (Fall 1980), p. 119.

53 See Chapter 7 below.

54 Internal colonialist approaches have tended to see the ghetto and barrio as colonized territory. See for example James Boggs, "The City is the Black Man's Land," in *idem, Racism and Class Struggle* (New York: Monthly Review Press, 1970); Barrera, Munoz and Ornelas, op. cit.

55 Burawoy, "Race, Class, and Colonialism," op. cit., pp. 526–7.

56 See Seymour Martin Lipset, *The First New Nation* (New York: Basic Books, 1963). There is plenty of room for conservative nationalism, though, of the jingoistic sort, and credulity beyond bounds for it as well.

Conclusion: Towards a racial formation perspective

1 William Julius Wilson, *The Declining Significance of Race*, 2nd edn (Chicago: University of Chicago Press, 1978); Harold M. Baron, "Racism Transformed: The Implications of the 1960s," forthcoming in *The Review of Radical Political Economics*.

Part II

4 Racial formation

1 *San Francisco Chronicle*, 14 September 1982, 19 May 1983. Ironically, the 1970 Louisiana law was enacted to supersede an old Jim Crow statute which relied on the idea of "common report" in determining an infant's race. Following Phipps's unsuccessful attempt to change her classification and have the law declared unconstitutional, a legislative effort arose which culminated in the repeal of the law. See *San Francisco Chronicle*, 23 June 1983.

2 The Mormon church, for example, has been heavily criticized for its doctrine of black inferiority.

3 Thomas F. Gossett notes:

Race theory . . . had up until fairly modern times no firm hold on European thought. On the other hand, race theory and race prejudice were by no means unknown at the time when the English colonists came to North America. Undoubtedly, the age of exploration led many to speculate on race differences at a period when neither Europeans nor Englishmen were prepared to make allowances for vast cultural diversities. Even though race theories had not then secured wide acceptance or even sophisticate formulation, the first contacts of the Spanish with the Indians in the Americas can now be recognized as the beginning of a struggle between conceptions of the nature of primitive peoples which has not yet been wholly settled. (Thomas F. Gossett, *Race: The History of an Idea in America* (New York: Schocken Books, 1965), p. 16.)

Winthrop Jordan provides a detailed account of early European colonialists' attitudes about color and race in *White Over Black: American Attitudes Toward the Negro, 1550–1812* (New York: Norton, 1977 [1968]), pp. 3–43.

4 Pro-slavery physician Samuel George Morton (1799–1851) compiled a collection of 800 crania from all parts of the world which formed the sample for his studies of race. Assuming that the larger the size of the cranium translated into greater intelligence, Morton established a relationship between race and skull capacity. Gossett reports that:

In 1849, one of his studies included the following results: The English skulls in his collection proved to be the largest, with an average cranial capacity of 96 cubic inches. The Americans and Germans were rather poor seconds, both with cranial capacities of 90 cubic inches. At the bottom of the list were the Negroes with 83 cubic inches, the Chinese with 82, and the Indians with 79. (Ibid., p. 74.)

On Morton's methods, see Stephen J. Gould, "The Finagle Factor," *Human Nature* (July 1978).

5 Definitions of race founded upon a common pool of genes have not held up when confronted by scientific research which suggests that the differences *within* a given human population are greater than those *between* populations. See L.L. Cavalli-Sforza, "The Genetics of Human Populations," *Scientific American* (September 1974), pp. 81–9.

6 Winthrop D. Jordan, op. cit., pp. 219–28.

7 Two recent histories of eugenics are Allen Chase, *The Legacy of Malthus* (New York: Knopf, 1977); Daniel J. Kelves, *In the Name of Eugenics: Genetics and the Uses of Human Heredity* (New York: Knopf, 1985).

8 Arthur Jensen, "How Much Can We Boost IQ and Scholastic Achievement?", *Harvard Educational Review*, vol. 39 (1969), pp. 1–123.

9 Ernst Moritz Manasse, "Max Weber on Race," *Social Research*, vol. 14 (1947), pp. 191–221.

10 Quoted in Edward D.C. Campbell, Jr, *The Celluloid South: Hollywood and the Southern Myth* (Knoxville: University of Tennessee Press, 1981), pp. 168–70.

11 Marvin Harris, *Patterns of Race in the Americas* (New York: Norton, 1964), p. 56.

12 Ibid., p. 57.

13 After James Meredith had been admitted as the first black student at the University of Mississippi, Harry S. Murphy announced that he, and not Meredith, was the first black student to attend "Ole Miss." Murphy described himself as black but was able to pass for white and spent nine months at the institution without attracting any notice (ibid., p. 56).

14 A. Sivanandan, "From Resistance to Rebellion: Asian and Afro-Caribbean Struggles in Britain," *Race and Class*, vol. 23, nos. 2–3 (Autumn-Winter 1981).

15 Consider the contradictions in racial status which abound in the country with the most rigidly defined racial categories – South Africa. There a race classification agency is employed to adjudicate claims for upgrading of official racial identity. This is particularly necessary for the "coloured" category. The apartheid system considers Chinese as "Asians" while the Japanese are accorded the status of "honorary whites." This logic nearly detaches race from any grounding in skin color and other physical attributes and nakedly exposes race as a juridicial category subject to economic, social and political influences. (We are indebted to Steve Talbot for clarification of some of these points.)

16 Gordon W. Allport, *The Nature of Prejudice* (Garden City, New York: Doubleday, 1958), pp. 184–200.

17 We wish to use this phrase loosely, without committing ourselves to a particular position on such social psychological approaches as symbolic interactionism, which are outside the scope of this study. An interesting study on this subject is S.M. Lyman and W.A. Douglass, "Ethnicity: Strategies of Individual and Collective Impression Management," *Social Research*, vol. 40, no. 2 (1973).

18 Michael Billig, "Patterns of Racism: Interviews with National Front Members," *Race and Class*, vol. 20, no. 2 (Autumn 1978), pp. 161–79.

19 "Miss San Antonio USA Lisa Fernandez and other Hispanics auditioning for a role in a television soap opera did not fit the Hollywood image of real Mexicans and had to darken their faces before filming." Model Aurora Garza said that their faces were bronzed with powder because they looked too white. " 'I'm a real Mexican [Garza said] and very dark anyway. I'm even darker right now because I have a tan. But they kept wanting me to make my face darker and darker' " (*San Francisco Chronicle*, 21 September 1984). A similar dilemma faces Asian American actors who feel that Asian character lead roles inevitably go to white actors who make themselves up to be Asian. Scores of Charlie Chan films, for example, have been made with white leads (the last one was the 1981 *Charlie Chan and the Curse of the Dragon Queen*). Roland Winters, who played in six Chan features, was asked by playwright Frank Chin to explain the logic of casting a white man in the role of Charlie Chan: " 'The only thing I can think of is, if you want to cast a homosexual in a show, and you get a homosexual, it'll be awful. It won't

be funny . . . and maybe there's something there . . .' " (Frank Chin, "Confessions of the Chinatown Cowboy," *Bulletin of Concerned Asian Scholars*, vol. 4, no. 3 (Fall 1972)).

20 Melanie Martindale-Sikes, "Nationalizing 'Nigger' Imagery Through 'Birth of a Nation'," paper prepared for the 73rd Annual Meeting of the American Sociological Association, 4–8 September 1978 in San Francisco.

21 Winthrop D. Jordan, op. cit., p. 95; emphasis added.

22 Historical focus has been placed either on particular racially defined groups or on immigration and the "incorporation" of ethnic groups. In the former case the characteristic ethnicity theory pitfalls and apologetics such as functionalism and cultural pluralism may be avoided, but only by sacrificing much of the focus on race. In the latter case, race is considered a manifestation of ethnicity. See Chapter 1 above.

23 The degree of antipathy for these groups should not be minimized. A northern commentator observed in the 1850s: "An Irish Catholic seldom attempts to rise to a higher condition than that in which he is placed, while the Negro often makes the attempt with success." Quoted in Gossett, op. cit., p. 288.

24 This analysis, as will perhaps be obvious, is essentially DuBoisian. Its main source will be found in the monumental (and still largely unappreciated) *Black Reconstruction in the United States, 1860–1880* (New York: Atheneum, 1977 [1935]).

25 Alexander Saxton argues that:

> North Americans of European background have experienced three great racial confrontations: with the Indian, with the African, and with the Oriental. Central to each transaction has been a totally one-sided preponderance of power, exerted for the exploitation of nonwhites by the dominant white society. In each case (but especially in the two that began with systems of enforced labor), white workingmen have played a crucial, yet ambivalent, role. They have been both exploited and exploiters. On the one hand, thrown into competition with nonwhites as enslaved or "cheap" labor, they suffered economically; on the other hand, being white, they benefited by that very exploitation which was compelling the nonwhites to work for low wages or for nothing. Ideologically they were drawn in opposite directions. *Racial identification cut at right angles to class consciousness.* (Alexander Saxton, *The Indispensable Enemy: Labor and the Anti-Chinese Movement in California* (Berkeley and Los Angeles: University of California Press, 1971), p. 1, emphasis added.)

26 Selig Perlman, *The History of Trade Unionism in the United States* (New York: Augustus Kelley, 1950), p. 52; emphasis added.

27 Whether southern blacks were "peasants" or rural workers is unimportant in this context. Some time during the 1960s blacks attained a higher degree of urbanization than whites. Before World War II most blacks had been rural dwellers and nearly 80 percent lived in the South.

28 See George Gilder, *Wealth and Poverty* (New York: Basic Books, 1981); Charles Murray, *Losing Ground* (New York: Basic Books, 1984) See Chapter 7 below.

29 A brilliant study of the racialization process in Britain, focused on the rise of "mugging" as a popular fear in the 1970s, is Stuart Hall *et al.*, *Policing the Crisis* (London: Macmillan, 1978).

30 The case of Vincent Chin, a Chinese American man beaten to death in 1982 by a laid-off Detroit auto worker and his stepson who mistook him for Japanese and blamed him for the loss of their jobs, has been widely publicized in Asian American communities. On immigration conflicts and pressures, see Michael Omi, "New Wave Dread: Immigration and Intra-Third World Conflict," *Socialist Review*, no. 60 (November–December 1981).

31 Milton Gordon describes this belief as "the liberal expectancy," in a treatment particularly relevant to ethnicity theory; see his *Human Nature, Class, and Ethnicity* (New York: Oxford University Press, 1964), pp. 69–70. Nathan Glazer has argued repeatedly that racial classification is but a temporary manifestation of hostility toward new immigrants whose eventual incorporation into the "American ethnic pattern" lays to rest the use of racial categories; see his "Government and the American Ethnic Pattern," in W.A. Van Horne and T.A. Tonneson, eds, *Ethnicity and Public Policy* (Madison: University of Wisconsin Press, 1982) p. 30; *idem, Affirmative Discrimination* (New York: Basic Books, 1975), chapter 1. Many other examples could be cited.

32   It is essential to destroy the widespread prejudice that philosophy is a strange and difficult thing just because it is the specific intellectual activity of a particular category of specialists or of professional and systematic philosophers. It must first be shown that all men [sic] are philosophers, by defining the limits and characteristics of the "spontaneous philosophy" which is proper to everybody. This philosophy is contained in: 1. language itself, which is a totality of determined notions and concepts and not just words grammatically devoid of content; 2. "common sense" . . .; 3. popular religion and, therefore, also in the entire system of beliefs, superstitions, opinions, ways of seeing things and of acting, which are collectively bundled together under the name of 'folklore.' (Antonio Gramsci, "The Study of Philosophy," *Selections from the Prison Notebooks*, Quentin Hoare and Geoffrey Nowell Smith, eds (New York: International Publishers, 1971) p. 323)

33 Samuel Bowles and Herbert Gintis, "On the Heterogeneity of Power" (unpublished MS, 1983), p. 17; emphasis original. In another paper, Bowles and Gintis define a "site" as "an arena of social activity with a characteristic set of social relations defining its specificity. . . . A site is defined not by what is *done* there, but by what imparts *regularity* to what is done there, its characteristic 'rules of the game' " (Herbert Gintis and Samuel Bowles, "Structure and Practice in the Labor Theory of Value," *Review of Radical Political Economics*, vol. 12, no. 4 (Winter

1981), p. 4; emphasis original). "Sites" such as families, state institutions, or realms of the economy obviously require further theorization as to their general characteristics. They are of interest here because they suggest the comprehensive character of racial meanings.

34 To cite only two controversial works on the subject: Daniel P. Moynihan, *The Negro Family: The Case for National Action*, in L. Rainwater and W. Yancey, eds, *The Moynihan Report and the Politics of Controversy* (Cambridge, Mass.: MIT Press, 1967); Herbert C. Gutman, *The Black Family in Slavery and Freedom, 1750–1925* (New York: Vintage, 1976).

35 Thus discrimination brings about a whole range of shifts in racial identities, not only of its victims but also of its perpetrators, a subject far too vast to address properly here. It may occasion family discord, guilt, or feelings of inferiority or superiority. It may structure attempts to "pass" or to deny racial belonging, or become generalized as a symbol of individual indignity; conversely, discrimination may generate individual or collective resentment and opposition.

36 We describe in Chapter 6 below how traditional elements of black identity provided the basis for political mobilization in the early civil rights movement.

37 This continuity might be described – to borrow a phrase from Foucault – as "regularity in dispersion." By this we mean that racial phenomena vary widely: among different racially defined groups, regionally, in respect to other variables such as class and gender, etc., but that they exhibit crucial equivalences and isomorphisms as well. The continuity of "micro-" and "macro-level" racial dynamics, for example, which holds true across all racial groups, illustrates this point. See Michel Foucault, *The Archaeology of Knowledge* (New York: Pantheon, 1972), pp. 37–8.

38 See Chapters 6 and 7 below. We argue that throughout the postwar period an expanded, *social* politics based on movement forms of mobilization has been supplanting the economically based politics characteristic of the early twentieth century and institutionalized in the political alignment of the New Deal.

39 Power structure theory and policy analysis have recognized for some years now that in certain situations power imbalances are so uneven that opposition is useless, and a conflictual "mobilization of bias" (Schattschneider) cannot be achieved. It follows that the very absence of conflict may indicate the presence of such an imbalance. See Peter Bachrach and Morton Baratz, *Power and Poverty* (New York: Oxford, 1970); Matthew Crenson, *The Unpolitics of Air Pollution* (Baltimore: Johns Hopkins University Press, 1971).

5 The racial state

1 Lance Liebman, "Anti-Discrimination Law: Groups and the Modern State," in Nathan Glazer and Ken Young, eds, *Ethnic Pluralism and*

Public Policy: Achieving Equality in the US and Britain (Lexington, Mass.: D.C. Heath, 1983) p. 13.

2 See Cynthia Enloe, "The Growth of the State and Ethnic Mobilization: The American Experience," *Ethnic and Racial Studies*, vol. 4, no. 2 (April 1981) p. 133.

3 See Mary Frances Berry, "Taming the Civil Rights Commission," *The Nation*, 2 February 1985, pp. 106–7.

4 Note that such movements can be egalitarian or counter-egalitarian, depending on the concepts of justice, equality, discrimination, etc., to which they adhere. For a theory of political change focused on this issue (drawing on German reference points), see Barrington Moore, *Injustice: The Social Bases of Obedience and Revolt* (White Plains, New York: Sharpe, 1978).

5 This does not mean that these channels are the sole province of reform-oriented movements or democratizing currents. They are also open to other uses and other interests, including those of reaction.

6 There are important continuities between present-day and past versions of racial ideology. Often, in the past, the dominant viewpoint about what race was and what race meant has been believed to represent the culmination of a long struggle to eliminate pre-existing "unenlightened" racial beliefs. Religious and scientific exponents of the dominant racial ideology, for example, have often made such claims. Thus it is all too easy to believe that in the present ("finally") the US has reached a stage at which racial oppression is largely a thing of the past, and that in the future race will play an ever-smaller role in determining the course of US political and social history. We obviously do not share that view.

7 A brief selection of sources: Eugene Genovese, *Roll, Jordan, Roll: The World the Slaves Made* (New York: Pantheon, 1974); Julius Lester, *To Be a Slave* (New York: Dial, 1968); Vincent Harding, "Religion and Resistance Among Antebellum Negroes, 1800–1860," in A. Meier and E. Rudwick, eds, *The Making of Black America*, 2 vols (New York: Atheneum, 1969); George Rawick, *From Sundown to Sunup: The Making of the Black Community* (Westport, Conn.: Greenwood, 1972); Herbert C. Gutman, *The Black Family in Slavery and Freedom, 1750–1925* (New York: Vintage, 1976); Robert Farris Thompson, *Flash of the Spirit: African and Afro-American Art and Philosophy* (New York: Random House, 1983).

8 Roxanne Dunbar Ortiz, "Land and Nationhood: The American Indian Struggle for Self-Determination and Survival," *Socialist Review*, no. 63–4 (May-August 1982).

9 Rodolfo Acuna, *Occupied America: A History of Chicanos*, 2nd edn (New York: Harper & Row, 1981); see also Leonard Pitt, *The Decline of the Californios* (Berkeley: University of California Press, 1966).

10 Our treatment here is necessarily very brief. The contemporary configuration of racial politics is a major subject later on in this work.

11 The ideological residue of these restrictions in naturalization and citizenship is the popular equation of the term "American" with "white." Other "Americans" are seen as black, Mexican, Oriental, etc.

12 For a comprehensive discussion of racial minorities in nineteenth-century California, see Tomas Almaguer, "Class, Race, and Capitalist Development: The Social Transformation of a Southern California County, 1848–1903," unpublished doctoral dissertation, University of California, Berkeley, 1979.

13 Harry P. Pachon and Joan W. Moore, "Mexican Americans," *Annals of the American Academy of Political and Social Science*, vol. 454 (March 1981).

14 They also set the stage for tragicomic attempts to manipulate this incomprehension. In 1979, for example, an Anglo named Robert E. Lee changed his name to Roberto E. Leon in order to qualify for affirmative action programs available to those with Spanish surnames. See David Haynes-Bautista, "Identifying 'Hispanic' Populations: The Influence of Research Methodology Upon Public Policy," *American Journal of Public Health*, vol. 70, no. 4 (April 1980) p. 355.

15 See Note 17 below.

16 State theory is undergoing something of a renaissance, especially in its Marxist (or neo-Marxist) variants. We have been influenced by Bob Jessop, *The Capitalist State* (New York: New York University Press, 1982); Theda Skocpol, "Bringing the State Back In: A Report on Current Comparative Research on the Relationship Between States and Social Structures," *Items*, vol. 36, nos. 1–2 (New York: Social Science Research Council, 1982).

17 Consider the conflicting 1960s activities of the federal courts and federal urban policies: the courts ordered school desegregation while urban renewal ("Negro removal") programs exacerbated residential segregation. Many similar conflicts in policy could be cited, not only at a given level of the state (i.e. federal, regional, local, etc. agencies), but also between different levels.

18 For a provocative treatment of the evolution of these "micro-political" measures, see Michel Foucault, *Discipline and Punish* (New York: Vintage, 1979), esp. pp. 135–6.

19 On "hegemonic projects," see Bob Jessop, "Accumulation Strategies, State Forms, and Hegemonic Projects," *Kapitalistate*, no.10–11 (1983).

20 On "rules of the game," see Herbert Gintis and Samuel Bowles, "Structure and Practice in the Labor Theory of Value," *Review of Radical Political Economics*, vol. 12, no. 4 (Winter 1981) p. 4. See also Chapter 4 above.

21 Thus in agriculture, for example, farm lobbying groups, the Agriculture Department, and the House and Senate agriculture committees together constitute the dominant policy-making mechanism. This concept has its origins in the work of Grant McConnell, and has been further refined by Gordon Adams. See Grant McConnell, *Private Power and American Democracy* (New York: Vintage, 1966); Gordon Adams, *The Politics of Defense Contracting: The Iron Triangle* (New Brunswick, New Jersey: Transaction, 1981).

22 The concept of civil society has a complex intellectual history, which originates in classical political economy, and comes via Hegel and Marx

to Gramsci. In Hegel's political philosophy, and still in the work of the early Marx, civil society is seen as the realm of "private" social relationships, and distinguished from that of the state. Economic relationships, understood in the classical sense of the "free market," are also located within civil society. Gramsci's conception is considerably more complicated, though built on these premises. Civil society for him is the terrain upon which hegemony is secured, the complex of social relationships whose existence depends upon the "consent" of their participants. Religion, education, linguistic practices, cultural and artistic life, trade unions and political organizations are thus included within it. Gramsci is well aware, though, that in the modern epoch there is no clear boundary between "private life" and the "life of the state." In a famous formulation, in fact, he includes civil society with a "political society" as part of the state. (See Antonio Gramsci, *Selections From the Prison Notebooks*, Quentin Hoare and Geoffrey Nowell Smith, eds (New York: International, 1971) p. 263.) In our view, the concept of hegemony, through which the dominant social forces acquire the consent of the subordinate ones, in itself presumes an autonomous civil society and a limited capacity for state "intervention" into the realm of "micro-politics," since this "consent" is not given stupidly or blindly but because the needs, interests and ideas of the subordinate groups are actively incorporated and taken into account in the organization of society.

23 See Theodore J. Lowi, "The New Public Philosophy: Interest-Group Liberalism," in T. Ferguson and J. Rogers, eds, *The Political Economy* (Armonk, New York: Sharpe, 1984).

24 This takes us into the realm of organizational theory, which is beyond the present scope. An interesting discussion of interagency relationships and their ability to frustrate innovative racial policy is Roland Warren *et al.*, *The Structure of Urban Reform* (Lexington, Mass.: D.C. Heath, 1973); on the autonomy of state officials see Fred Block, "Beyond Relative Autonomy: State Managers as Historical Subjects," *New Political Science*, no. 7 (Winter 1981).

25 Claus Offe has developed some interesting approaches to these issues in his concepts of "selection mechanisms" by which political demands are rendered salient to state institutions, and of "allocative" vs. "productive" types of state policies, which are brought into play to deal with different rules of state decision-making. See, respectively, Offe, "Structural Problems of the Capitalist State," in K. von Beyme, ed., *German Political Studies*, vol. 1 (Beverly Hills: Sage, 1974), and *idem*, "The Theory of the Capitalist State and the Problem of Policy Formation," in L. Lindberg *et al.*, eds, *Stress and Contradiction in Modern Capitalism* (Lexington, Mass.: Heath, 1975).

26 See for example Gramsci's remarks on parliamentary democracy, op. cit., p. 80n.

27 These are aspects of hegemony which are beyond our present scope, but consider for example Roosevelt's failure to "pack" the Supreme Court (which constitutionally may have as many as fifteen justices); or the

outcry at Nixon's so-called "Saturday Night Massacre" (his firings of Cox, Richardson and Ruckelshaus were perfectly legal). On the oppositional side, there are enormous difficulties involved in breaking with the supposedly "consensual" aspects of US politics: the logic and justice of the "free enterprise system," anti-communism, the morality and truthfulness of government ("We stand for freedom," etc.). These are examples of a hegemonic domain from which challenges are effectively excluded – and within which basic political unity is therefore preserved.

28 The following discussion assumes the kinds of general racial conditions that have existed in the postwar US: what we have termed racial war of position (e.g. the availability of "normal" political channels for racial politics), and the open existence of racial civil society (e.g. the possibility of minority cultural autonomy, political institutions, observance of traditional customs, linguistic practices, etc.) Obviously these conditions have not existed at all times and all places; indeed the civil rights phase of the black movement was concerned precisely with extending and institutionalizing them in the South. The very success of the southern struggle shows, though, that at least on a national level, these conditions did already obtain. See Chapter 6 below.

29 Gramsci, op. cit., p. 182.

30 The main means available to the state for the equilibration of conflicting interests is precisely their incorporation into the state in the form of policies, programs, patronage, etc. Gramsci argues that various forms of hegemony flow from this process of incorporation: "expansive" hegemony if state-society relations display sufficient dynamism and are not inordinately plagued by crisis conditions; "reformist" hegemony (what he calls "transformism") if political stability requires continuing concessions to competing forces. See also our discussion of "absorption" and "insulation" below.

31 Racially subordinated groups may not be permitted access to the political system; if they are represented, this will take the form of racially defined political organizations, or by organizations which have racially explicit projects and programs.

32 We use this term in the Gramscian sense of social actors whose position and training permits them to express the worldviews, ideas and sense of social identity of various social actors. Priests, teachers, artists and entertainers fit in this definition, which is not the same as the standard usage of "intelligentsia."

33 Lack of success terminates the crisis. The result may be a restoration of the previous pattern of unstable equilibrium, or the consolidation of a counter-reformist agenda. On cyclical patterns in contemporary movement politics, see Frances Fox Piven and Richard A. Cloward, *Poor People's Movements: How They Succeed, Why They Fail* (New York: Vintage, 1979).

34 As seen from a movement standpoint. From the standpoint of the state, these are reform policies.

35 "The Mexican Americans now view the political system as an Anglo system. They feel that only a Mexican American political system can

serve their needs. . . . ." Jose Angel Gutierrez, "La Raza and Revolution" [1968], in Meier and Rivera, eds, *Reading on La Raza* (New York: Hill & Wang, 1974) p. 231.

36 Charles V. Hamilton, "Black Social Scientists: Contributions and Problems," in Joyce Ladner, ed., *The Death of White Sociology* (New York: Vintage, 1973) pp. 472–3.

37 Michael Novak, *The Rise of the Unmeltable Ethnics* (New York, Macmillan: 1972); Nathan Glazer, *Affirmative Discrimination* (New York: Basic Books, 1975).

38 For example, see Gutierrez, op. cit., p. 232. These organizations had often played a challenging role in a previous phase of the reform trajectory; their leaders had been, in many cases, the militants of their generation. We discuss the concept of "trajectories" of reform movements below.

39 Malcolm X (with Alex Haley), *The Autobiography of Malcolm X* (New York: Grove Press, 1965) pp. 53–6.

40 A good example is the incorporation of the Gandhian concept of nonviolence into the civil rights movement. See Chapter 6 below.

41 The dislocation of white identity, of the meaning of "whiteness" in contemporary racial conflicts, has received relatively little attention. Some social psychological studies have been directed at the identity crisis experienced by whites in the face of minority demands for equality, political rights, cultural/organizational autonomy, etc. The idea that the great Western societies are somehow fundamentally white – which today is espoused by explicitly racist groups like the Ku Klux Klan and the National Front in Britain – seems to us to be an attempt to keep the formerly unquestioned (or barely questioned) subjective coherence of "whiteness" alive. See for example Michael Billig, "Patterns of Racism: Interviews With National Front Members," *Race and Class*, vol. 20, no. 2 (Autumn 1978), pp. 161–79.

Part III

6 The great transformation

1 By *racism* we mean those social practices which (explicitly or implicitly) attribute merits or allocate values to members of racially categorized groups, solely because of their race.

2 This phrase, of course, is Karl Polanyi's term for the introduction of market society in pre-capitalist England. We have appropriated it, with apologies to Polanyi, to indicate the epochal character of the shift to a *socially* based politics in the contemporary US.

3 David Edgar, "Reagan's Hidden Agenda: Racism and the New Right," *Race and Class*, vol. 22, no. 3 (Winter 1981), p. 222.

4 See Chapter 1 for more detailed discussion of this point.

5 Nathan Glazer, *Affirmative Discrimination: Ethnic Inequality and Public Policy* (New York: Basic Books, 1975) p. 3.

6 Use of the term "elite" is not meant pejoratively. Although the prewar

civil rights movement included some episodes of "direct action" and mass mobilization (notably during Reconstruction and in the aftermath of World War I, e.g. the Garvey movement), these were infrequent and antagonistic to moderate programs. Reform strategies concentrated, for reasons of necessity, on lobbying, use of the courts, and appeals to enlightened whites, tactics which depend on knowledgeable elites for leadership and may render mass participation counterproductive. In addition, the straitened conditions facing blacks in the prewar period generated a survival-oriented ideology which did not adapt itself well to mass mobilization. (See below.) For a good history of the black struggle in the 1930s, see Nancy J. Weiss, *Farewell to the Party of Lincoln: Black Politics in the Age of FDR* (Princeton: Princeton University Press, 1983).

7 Douglas McAdam, *Political Process and the Development of Black Insurgency* (Chicago: University of Chicago Press, 1984).

8 Aldon D. Morris, *The Origins of the Civil Rights Movement: Black Communities Organizing for Change* (New York: Free Press, 1984).

9 For representative statements, see Robert A. Dahl, *Pluralist Democracy in the United States* (Chicago: Rand McNally, 1967); Arnold Rose, *The Power Structure* (New York: Oxford University Press, 1967). Good critiques are Theodore J. Lowi, *The End of Liberalism* (New York: Norton, 1969); Peter Bachrach and Morton Baratz, *Power and Poverty* (New York: Oxford University Press, 1970); Steven Lukes, *Power: A Radical View* (London, Macmillan, 1974).

10 Southern loyalty to the Democrats was assured by the national Party's acquiescence in segregation, and specifically in the disenfranchisement of southern blacks.

11 *Rearticulation* is a practice of discursive reorganization or reinterpretation of ideological themes and interests already present in the subjects' consciousness, such that these elements obtain new meanings or coherence. This practice is ordinarily the work of "intellectuals." Those whose role is to interpret the social world for given subjects – religious leaders, entertainers, schoolteachers, etc. – may on this account be "intellectuals."

12 For a startling and vivid evocation of that rhetorical toolkit, see Zora Neale Hurston, "The Sermon," in *idem, The Sanctified Church* (Berkeley: Turtle Island, 1984).

13 Cornel West, *Prophesy Deliverance! Toward A Revolutionary Afro-American Christianity* (Philadelphia: Westminster, 1982).

14 Robert Moses drew important inspiration from Camus, for example.

15 Eugene Genovese, among others, has argued that religious and cultural forms operating during slavery constituted "pre-political" forms of black resistance. See Genovese, *Roll, Jordan, Roll: The World the Slaves Made* (New York: Pantheon, 1974).

16 Martin Luther King, quoted in Harvard Sitkoff, *The Struggle for Black Equality* (New York: Hill & Wang, 1981), p. 61.

17 See, for example, Julius Lester, *Look Out Whitey! Black Power's Gon Get Your Mama!* (New York: Dial, 1968).

18 Quoted in William Julius Wilson, "The Black Community in the 1980s: Questions of Race, Class, and Public Policy," *The Annals of the American Academy of Social and Political Science*, vol. 454 (March 1981), p. 28.

19 The march had been planned as a unified effort to demonstrate black and liberal support for national civil rights legislation. The SNCC speaker, John Lewis, was forced to censor his remarks by white and black moderates, but even the rewritten speech contrasted sharply with the self-congratulatory tone of the rest of the event: "The party of Kennedy is also the party of Eastland . . . the party of Javits is also the party of Goldwater. Where is our party?" Quoted in Clayborne Carson, *In Struggle: SNCC and the Black Awakening of the 1960s* (Cambridge, Mass.: Harvard University Press, 1981), p. 94.

20 The white violence culminated a month after the campaign's end in the bombing of the 16th Street Baptist Church (15 September 1963), which killed four black children in the institution which had been the center of the Birmingham movement. Sources on Birmingham are numerous. A few good ones are David Lewis, *King: A Critical Biography* (New York: Praeger, 1970) pp. 171–209; Martin Luther King, Jr, *Why We Can't Wait* (New York: Signet, 1964); Stanley B. Greenberg, *Race and State in Capitalist Development* (New Haven: Yale University Press, 1980) pp. 235–42; Aldon D. Morris, op. cit., pp. 229–74.

21 At first promised and then denied white liberal support, the MFDP challengers left the convention profoundly disillusioned. On the MFDP, see Clayborne Carson, op. cit., pp. 108–9, 123–9, 185–6.

22 The "long hot summers" of the middle 1960s were viewed by many blacks (and by the US police at all levels) as a proto-revolutionary situation. Many activists saw the black underclass as "voting with shopping carts," taking what was deservedly theirs, and accelerating the unacceptably slow pace of reform. Moderates, by contrast, questioned the effectiveness of disruption and argued that riots discredited efforts to achieve political reforms. In retrospect we may discount the more extreme claims made by all sides during these years, but during the 1967–68 period alone, some 384 "racial disorders" were recorded in 298 cities, and these can hardly be considered as unrelated to the atmosphere of black protest which after 1964 engulfed the nation, not just the South. (Data are from McAdam, op. cit., p. 227.) Other good sources are Joe R. Feagin and Harlan Hahn, *Ghetto Revolts: The Politics of Violence in America's Cities* (New York: Macmillan, 1973); James W. Button, *Black Violence* (Princeton: Princeton University Press, 1978); Frances F. Piven and Richard A. Cloward, *Poor People's Movements: Why They Succeed, How They Fail* (New York: Vintage, 1979) pp. 248, 272–3. It should be remembered that measurements and statistics are notoriously unreliable on the subject of riots. For the moderate response, see Bayard Rustin, "The Lessons of the Long Hot Summer," *Commentary* (October 1967); Lewis M. Killian, *The Impossible Revolu-*

tion, Phase II: Black Power and the American Dream (New York: Random House, 1975).

23 This trend was most spectacularly demonstrated by the appearance in the national spotlight of George Wallace, the arch-segregationist Governor of Alabama. "Backlash" also took the form of white counter demonstrations and violence against civil rights marches. Many movement radicals viewed white resistance (especially white resistance in the North) as decisive proof that nonviolent strategy was ineffective in its efforts to lead not only blacks but also whites toward greater racial equality and harmony. The "backlash" phenomenon, and Wallace in particular, are considered in greater depth in Chapter 7 below.

24 On 7 March, some 2000 marchers had been ferociously attacked on the Pettus Bridge at Selma. For good analyses of the complexities of the Selma situation, which many see as the point at which southern intransigence was finally ruptured, see Carson, op. cit., pp. 157–62; Lewis, *King*, op. cit., especially pp. 375–81; David Garrow, *Protest at Selma: Martin Luther King Jr and the Voting Rights Act of 1965* (New Haven: Yale University Press, 1978).

25 Many commentators date the black power phase of the movement from the "Meredith march" of June 1966, though this is clearly a somewhat arbitrary periodization.

26 Roy Wilkins, quoted in Robert Allen, *Black Awakening in Capitalist America: An Analytic History* (Garden City, New York: Doubleday, 1969) p. 78.

27 See Nathan Glazer and Daniel P. Moynihan, *Beyond the Melting Pot* (Cambridge, Mass.: MIT Press, 1970), p. x.

28 Allen, *Black Awakening*, op. cit., p. 50; see also Stokely Carmichael and Charles V. Hamilton, *Black Power: The Politics of Liberation in America* (New York: Vintage, 1967) p. 44.

29 See Chapter 7 below.

30 (New York: Random House, 1967.) This work certainly did not burn its moderate bridges. Robert Allen wrote that *Black Power* ". . . was largely an essay in liberal reformism . . ." (Allen, *Black Awakening*, op. cit., p. 247), a judgment based on the authors' lack of "revolutionary" political program. The book is better interpreted as one of the first postwar efforts – after those of Cruse and Malcolm X – to understand black oppression in a global context. The authors wish to break with the ethnicity paradigm, but not with the mainstream aspirations of US blacks.

31 James Boggs, *Racism and Class Struggle* (New York: Monthly Review Press, 1970).

32 See his speech "The Ballot or the Bullet," in *Malcolm X Speaks* (New York: Grove, 1966).

33 See George Breitman, ed., *The Last Year of Malcolm X* (New York: Pathfinder, 1967).

34 Malcolm's chief bodyguard was later revealed to be a police agent.

35 See John Brown Childs, "Afro-American Intellectuals and the People's Culture," *Theory and Society* 13 (1984).

36 Some good sources here are Mark Naison, *Communists in Harlem During the Depression* (Urbana: University of Illinois Press, 1983); Cedric J. Robinson, *Black Marxism: The Making of the Black Radical Tradition* (London: Zed, 1983).

37 See Allen, *Black Awakening*, op. cit., pp. 153–64, 210–38.

38 Elsewhere in this work we have referred to the "trajectory" of movement/state relationships (see Chapter 5, for example). In respect to the racial history of the postwar period, we understand this trajectory to include both the encounter discussed here – a "rising phase," so to speak, of the racial minority movements – and that considered in the following chapter as a period of "reaction." See Chapter 7 below.

39 This formulation derives from Marxist state theory. The state provides a political framework for interest concertation – understood in the traditional economically determined meaning of classes, of course, but this is not important for our argument here – which is unavailable to particularistic interests interacting directly. For present purposes the state may be seen as the institutions, policies, conditions, and rules through which the racial order is organized, enforced and transformed. For an erudite reading of the Marxist literature on the "factor of cohesion" formulation, see Bob Jessop, *The Capitalist State* (New York: New York University Press, 1982). pp. 16–20. These points are considered in more detail in Chapter 5 above.

40 Two good sources here are Allen, *Black Awakening*, op. cit.; Manning Marable, "Black Nationalism in the 1970s: Through the Prism of Race and Class," *Socialist Review*, no. 50/51 (March-June 1980). See also the concluding section of this chapter.

41 Radical black organizations like SNCC opposed the war, while moderate groups like the Urban League supported it.

42 Huntington has analyzed the black movement as an "ideals vs. institutions" conflict. He dates the onset of this new upsurge from the Greensboro student sit-ins of February 1960, which seems to us too late. See Samuel P. Huntington, *American Politics: The Promise of Disharmony* (Cambridge, Mass.: Harvard University Press, 1978).

43 See Chapter 5 above.

44 Consider the transformation of the United Farmworkers into an organized lobbying group for Agricultural Labor Relations Act passage and enforcement, which tended to weaken the Union's ability to mobilize a national support network, and diverted it from servicing and organizing farmworker members.

45 For example a SNCC worker's 1962 letter to President Kennedy: "The People of Ruleville . . . wonder why protection can be given to people 6000 miles away and not be given to American citizens in the South" (Charles McLaurin, cited in Carson, op. cit., p. 85).

46 The CRS was later to be transformed once again into an *agent-provocateur* center. See Pat Bryant, "Justice vs. the Movement," *Southern Exposure*, vol. 8, no. 2 (Summer 1980) pp. 79–80.

47 James O'Connor, "The Democratic Movement in the United States," *Kapitalistate*, no. 7 (1978); Robert R. Alford and Roger Friedland,

"Political Participation and Social Policy," *Annual Review of Sociology*, 1975.

48 None of these currents is by any means exclusive. Specific perspectives often contain elements of more than one current. Internal colonialism, for example, can be expressed in nationalist or socialist terms. The categories we employ are "ideal types" – they permit the classification of diverse tendencies for analytical purposes.

49 See Rodolfo Acuna's account of the LRUP's trajectory in *Occupied America: A History of Chicanos*, 2nd edn (New York: Harper & Row, 1981) pp. 387–91; see also Mario Barrera, "The Historical Evolution of Chicano Ethnic Goals" (MS, 1984), pp. 31–2; David Montejano, "The Demise of 'Jim Crow' for Texas Mexicans, 1940–1970" (MS, 1984), pp. 30–4; John Shockley, *Chicano Revolt in a Texas Town* (Notre Dame: Notre Dame University Press, 1974).

50 See Carson, op. cit., pp. 167–8.

51 The history of recent minority Marxism-Leninism is interesting as an organizational process. Several of the currently active M-L organizations with substantial minority membership – for example, the League for Revolutionary Struggle, the Communist Workers Party – were formed when racially exclusive groups merged and composed "multiracial" organizations, parties or "pre-parties." The LRS, for example, was formed by a merger of the I Wor Kuen, an Asian American (largely Chinese American) group, with the August Twentyninth Movement, a largely Chicano group. Other M-L organizations began as white "new left" groups and have since incorporated substantial numbers of minority members: the Revolutionary Communist Party, Communist Labor Party, and the Democratic Workers Party. These groups remain by and large white-dominated, in our view. (This brief survey does not take into account the "old left" groups which can also stake a claim on Marxism-Leninism, such as the Communist Party or Socialist Workers Party; the CP in particular has significant minority membership. Nor do we discuss here the various social democratic currents).

52 The first "stage" is the creation of a multi-class united front to liberate the colony; the second "stage" is the subsequent pursuit of socialist reconstruction and, presumably, class struggle. The internal colonialist orientation of the 1960s was often explicitly Maoist, as were many other Marxisms of the period.

53 Land struggles were most strenuously pursued by the *Alianza Federal de Mercedes*, founded in 1963 by Reies Lopez Tijerina. The *Alianza* (later renamed *La Confederacion de Pueblos Libres*) sought to restore lands originally held by Mexican Americans in northern New Mexico under grants dating from the conquest, and built upon regional traditions of struggle dating from the nineteenth century. See Reies Lopez Tijerina, *Mi Lucha Por La Tierra* (Mexico, DF: Fondo de Cultura Economica, 1978); Peter Nabokov, *Tijerina and the Courthouse Raid* (Albuquerque: University of New Mexico Press, 1969). Tijerina's politics have been the subject of some debate. His personalistic and confrontational style and his focus on the tactics of land occupation

place him in a venerable Mexican revolutionary tradition. But Tijerina built upon and altered this legacy in the attempt to address modern US conditions. He ran for Governor of New Mexico in 1968, joined Martin Luther King Jr's Poor People's Crusade, and espoused a Pan American and Third Worldist revolutionary philosophy. After extensive harassment, Tijerina was jailed in 1969, and his movement dispersed.

54 Important regional distinctions also affect Mexican American politics in the Southwest. Andres Jimenez identifies four regions – the lower Rio Grande valley (incorporating the frontier zone with the Mexican states of Nuevo Leon, Tamaulipas, and Coahuila), the upper Rio Grande corridor (extending from the state of Chihuahua north into New Mexico), the Arizona area (incorporating the frontier with the state of Sonora), and California (including the Baja California border area) – each with its particular history of political development, incorporation in the US (and global) economy, and cultural traditions. This obviously leaves aside important concentrations such as Colorado, the Pacific Northwest, and the Midwest. Chicago today is one of the largest "Mexican" cities in the world. (Andres Jimenez, personal communication, July 10, 1985.)

55 For the nineteenth century heritage, see Acuna, op. cit.; Matt S. Meier and Feliciano Rivera, *The Chicanos: A History of Mexican Americans* (New York: Hill & Wang, 1972) pp. 54–95; Mario Barrera, *Race and Class in the Southwest* (Notre Dame: University of Notre Dame Press, 1979). Interestingly, Barrera suggests that "The system of colonial labor appears to have been based on racial rather than ethnic distinctions" (ibid., p. 49), which is consistent with our argument (in Chapter 3 above) that a racial logic structured North American colonialism and was not merely an outcome of that system.

56 Groups such as the Brown Berets, The Crusade for Justice, El Movimiento Estudiantil Chicanos de Aztlan (MEChA), and the Mexican American Youth Organization (MAYO) originated at this time. Through asserting their *Chicanismo*, most groups adopted a Mexicanized political style, setting forth their demands in *Planes*, for example. MEChA enunciated its program in *El Plan de Santa Barbara*; Rodolfo "Corky" Gonzales launched *El Plan Espiritual de Aztlan* at a Chicano Youth Conference held in Denver in 1969. Many other groups developed their demands in this manner. See Barrera, "The Historical Evolution. . . ," op. cit., pp. 27–31; Acuna, op. cit., pp. 357–60.

57 Commitment to the struggle for Chicano Liberation is the operative definition of the ideology used here. Chicanismo involves a crucial distinction in political consciousness between a Mexican American and a Chicano mentality. The Mexican American is a person who lacks respect for his [sic] cultural and ethnic heritage. Unsure of himself, he seeks assimilation as a way out of his "degraded" social status. . . . In contrast, Chicanismo reflects self-respect and pride in one's ethnic and cultural background. . . . Mexican Americans must be viewed as potential Chicanos. . . . Chicano Liberation is a means of total Chicano liberation." ("El Plan de Santa Barbara," quoted ibid., p. 34)

58 These conflicts often revealed important class dimensions within Asian American communities – dimensions which were played up by Marxist-Leninist groups and played down by "entrists" and more moderate nationalists. For example, Asian entrepreneurs were sometimes branded an indigenous "national" bourgeoisie, whose "class interests" conflicted with those of other class forces.

59 *El Grito, Aztlan, El Tecolote,* and *La Raza* were some of these.

60 Paul Wong notes: "The most widely accepted slogans in the white antiwar movement have been 'Give peace a chance' and 'Bring the GIs home.' The Asian-American movement, in contrast, emphasized the *racist* nature of the war, using such slogans as 'Stop killing *our* Asian brothers and sisters,' and 'We don't want *your* racist war.' Paul Wong, "The Emergence of the Asian-American Movement," *Bridge*, vol. 2, no. 1 (September/October 1972), pp. 35–6.

61 Republican "entrism" has also come into being among minorities long considered to be in the Democratic column, especially since the election of Reagan.

62 Some campaigns led by community organizations continued into the 1970s with varying degrees of success. In San Antonio, where the Communities Organized for Public Service (COPS) was active, a moderate Chicano mayor was eventually elected with a strong community base. Local organizing by Chicano moderates has also continued to flourish or at least survive in Los Angeles and Denver.

63 Of a voluminous literature, see for example Guillermo Flores, "Internal Colonialism and Racial Minorities in the US: An Overview," in Frank Bonilla and Robert Girling, eds, *Structures of Dependency* (Stanford, Cal.: Stanford University Press, 1973); Robert Blauner, *Racial Oppression in America* (New York: Harper & Row, 1972) pp. 82–110; see also Chapter 3 above.

64 See Chapter 3 above.

65 Consider the history of Indian education, for example, or the perverse hyperpatriotism of the "relocation camps" – Manzanar, Tule Lake, Gila River – in which Japanese Americans were imprisoned during World War II.

66 The internal colonialism framework made more sense in dealing with relatively homogeneous concentrations of minorities, for example New York's Ocean Hill-Brownsville and Bedford-Stuyvesant ghettos (both heavily black), or South Bronx (Puerto Rican). It was less useful where given minority groups were insufficiently concentrated geographically, or where minority communities were more heterogeneous. Homogeneity, of course, is never more than relative. See Chapter 1 above.

67 See, for example Carlos Moore, "Marxism: A Prolet-Aryan Outlook," *Berkeley Journal of Sociology*, vol. XIX (1974–75).

7 Race and reaction

1 *San Francisco Chronicle*, 8 March 1985.
2 In April 1985, the black unemployment rate was 16.3 percent compared to the overall unemployment rate of 7.3 percent (Department of Labor, Bureau of Labor Statistics). The Center on Budget and Policy Priorities reported that the poverty rate among blacks is almost 36 percent, the highest proportion since 1968. The Center also noted that while long-term unemployment among whites has increased 1.5 percent since 1980, among blacks it has increased by 72 percent. Cited in Roger Wilkins, "Smiling Racism," *The Nation*, vol. 239, no. 14 (3 November 1984).
   While the overall infant mortality rate has steadily declined (11.2 per 1000 in 1982), the rate for blacks has been rising. In 1981, the infant mortality rate in black neighborhoods of Chicago was 55 per 1000; in central Harlem it was 28 per 1000; and in areas of Baltimore, 59.5 per 1000. See Michael Robin, "Black Babies: A Right to the Tree of Life," *The Nation*, vol. 238, no. 22 (9 June 1984).
   For additional indicators and trends, and a discussion of their meaning, see Alphonso Pinkney, *The Myth of Black Progress* (Cambridge and New York: Cambridge University Press, 1984) and Reynolds Farley, *Blacks and Whites: Narrowing the Gap?* (Cambridge, Mass.: Harvard University Press, 1984).
3 Barry Bluestone and Bennett Harrison, *The Deindustrialization of America: Plant Closings, Community Abandonment, and the Dismantling of Basic Industry* (New York: Basic Books, 1982).
4 Howard J. Sherman, *Stagflation* (New York: Harper & Row, 1976).
5 James O'Connor, *The Fiscal Crisis of the State* (New York: St Martin's Press, 1973).
6   The advantages for the US of this dollar-based system were formidable. Essentially, it created a unique, built-in demand for dollars, independent of the demand for US products. This need for dollars meant the US could buy more than it sold abroad without fearing that the oversupply of dollars would cause the value of the dollar to drop. US multinationals and banks were in a strong position to invest abroad, since the dollars they were spending were in such demand. This in turn encouraged US military expansion worldwide by allowing the US to keep spending the money needed to support its troops overseas. In short, it was precisely through the enthronement of the dollar at Bretton Woods that the US was able to finance the postwar Pax Americana." ("Bretton Woods: The Rise and Fall of an International Monetary System," *Dollars & Sense*, no. 102, December 1984)
   See also Fred Block, *The Origins of International Economic Disorder* (Berkeley: University of California Press, 1977).
7 In 1984, the US trade deficit with Canada was $20 billion, second only to the nation's $37 billion trade deficit with Japan. In spite of this, no Americans hold the same degree of negative attitudes towards Canada

for the trade imbalance and for heavily protecting her industries from US exports.

8 Republican Senator John Heinz during a Congressional debate over US-Japan trade relations stated that "In category after category they [the Japanese] are slicing us neatly and thinly off like a piece of sushimi [sic], which they so elegantly do." At a 8 March 1985 hearing, Sen. Heinz noted that when the "Japanese get their little fork into us – or chopsticks . . . they really do stick it to us." During a 20 March 1985 hearing, Democratic Senator Ernest Hollings said the Japanese "love all those bowings – they have been doing that for 25 years and getting away with it" (cited in *Hokubei Mainichi*, 16 April 1985).

9 Laura Chin and Ada Kan, *Where We Stand in America: A Report on Anti-Asian Violence and Anti-Foreign Sentiments* (Washington, DC: The Organization of Chinese Americans, August 1984). In 1982 Vincent Chin, a Chinese American man, was beaten to death in Detroit by a laid-off plant foreman and his stepson who mistook their victim for Japanese and blamed him for the loss of their jobs. The incident further outraged Asian American communities when Wayne County Circuit Court Judge Charles Kaufman allowed the two men to plead guilty to manslaughter (the original charge had been second-degree murder), placed them on three years' probation, and fined them $3,780 each.

10 "Illegal aliens" are equated with "Mexicans" or the "brown flood" in general, even though undocumented workers from Mexico constitute at most 60 percent of the "illegal population." It is estimated that of the 1,086,000 undocumented workers in California between 1970 and 1980, 589,000 were from Mexico. See Thomas Muller, *The Fourth Wave: California's Newest Immigrants* (Washington, DC: The Urban Institute Press, 1984). Despite the numbers, the US Immigration and Naturalization Service directs its enforcement activities at Mexicans. More than 90 percent of the arrests of "illegal aliens" are made along the US border with Mexico. See Ann Cooper, "Hazy Numbers Complicate the Debate Over How to Slow Illegal Immigration," *National Journal*, 8 June 1985.

11 A Gallup poll conducted in May 1980 revealed that 91 percent of the people interviewed felt that *all* immigration to the United States should be halted until the national unemployment rate dropped to 5 percent.

12 Geoffrey Rips, "The Simpson-Mazzoli Bill: Supply-Side Immigration Reform," *The Nation*, vol. 237, no. 10 (8 October 1983).

13 See, among a host of similar works, Charles Murray, *Losing Ground: American Social Policy 1950–1980* (New York: Basic Books, 1984). For a good critique of Murray's book, see Sar A. Levitan's review in *Society*, vol. 22, no. 4 (May-June 1985); see also the debate between Murray and Levitan in *Political Science Quarterly*, vol. 100, no. 3 (Fall 1985).

14 David Edgar has suggested that "California's tax-cutting referendum Prop. 13 was as much a vote against black welfare as it was a vote for lower taxes." David Edgar, "Reagan's Hidden Agenda: Racism and the New American Right," *Race & Class*, vol. XXII, no. 3 (Winter 1981), p. 231.

15 In 1982, Metzger ran for the US Senate in the Democratic primary and

placed fourth in a field of eleven candidates, garnering 73,987 votes. Bill Wallace, "Racist Group Using Computers and TV to Recruit in Bay Area," *San Francisco Chronicle*, 5 March 1985.

16 "Violence on the Right," *Newsweek*, 4 March 1985, p. 25.

17 Note the ecological language. Some far right groups, perhaps via survivalism, are rearticulating environmentalist themes. The original notion of race-mixing, which occasionally used similar terms, was not nearly as holistic or totalizing. Its frame of reference was eugenicist (i.e. Darwinian) or even Linnaean/Aristotelian.

18 "Jesus Christ Christian" means rejection of the Jewishness of Jesus, an important interpretation for far-right anti-semites.

19 *Newsweek*, op. cit.

20 Tom Metzger himself has suggested this:

> . . . [T]he only time you can get a white person's attention, a working person, is when things get tight. Then you can get him to sit down and listen. While he's got his beer, and got his dune buggy, and everything's going good, and he's got a job, he won't listen to you. Once things start to get tight, he starts looking around, what's the problem, and then you can get a foot in the door. (ABC News Closeup, "Wounds From Within" with Marshall Frady, broadcast 18 October 1981)

21 Bruce Maxwell, "Radical Rightist Groups Feed on Rural Despair," *San Francisco Examiner*, 5 March 1985.

22 Ethnic, class, national and religious dimensions of "whiteness" have all been explored by the far right. See Patsy Sims, *The Klan* (New York: Stein & Day, 1978).

23 ABC News Closeup, op. cit.

24 Vincent Ryan, managing editor of the far-right publication *The Spotlight*, said his paper's circulation has been cut almost in half, to 166,000, without "a Carter to push around." *Newsweek*, op. cit.

25 In 1984, the Anti-Defamation League of B'nai B'rith suggested the Ku Klux Klan membership has dropped about 35 percent in the past two years. Cited in *The Pacific Citizen*, 16 November 1984.

26 Sara Diamond, "Neo-Nazis in America," *The Daily Californian*, 30 April 1985.

27 Jeff Bale says that "highly visible hate groups like the Klan and Aryan nations serve to *distract* attention away from the far more dangerous activities of the 'respectable' authoritarians in positions of real power." Quoted in Diamond, op. cit.

28 Ironically the only other analogy in recent US history comes from the far left. The Weather Underground, the SLA and the Black Liberation Army have played a similar role as "fringe groups" in American politics.

29 Walter Dean Burnham, "Post-Conservative America," *Socialist Review*, no. 72 (November-December 1983), p. 125.

30 Of particular importance was the feminist movement which critiqued the patriarchial family, inequities in sex/gender relations, and women's

lack of control over their own bodies.

31 Gillian Peele, *Revival and Reaction: The Right in Contemporary America* (Oxford: Oxford University Press, 1984), p. 52.

32 Alan Crawford, *Thunder on the Right: The "New Right" and the Politics of Resentment* (New York: Pantheon Books, 1980), p. 5.

33 The collapse of the family and the decline of traditional values and forms of authority are often cited by the new right as the causes of domestic ills and the decline of the American hegemony in the world. The new right's agenda is therefore filled with anti-abortion platforms, social prayer amendments and other "pro-family" issues.

34 See Lillian Rubin, *Busing and Backlash* (Berkeley and Los Angeles: University of California Press, 1972).

35 More complex scientistic ideologies of racial inferiority are a different matter, and here the new right is actively engaged. See L. Kamin, R. Lewontin and Stephen Rose, *Not In Our Genes* (New York: Pantheon, 1984) for an excellent account of the modern application of biologism to social and political categories such as race.

36 As a young Alabama politician, Wallace was seen as something of a moderate. But after losing a close election early in his career he made a public vow to "never be outniggered again." He then rose to his second last stand, when as Governor of Alabama in 1962 he "stood in the schoolhouse door" to prevent integration. His third incarnation, as Presidential candidate, required him to moderate his white supremacy and to experiment with "code words." His fourth and current identity, which appeared in the aftermath of the Voting Rights Act and of a 1972 assassination attempt, is once again "moderate."

37 Kevin Phillips, *The Emerging Republican Majority* (New York: Anchor, 1970).

38 Conservative egalitarianism was the principle advocated by ethnicity theorists (of whom Moynihan was a leading personage) in policy matters. Ethnicity theory, as we have argued above (Chapter 1) was and remains the dominant racial theory in the US.

39 The "Republicanized" version of minority politics strictly distinguished between moderate and radical features of the 1960s racial movements. Those which had challenged such anachronistic and inessential forms of racial inequality as legalized segregation and discriminatory employment practices (i.e. explicit discrimination against individuals) were easily jettisoned. Those features of the minority movements which had questioned the role of race in shaping the US social structure, however, were rejected and marginalized. Collective demands, "institutionalized racism": these issues the Republicans opposed or ignored.

40 See Burnham, op. cit.

41 The charge of "secular humanism" is directed at liberals in general, and the welfare state in particular, mainly by new right activists oriented to Protestant fundamentalism. The chief complaint seems to be that liberal (and radical) ideologies have desacralized morality, placing "values" on the same rationalistic terrain as politics, and subjecting them to the "culture of critical discourse." There are also important ties

between the critique of "secular humanism" and new right/ neoconservative hostility to the "new class" of knowledge workers. For an academically based statement of this critique, see Peter L. Berger, "The Worldview of the New Class: Secularity and Its Discontents," in B. Bruce Briggs, ed., *The New Class?* (New Brunswick, New Jersey: Transaction, 1979), p. 50; the concept of a "culture of critical discourse" fundamental to the ideology of the "new class" originates in Alvin Gouldner's *The Future of Intellectuals and the Rise of the New Class* (New York: Seabury, 1979). Gouldner's perspective, of course, is quite different from that of the right-wing "new class" theorists.

42 Crawford, op. cit., pp. 311–12.

43 Ibid., p. 5.

44 The concept of "status revolution" has its origins in the liberal historian Richard Hofstadter's rejection of the class-based categories of Charles Beard and others whose work on US social movements had reached its high point in the 1930s. See Hofstadter, *The Age of Reform: From Bryan to FDR*, 2nd edn (New York: Alfred A. Knopf, 1965).

45 Crawford, op. cit., p. 148.

46 Linda Gordon and Allen Hunter, "Sex, Family and the New Right: Anti-Feminism as a Political Force," *Radical America*, vol. 11, no. 6 and vol. 12, no. 1 (November 1977-February 1978), p. 12. See also Jonathan Rieder, *Canarsie: The Jews and Italians of Brooklyn Against Liberalism* (Cambridge, Mass.: Harvard University Press, 1985).

47 Rowland Evans and Robert Novak, "Ed Davis, Toned-Down Favorite," *Washington Post*, 3 February 1978, cited in Crawford, op. cit., p. 104.

48 The term "Third World state" is from Phillips who uses it to describe states which have an increasing racial minority population. Phillips writes, 'Retention of the Electoral College would probably guarantee a minority-oriented presidential selection process for the 1980s' (Kevin Phillips, "Abolish the Electoral College!" *Morgantown Dominion-Post*, 15 July 1977, cited in Crawford, op. cit., p. 324).

49 These charges had their origins in the FBI's campaigns to discredit King, in which Robert Kennedy was also involved.

50 Patrick J. Buchanan, "GOP Vote Search Should Bypass Ghetto," *Charleston Daily Mail*, 16 February 1977, cited in Crawford, op. cit., p. 258.

51 Crawford, op. cit., p. 145.

52 William Rusher, *The Making of a New Majority Party* (Ottawa, Ill.: Greenhill Publications, 1975), p. 31.

53 We also wonder if the "liberal verbalist elite" is not implicitly Jewish.

54 Gordon and Hunter, op. cit., p. 11.

55 Certain left groups allied themselves with the anti-busing forces, arguing that the issue was one of class, rather than race. Others withdrew in confusion. See the articles in *Radical America*, vol. 8, no. 6 (1974) and vol. 9, no. 3 (1975).

56 In attempting to portray diversity, the nearly absolute attention which textbooks had formerly paid whites had perhaps been "diluted,"

though hardly to the extent some groups claimed. Interestingly, a study by the National Council of Teachers in 1978 found that parent protesters were most concerned with books that presented attitudes and lifestyles of those of "different" cultural backgrounds. See Crawford, op. cit., pp. 155–8.

57 Lyndon B. Johnson, "To Fulfill These Rights," delivered at Howard University on 4 June 1965; in L. Rainwater and W. Yancey, *The Moynihan Report and the Politics of Controversy* (Cambridge, Mass.: MIT Press, 1967), p. 126.

58 Nathan Glazer, "The Peoples of America," *Ethnic Dilemmas, 1964–1982* (Cambridge, Mass.: Harvard University Press, 1983) p. 27. This, of course, was the underside of the ideal of tolerance: implicit threats toward groups which failed to conform. It was precisely these kinds of formulations which led blacks to mistrust white liberals and to preserve "group interests."

59 Glazer, *Affirmative Discrimination*, op. cit., p. 220.

60 Glazer even went so far as to suggest that if affirmative action programs were effective he might support them out of pragmatic commitment to equality.

> For me, no consideration of principle – such as that merit should be rewarded, or that governmental programs should not discriminate on the grounds of race or ethnic group – would stand in the way of a program of preferential hiring if it made some substantial progress in reducing the severe problems of the low-income black population and of the inner cities. (ibid., p. 73)

61 A typical polemic is Morris Abram, "What Constitutes a Civil Right?" *New York Times Magazine*, 10 June 1984. In a thoughtful reconceptualization, Lewis M. Killian argues that "From its inception, the Civil Rights movement was fundamentally and unrelentingly 'assimilationist.' " On the other hand, "Black power treated Blacks in the United States as a community, not as a category of individual Americans handicapped and stigmatized on the basis of their color." This distinction corresponds to our argument that the civil rights movement operated largely within the dominant *ethnicity* paradigm of race, while black power broke with the dominant view, invoking the *nation-based* (and, to a lesser extent, the class-based) paradigms of race. If this distinction is recognized, neoconservatism emerges clearly as a reaction to the radical currents of the "great transformation," an attempt to confine racially based demands to an ethnicity-oriented model of politics. See Killian, "Black Power and White Reactions: The Revitalization of Race-Thinking in the United States," *The Annals of The American Academy of Political and Social Sciences*, no. 454 (March 1981), pp. 43, 47.

62 Abram, op. cit, p. 60. Of course, many opponents of affirmative action are also "right-to-work" advocates who find the same kinds of faults with the labor laws that those who charge "reverse discrimination" do with affirmative action. At the heart of the right-wing agenda, as James

O'Connor has recently argued, is always an ideology of individualism. See O'Connor, *Accumulation Crisis* (New York: Blackwell, 1984).

63 Philip Green, *The Pursuit of Inequality* (New York: Pantheon, 1981).

64 The key work here is Glazer's, particularly *Affirmative Discrimination*, op. cit., and the later essays in *Ethnic Dilemmas*, op. cit. Many of the interpretive essays in the massive *Harvard Encyclopedia of American Ethnic Groups* (Cambridge, Mass.: Harvard University Press, 1982) also share the neoconservative perspective.

65 In our view this threat reflected not so much the radical nature of the 1960s minority upsurge or the reforms it won, but indeed their fundamentally moderate and half-hearted character. A more comprehensive series of reforms, for example, might have extended to redistribution initiatives and full employment commitments, which could have cushioned the blow that whites located in marginal neighborhoods, school districts, jobs, etc. received when affirmative action and similar programs increased competition for semi-skilled work, public education and affordable housing. But as it was, the threat was real enough.

66 As Rieder demonstrates, however, white ethnic appeals to "fairness" often segue into overt racism, especially as the perceived threats to community, family and "way of life" increase. For one example among many provided in this work, see Rieder, op. cit., p. 245.

67 Cited in Robby Cohen, "Reagan: A 'Neo-Segregationist,' " *The Daily Californian*, 18 October 1984.

68 Ibid.

69 *San Francisco Chronicle*, 18 February 1980. Her remark was made during a telephone conversation with Mr Reagan broadcast over loudspeakers for the benefit of the diners. Flustered, Mrs Reagan tried to correct herself by saying, ". . .all the beautiful black and white people." Unfortunately, there were no blacks in the room. Reported in Michael Kilian, "GOP Genie Rescues Reagans," *Chicago Tribune*, 25 February 1980.

70 "White Men Were Key to Reagan Landslide," *San Francisco Chronicle*, 27 December 1984.

71 Ibid.

72 Kirk made his remark on 3 February on NBC's "Meet the Press." This may be in direct response to Kevin Phillips's hostile advice to the Democrats:

> "If you Democrats do anything, try to get rid of the party's
> pervasive image of being the vehicle of every kind of cultural,
> sexual and ethnic fringe group with a letterhead and stationery.
> Jettisoning special-interest group caucuses would be a start."
> (Cited in J.K. Yamamoto, "Democratic National Committee Chair
> Questions Need for Asian/Pacific Caucus," *Pacific Citizen*, 8
> March 1985)

73 He argued that their persistence was merely a function of a self-serving bureaucracy:

> I think there are, there is a tendency of some individuals who have

positions in organizations that have been created for whatever purpose but for some purpose to rectify some ill, that then once that gets going they're reluctant to admit how much they've achieved, because it might reveal then that there's no longer a need for that particular organization, which would mean no longer a need for their job. (Taken from a radio interview with seven correspondents on 26 January 1985. Cited in "Rights Groups Unneeded, Reagan Says," *Pacific Citizen*, 1 February 1985)

74 "Justice Dept. Taking A City to Court Over Hiring Quotas," *San Francisco Chronicle*, 30 April 1985.
75 "Race Questions Cut From Federal Forms," *San Francisco Chronicle*, 25 March 1985. "Jerry McMurry, staff director for the housing subcommittee of the House Banking Committee, said the Reagan administration 'would rather not know' the racial composition of its programs so it cannot be challenged on its civil rights record." An early policy recommendation along these lines was the Heritage Foundation report "Agenda '83," a new right blueprint for the President. One of its major points was an attack on affirmative action – "Agenda '83" argued for a challenge to court-ordered quotas in hiring and promotion and for a new definition of discrimination.
76 Mary Frances Berry, "Taming the Civil Rights Commission," *The Nation*, 2 February 1985.
77 The bible in this regard is Charles Murray, op. cit. See also George Gilder, *Wealth and Poverty* (New York: Basic Books, 1981).
78 See Gary Delgado, "Reverse Distribution: Fiscal Crisis and Black Resistance," *Critical Perspectives of Third World America*, vol. 1, no. 1 (Fall 1983).
79 In contrast to the new racists, Pendleton stated that Reagan supporters "are performing corrective surgery on the disfigured civil rights laws." *New York Times*, 6 March 1985.
80 Roger Wilkins, "Smiling racism," *The Nation*, 3 November 1984.
81 Cohen, op. cit.
82 Black's remarks were made in an interview with Haynes Johnson of *The Washington Post*. Cited in Wilkins, op. cit.

Conclusion

1 At stake was who represented the legitimate voice of "the People." Community activists who were absorbed into the various state-sponsored bureaucracies were derided as "poverty pimps" who had been "coopted" by "the system" and now sought to preserve their jobs and expand their influence by making the community increasingly dependent upon them. College students were faulted for their often sporadic commitment (revolution according to the academic calendar) and their potentially upwardly mobile status. The "lumpenproletariat" was either glorified as the "vanguard" of Third World struggles in the

US or denounced as criminal elements and/or "street people" with little collective political consciousness.

2 Samuel P. Huntington, 'Chapter III: The United States," in Michel Crozier, Samuel P. Huntington and Joji Watanuki, *The Crisis of Democracy: Report on the Governability of Democracies to the Trilateral Commission* (New York: New York University Press, 1975).

3 Jonathan Rieder, *Canarsie: The Jews and Italians of Brooklyn Against Liberalism* (Cambridge, Mass.: Harvard University Press, 1985) p. 6; see also Kevin Phillips's newsletter, *The American Political Report* (Bethesda, Maryland: The American Political Research Group), 17 May 1985, pp. 4–5.

4 Stuart Hall has used this term to characterize the Thatcher regime in Britain; it has obvious resonance on American shores as well. See Hall, "The Great Moving Right Show," *Socialist Review*, no. 55 (January–February 1981).

5 Such a program would probably rearticulate racial theory in terms of a biologistic conception of race which would locate inequality in racial differences themselves. Some preliminary steps have been taken in this direction, for example in the uses of "sociobiology," but intellectual acceptance of a new biologistic racism has thus far not materialized.

6 According to the present version, state anti-discrimination activity is only justified when the practice of intentional discrimination on racial grounds can be demonstrated. This theory, however, still bears the marks of its liberal origins. For example, Nathan Glazer claims that he would favor more extensive state anti-discrimination activity, even in the face of principle, if on pragmatic grounds it could be shown to be effective. See Glazer, *Affirmative Discrimination* (New York: Basic Books, 1975) p. 73.

7 Orlando Patterson has described this solution with respect to the black community:

> Ideally the proto-fascist scenario calls for the containment of the black poor in concentrated areas and the use of their labor for the menial but essential tasks that will remain even in the most highly advanced, post-industrial utopia: street cleaning and general sanitation, sewage disposal, hospital attendants, the less technical aspects of the transportation industry, and the filthier and more hazardous types of blue collar jobs.

He doubts such a scenario could be implemented due to the "counter-leviathan power of the urban poor." Orlando Patterson, "The Black Community: Is There a Future?", in Seymour Martin Lipset, ed., *The Third Century* (Stanford, Cal.: Hoover Institution Press, 1979), pp. 280–1.

8 William J. Wilson's *The Declining Significance of Race*, 2nd edn. (Chicago: University of Chicago Press, 1978) played an important role in catalyzing these debates. Wilson's title is actually a bit deceptive (though it does make for provocative copy). His work really focuses on

"the increasing significance of class" in determining the life chances of blacks.

9 The same is true for Latinos (a.k.a "Hispanics"), a category broad enough to include Salvadorans, Argentines, Brazilians, Cubans, Mexicans and Mexican Americans, among others.

Index

Index